The Liturgy of the Gospel

WORD AND SPIRIT
PENTECOSTAL INVESTIGATIONS IN THEOLOGY AND HISTORY

The *Word and Spirit* series will make space for the pneumatological emphasis typical of Pentecostal/charismatic approaches to theology without eclipsing the discernment that comes with the Word of God (that is the Word both christological and scriptural). This series will not be narrowly *Pentecostal* but will include other approaches deemed charismatic as well. Furthermore, the series will also have an ecumenical horizon. Contributors will be encouraged to write in a way that would make these books relevant to other denominational traditions. These books are *Investigations* in that they are scholarly treatments of topics that will seek to remain accessible to pastors as well as seminary and upper division college readers. *Theology* in the series name signals that these are constructive works engaging biblical, systematic, and historical theological discourse, with an eye towards offering contributions of contemporary relevance to the church.

The series will contract academic monographs that offer a solid Pentecostal and ecumenical discussion of key loci, but also of key trajectories in Pentecostal thought and experience.

EDITORS:

FRANK D. MACCHIA: Professor of Systematic Theology at Vanguard University of Southern California

DALE M. COULTER: Professor of Historical Theology at the Pentecostal Theological Seminary

ASSOCIATE EDITORS:

DAVID D. DANIELS III: Henry Winters Luce Professor of World Christianity at McCormick Theological Seminary

LISA P. STEPHENSON: Associate Professor of Systematic Theology at Lee University

NÉSTOR MEDINA: Director of Master of Theological Studies and Associate Professor of Religious Ethics and Culture at Emmanuel College of Victoria University in the University of Toronto

"Framed by a fresh introduction and conclusion, Vondey includes essays published over twenty-five years, exploring aspects of Pentecostal theological hermeneutics related to embodying the full gospel. He demonstrates that the nature of Pentecostal hermeneutics functions as a liturgy of the full gospel. He does this by examining the dynamic and playful liturgical hermeneutic interaction of fusion and fission within interpretive horizons, with the altar metaphor serving as a key site for the merging and dividing of hermeneutical horizons. I strongly recommend this ecumenically engaging, intellectually stimulating, and spiritually nourishing collection of essays as a significant contribution to Pentecostal theological hermeneutics."

—**Kenneth J. Archer**, Professor of Theology and Pentecostal Studies, Trinity Bible College and Graduate School, North Dakota

"Wolfgang Vondey is one of the most accomplished doctrinal theologians to have emerged from the Pentecostal movement. The essays collected here demonstrate the development of his systematic thinking over the course of two decades, particularly as working out his theology of the full gospel. The new introductory and concluding book ends to the volume recast Vondey's liturgical imagination in dialogue with Gadamer's general hermeneutics and suggest instead a 'this-is-and-is-not-that' both fusion and fission of horizons generated playfully, unpredictably, and non-conformationally from altar encounters with the divine Spirit. The result is a transformation-of-life interpretive posture that not only names what happens through Pentecost events but also deserves broader methodological and hermeneutical consideration befitting Vondey's stature as an internationally renowned ecumenical theologian."

—**Amos Yong**, Professor of Theology and Mission, Fuller Seminary

"Wolfgang Vondey is one of those rare thinkers that scholars go to when they want to engage Pentecostal theology at its most astute theoretical dimension, mine it at its systematic theology motherlode, and participate in the effects of its most siring hermeneutics. Vondey in this text does not disappoint his most brilliant and discerning readers. This book—in a robust display of careful reasoning and nuanced familiarity with Pentecostal sensibility—masterfully argues that liturgy, not language, is the medium of Pentecostal hermeneutics."

—**Nimi Wariboko**, Walter G. Muelder Professor of Social Ethics, Boston University

"Few have been more helpful than Wolfgang Vondey in framing how to think through the vast and diffuse tradition that constitutes contemporary Pentecostalism. This collection of Vondey's writings is a rich source for (re)considering the way Pentecostalism interprets life from one of the leading Pentecostal theologians in the world. It also provides an education in the important subject of theological hermeneutics. This volume is immediately a leading work in theological hermeneutics and Pentecostal theology."

—L. William Oliverio Jr., Editor-in-Chief, *Pneuma: The Journal for the Society of Pentecostal Studies*

The Liturgy of the Gospel

Theological Hermeneutics in Pentecostal Perspective

WORD AND SPIRIT: PENTECOSTAL INVESTIGATIONS
IN THEOLOGY AND HISTORY

WOLFGANG VONDEY

CASCADE *Books* · Eugene, Oregon

THE LITURGY OF THE GOSPEL
Theological Hermeneutics in Pentecostal Perspective

Word and Spirit: Pentecostal Investigations in Theology and History

Copyright © 2025 Wolfgang Vondey. All rights reserved. Except for brief quotations in critical publications or reviews, no part of this book may be reproduced in any manner without prior written permission from the publisher. Write: Permissions, Wipf and Stock Publishers, 199 W. 8th Ave., Suite 3, Eugene, OR 97401.

Cascade Books
An Imprint of Wipf and Stock Publishers
199 W. 8th Ave., Suite 3
Eugene, OR 97401

www.wipfandstock.com

PAPERBACK ISBN: 979-8-3852-5078-3
HARDCOVER ISBN: 979-8-3852-5079-0
EBOOK ISBN: 979-8-3852-5080-6

Cataloguing-in-Publication data:

Names: Vondey, Wolfgang, author.

Title: The Liturgy of the Gospel: Theological Hermeneutics in Pentecostal Perspective / by Wolfgang Vondey.

Description: Eugene, OR: Cascade Books, 2025. | Word and Spirit: Pentecostal Investigations in Theology and History. | Includes bibliographical references and index.

Identifiers: ISBN 979-8-3852-5078-3 (paperback). | ISBN 979-8-3852-5079-0 (hardcover). | ISBN 979-8-3852-5080-6 (ebook).

Subjects: LCSH: Pentecostalism. | Bible—Hermeneutics. | Pentecostal hermeneutics. | Hermeneutics—Religious aspects—Pentecostal churches.

Classification: BX8762 V66 2025 (print). | BX8762 (ebook).

VERSION NUMBER 09/08/25

Scripture quotations are from New Revised Standard Version Bible, copyright © 1989 National Council of the Churches of Christ in the United States of America. Used by permission. All rights reserved worldwide.

To my teachers
at the Pentecostal Theological Seminary,
pioneers of hermeneutics in Pentecostal perspective

Contents

Acknowledgments ix

Introduction 1

PART I | THE QUESTION OF TRUTH IN THE PENTECOSTAL TRADITION

1 The Unity and Diversity of Pentecostal Theology 11

2 The Hierarchy of Truths and Pentecostal Identity 35

3 Pentecostalism as a Theological Tradition 50

PART II | THE EXTENSION OF THE QUESTION OF TRUTH TO HERMENEUTICAL EXPERIENCE

4 The Symbolic Turn in the Liturgy of Pentecostalism 67

5 Worship, Spirituality, and the Making of a Black Liturgy 90

6 Religion at Play and the Transformation of a Secular Age 108

PART III | THE ONTOLOGICAL SHIFT OF PENTECOSTAL HERMENEUTICS GUIDED BY LITURGY

7 Gospel as Principle of Pentecostal Theology 129

8 Sacramentality and the Hermeneutic of the Altar 144

9 The Materiality of Pentecostal Theology 160

10 A Liturgical Hermeneutic of Pentecost   175

Conclusion   189

Bibliography   197

Index   225

Acknowledgments

FRAMED BY A NEW introduction and conclusion, the remaining chapters in this book have been previously published over the past twenty-five years. I thank the editors and publishers for permission to reuse the following essays:

Chapter 1: "The Unity and Diversity of Pentecostal Theology: A Brief Survey for the Ecumenical Community in the West." *Ecclesiology* 10 (2014) 76–100.

Chapter 2: "Christian Amnesia: Who in the World Are Pentecostals?" *Asian Journal of Pentecostal Studies* 4 (2001) 21–39.

Chapter 3: "Pentecostalism as a Theological Tradition: An Ideological, Historical, and Institutional Critique." *Pneuma: The Journal of the Society for Pentecostal Studies* 42 (2020) 521–35.

Chapter 4: "The Symbolic Turn: A Symbolic Conception of the Liturgy of Pentecostalism." *Wesleyan Theological Journal* 36 (2001) 223–47.

Chapter 5: "The Making of a Black Liturgy: Pentecostal Worship and Spirituality from African Slave Narratives to Urban City Scapes." *Black Theology* 10 (2012) 147–68.

Chapter 6: "Religion at Play: Pentecostalism and the Transformation of the Secular Age." *Pneuma: Journal of the Society for Pentecostal Studies* 40 (2019) 17–36.

Chapter 7: "Full Gospel or Pure Gospel: Principles of Lutheran and Pentecostal Theology." *Dialog: A Journal of Theology* 55 (2016) 324–33.

Chapter 8: "Pentecostal Sacramentality and the Theology of the Altar." In *Scripting Pentecost: A Study of Pentecostals, Worship, and Liturgy*, edited by Mark J. Cartledge and A. J. Swoboda, 94–107. Aldershot, UK: Ashgate, 2016.

Chapter 9: "Embodied Gospel: The Materiality of Pentecostal Theology at the Altar." In *Pentecostals and the Body*, edited by Michael Wilkinson and Peter Althouse, 46–72. Annual Review of the Sociology of Religion 8. Leiden: Brill, 2017.

Chapter 10: "The Full Gospel: A Liturgical Hermeneutic of Pentecost." In *The Routledge Handbook of Pentecostal Theology*, edited by Wolfgang Vondey, 173–82. London: Routledge, 2020.

The chapters in this volume demonstrate the development of the book's thesis over the course of more than two decades and a journey measured by different continents, languages, schools, and individuals who have shaped my understanding of Pentecostal hermeneutics. I am grateful to Michael Thomson at Wipf and Stock for seeing the value in this collection, for his professional advice and support, and to Dale M. Coulter and Frank D. Macchia for including this volume in the series *Word and Spirit: Pentecostal Investigations in Theology and History*. The chapters in this volume have had many teachers who took the time to model the meaning of theological method and hermeneutics for Pentecostals. I have greatly benefited from discussions with students who read the essays from critical global experiences at the Center for Renewal Studies of Regent University (2005–2015) and at the Centre for Pentecostal and Charismatic Studies at the University of Birmingham since 2015. The book is dedicated to my teachers at the Pentecostal Theological Seminary, whose combined vision for theological education in the 1990s pioneered a new generation of Pentecostal scholars: Delton L. Alford, French L. Arrington, James M. Beaty, Ron Cason, David D. Franklin, R. Hollis Gause, David Sang-Ehil Han, Cheryl Bridges Johns, Jackie D.

Johns, Cecil B. Knight, Steven J. Land, Lee Roy Martin, F. J. May, Lloyd Grant McClung, Rickie D. Moore, David Roebuck, Douglas W. Slocumb, John Christopher Thomas, and Rick Waldrop. Thank you for shaping and modeling the altar hermeneutic described in this volume.

Birmingham, United Kingdom

Introduction

THEOLOGICAL HERMENEUTICS HAS PLAYED a critical role in the rise of Pentecostalism as a theological tradition. At face value, the importance of interpretation for specifically and explicitly theological reasons is grounded in the Pentecostal concern for the understanding of the Christian scriptures. Reading the scriptures as Christians, Pentecostals have naturally been interested in understanding the meaning of the biblical texts. But as Pentecostals—motivated by their transformative experiences of the Holy Spirit—these Christians have approached the Scriptures with a hermeneutical perspective interested less in the texts than in the events (and the corresponding effects) motivating the biblical records.[1] More precisely, what has made Christian hermeneutics "Pentecostal" is what Hans-Georg Gadamer has called a "fusion of horizons" found in any hermeneutical task.[2] Pentecostals have articulated "their" particular fusion most prominently in terms of a hermeneutical consciousness borrowed from the apostle Peter's argument that the events on the day of Pentecost were the fulfillment of biblical prophecy: "Indeed, these are not drunk, as you suppose, for it is only nine o'clock in the morning. No, this is what was spoken through the prophet Joel" (Acts 2:15–16). Adopting the apostle's "this-is-that" fusion of horizons, modern-day Pentecostals have claimed that their own contemporary experiences were "what was spoken" in the biblical records of Pentecost.[3] At the same time, I have argued that Pentecostals have also adopted Peter's corresponding (and preceding!) rejection of the dominant hermeneutical horizon (v. 15), or

1. See my larger argument in Vondey, *Beyond Pentecostalism*, 47–77.
2. Gadamer, *Truth and Method*, xx.
3. See Land, *Pentecostal Spirituality*, 71–81.

what may be called a "this-is-*not*-that" hermeneutic.[4] Pentecostals are acutely aware that the claim of their interpretive horizon is tempered by a rejection of the dominant descriptive mechanisms necessary to understand and interpret the Pentecostal fusion of horizons. How this tension in the hermeneutical history of Pentecostal theology is resolved and contributes to the emergence of Pentecostalism as a hermeneutical tradition is the subject of the present study.

The fusion of horizons has led Pentecostals from a predominant occupation with biblical hermeneutics, and the methods of interpreting Christian scripture, to the wider concerns of theological hermeneutics. In this volume I narrate this shift as necessitated by hermeneutical questions that corresponded to but did not originate from the concerns of biblical exegesis: the formation of the Pentecostal self-awareness as a distinctive horizon of interpretation. The title of this volume submits that theological hermeneutics in Pentecostal perspective is the interpretation of the world explicitly and specifically informed by *the liturgy of the gospel*. My concern here is to identify how this horizon emerged not only thematically and historically but experientially and subjectively as a fusion of horizons, or again in Gadamer's terms, as "the range of vision that includes everything that can be seen from a particular vantage point" without "being limited to what is nearby but being able to see beyond it."[5] Along with others, I have argued consistently that the distinctive vantage point of Pentecostal hermeneutics is the event of Pentecost. Central to the ability to look beyond is that this interpretive horizon moves and develops with the hermeneutical task, and to speak of Pentecost as a horizon means not to obtain a fixed position but a critical and dynamic positioning *between* the past event and its various present interpretations. The following essays show that this dynamic hermeneutical positioning among Pentecostals originated and continues to be shaped liturgically.

At least initially, Gadamer presents a helpful approach to identify the positioning of liturgical hermeneutics, because he offers no particular hermeneutical theory but aims at a foundational explanation of the general structure of hermeneutics. While Gadamer did not pursue a specifically theological hermeneutics, he is acutely aware that faith begins with the proclamation of the gospel and that its continuous reinforcement

---

4. See Vondey, *Scandal of Pentecost*; Vondey and Green, "Between This and That," 243–64.

5. Gadamer, *Truth and Method*, 301. He attributes the notion to Nietzsche, Husserl, and James (*Truth and Method*, 237–38, 264–65, 301).

through "the work of the religious rite" serves precisely "to mediate between past and present, and that it therefore comes to play a leading role in the problem of hermeneutics."[6] Gadamer's particular concern for "truth and method" (the title of his seminal study) holds special significance for determining the liturgical horizon among Pentecostals: the experience of encountering God with the manifestation of spiritual gifts believed to have ended with the apostolic age and the corresponding scrutiny and criticism Pentecostals have endured (both internally and externally) has warranted a sustained debate concerning the nature of the Christian life.

Gadamer highlights that the integrity of the ever-expanding hermeneutical circle demands the development of a historically effected consciousness that warrants the *correspondence* of truth and method.[7] For Pentecostals, this correspondence means that the act of interpretation is both participation in the effects of the history of Pentecost *and* the ability to rise above it. Gadamer expresses the concern we also find at the heart of the anti-intellectualism that once occupied Pentecostal history: that the hermeneutical task is dissolved "into a mere reflective reality"[8] where the interest is in only the consciousness of but not the experience and participation in the effect. With Gadamer, Pentecostal hermeneutics can argue that it is "concerned to conceive a reality that limits and exceeds the omnipotence of reflection."[9] I have suggested elsewhere that the emergence of a reflective Pentecostal hermeneutical consciousness leads not only toward but also beyond Pentecostalism.[10] However, while Gadamer points to the experience of understanding that is both historically and linguistically conditioned,[11] Pentecostals appeal to Pentecost as the event that defines their self-understanding precisely for its hermeneutical "breaking" with tradition and its language. In turn, whereas Gadamer is interested primarily in the fusion of horizons, Pentecostal hermeneutics includes also a necessary fission or separation.[12] A further feature of this book is therefore a closer examination of the nature of this hermeneutical break, both analytically and constructively, by modifying the structure of

6. Gadamer, *Truth and Method*, 123.

7. Gadamer, *Truth and Method*, 336–41. That this is neither antithesis nor synthesis was suggested by Weinsheimer, *Gadamer's Hermeneutics*, 36.

8. Gadamer, *Truth and Method*, 338.

9. Gadamer, *Truth and Method*, 338.

10. Vondey, *Beyond Pentecostalism*, 2–8.

11. See Risser, "Philosophical Hermeneutics," 93–116.

12. See Land, *Pentecostal Spirituality*, 103–10.

Gadamer's pursuit and applying the correlation of fusion and fission to the historical narrative of Pentecostal hermeneutics.

Adapting the three main sections in Gadamer's *Truth and Method*, the essays in this volume begin with (1) the question of truth in the Pentecostal tradition, then move to (2) the extension of the question of truth to hermeneutical experience and conclude with a discussion of (3) the ontological shift of Pentecostal hermeneutics guided by liturgy. The direction of this approach offers original reflections on the constellation of theological hermeneutics that both modifies Gadamer's philosophical hermeneutics and contrasts with the stereotype that Pentecostals belong to a non- or anti-liturgical stream of Christianity.[13] On the contrary, we can employ "liturgy," not only in the traditional sense as the customary public worship of Pentecostals but as the primary normative horizon for Pentecostal self-reflection and theological interpretation. This argument proceeds from the liturgical dimension identified in the first part as a question of truth via the formation of the liturgy of Pentecostalism to the identity of this liturgical hermeneutic in the form of the full gospel.

Gadamer would argue that the quest for a distinctive Pentecostal hermeneutic must begin with the question of truth. However, the definition and boundaries of truth claims in the Pentecostal tradition have not been subject to much exploration.[14] A common historical perspective is that Pentecostals arrived at their claims by appealing to "a coherent set of assumptions about the sources of authority."[15] But this argument neglects Gadamer's valid concerns for the unreflective presuppositions that inform the historical consciousness of any hermeneutical tradition, particularly of those still in the process of their original formation. The goal of the first section is therefore to stake the boundaries that identify the historically effected consciousness responsible for the correspondence of truth and method in Pentecostal hermeneutics. This section opens the liturgical horizon through a sustained discussion of the relationship of experience and doctrine in the history of effects of Pentecost. The first chapter introduces the challenges confronting both the unity and diversity of Pentecostal theology by marking the movement's inherent struggle

13. See Alexander, "Liturgy," 158–93; Albrecht, "Pentecostal Spirituality," 107–25.

14. The traditional notions of truth are a concern for the pneumatological imagination developed in Yong, *Spirit-Word-Community*, 164–75. See also Yong, "Demise of Foundationalism," 563–88; Yong, "'Tongues of Fire,'" 39–65.

15. See, e.g., Wacker, *Heaven Below*, 70–86, although he suggests that not every Pentecostal was sufficiently self-conscious (70).

for both doctrinal distinctiveness and ecumenical integration. The second chapter proposes that, rather than a hierarchy of truths, a Pentecostal theological hermeneutics is situated along a body of truths that values truth claims in terms of their centrality to Pentecostal experience rather than their foundational placement in a hierarchical system of doctrines. The third chapter critically identifies and discusses the foundational patterns of Pentecostalism as a "tradition" by placing a formulaic conception of truth at the center of its collective memory, its ritual expression, the guardians of the tradition, and its normative content.

The second part echoes Gadamer's extension of the question of truth to hermeneutical experience. Gadamer's approach is framed by an extensive critique of the human sciences.[16] Situating Pentecostalism in this critique is beyond the scope of this volume. However, like Gadamer, I am interested in the recovery of the fundamental hermeneutical problem.[17] That is, Gadamer raises the constitutive significance of the *question* for the hermeneutic process. Similarly, and at a more basic level, part two pursues the nature of the question that has come to identify Pentecostalism as a Christian hermeneutical tradition. Distinct from Gadamer, who concludes "that the essence of tradition is to exist in the medium of language,"[18] the essays in this part show that the Pentecostal question emerges rather in resistance to the dominance of this medium. Chapter 4 identifies how an irreversible symbolic turn initiated the rise of Pentecostal hermeneutics that is more readily expressed in a theology of liturgy than of language. Chapter 5 continues this proposal by tracing the rise of a Black liturgy from the plantation prayer grounds of African slaves and the camp meetings of the American South to the rise of twentieth-century Pentecostalism in North America. Chapter 6 places this alternative liturgy in the broad, dominant narrative of the secular age and contends that the Pentecostal hermeneutical horizon engages with the secular without accepting its authority. This dynamic tension of both fusion and fission characteristic to the Pentecostal liturgical consciousness is identified as play.

Play also constitutes an important element in Gadamer's project, although he places its discussion primarily in the context of ontological explanation in reference to the experience of art.[19] For Gadamer, play

16. Gadamer, *Truth and Method*, 172–266.
17. Gadamer, *Truth and Method*, 305–34.
18. Gadamer, *Truth and Method*, 391.
19. See Gadamer, *Truth and Method*, 102–30; Gadamer, *Relevance of the Beautiful*,

is a primordial mode of being, a process, and, eventually, a structure of total mediation.[20] Play is significant for hermeneutics insofar as the object of interpretation no longer "stands over against a subject for itself" but "becomes an experience that changes the person who experiences it."[21] Gadamer's insistence that the fusion of horizons exists "between" rather than toward either end is achieved by the freedom of the movement of play.[22] It is through the intended yet nonpurposive activity of play that we can dissolve the distinction between subject and object and arrive with the fusion of horizons at the transformation of reality into truth.[23] Gadamer's illustration of play with the help of Christian ritual reflects the significance placed on liturgy as a playful hermeneutical activity more widely.[24] However, his interest in liturgy is only tangential to his underlying concerns for the aesthetic consciousness and its hermeneutical significance for understanding the text, and Gadamer ultimately shifts to language as the medium of this hermeneutical experience. For Pentecostals, on the other hand, play exists not only in the fusion but also in the fission of interpretative horizons, precisely because it is a liturgical hermeneutic not dominated by language.

The final part of this book completes the argument that liturgy, not language, is the medium of Pentecostal hermeneutics. Pentecostals share with Gadamer the concern for practical over theoretical and technical knowledge and for transformation as the outcome of the fusion of horizons, although they disagree with him as to the conditions of our knowledge.[25] While Gadamer views language as the necessary horizon of a hermeneutical ontology and insists "*that this whole process is verbal*,"[26] Pentecostals claim that understanding through language as the universal medium of our experience of the world is challenged and transformed with the outpouring of the Spirit at Pentecost. The

---

esp. 116–22, 123–30. See also Vilhauer, "'Fusion of Horizons,'" 359–64.

20. Nielsen, "Gadamer on Play," 139–54.

21. Gadamer, *Truth and Method*, 103.

22. Gadamer, *Relevance of the Beautiful*, 24. See Eberhard, *Middle Voice*, 62–94.

23. Chiurazzi, "Truth," 100.

24. See, more recently, Williams, "Playing Church," 323–36; Stringer, "Text, Context, and Performance," 365–79; Flanagan, "Liturgy as Play," 346–72. For my broader exposition of Gadamer and play see the introduction to Vondey, *God and Play*.

25. See Oliverio, *Pentecostal Hermeneutics*, 17–18; Nel, "Distinctive Pentecostal Hermeneutic."

26. Gadamer, *Truth and Method*, 385 (emphasis original).

theological narrative of this transformation among Pentecostals is the so-called full gospel, most prominently known in the fivefold proclamation of salvation, sanctification, Spirit baptism, divine healing, and the coming kingdom of Jesus Christ.

Chapter 7 offers a historical and theological study of the notion of the full gospel and identifies its hermeneutical commitments in conversation with Lutheran theology. The goal of this chapter is to refine the notion of the "gospel" in Pentecostal hermeneutics by contrasting its emphasis on the fullness of the gospel with the Lutheran idea of the purity of the gospel. Chapter 8 argues in conversation with Roman Catholic theology that the liturgical center of this gospel hermeneutic is the altar where the fusion and fission of hermeneutical horizons takes place. The consequences of this correlation are then presented in chapter 9 by outlining the kinesthetic contours of embodied practices that identify theological hermeneutics in Pentecostal perspective experientially as an embodied gospel. The final chapter offers a concluding theological analysis of the full gospel as a liturgical hermeneutic of Pentecost that aims at understanding and perpetuating the transformative encounter with God as the ultimate horizon.

PART I

The Question of Truth
in the Pentecostal Tradition

1

The Unity and Diversity of Pentecostal Theology

PENTECOSTALISM IS A PERPLEXING phenomenon.[1] Beginning as a fringe movement at the margins of the Christian world, the modern-day Pentecostal movement has become one of the fastest growing religious movements of the twenty-first century. Today's Pentecostalism is a global phenomenon, an ecumenical melting pot, a theological puzzle consisting of a multiplicity of voices and positions, and a major factor in the shaping of late-modern Christianity.[2] Since the widely recognized revivals that mark the historical origins of classical Pentecostalism at the beginning of the twentieth century, the movement has endured unprecedented changes in its global representation, doctrinal composition, ecumenical participation, organizational structures, liturgical makeup, religious ethos, sociocultural significance, and political participation. The dramatic development of Pentecostalism has made it necessary to distinguish between different types of Pentecostalism on a large scale. The most common distinction is between the so-called classical Pentecostals connected with the revival at the Azusa Street Mission in Los Angeles (1906–1915), the members of the so-called

1. Parts of this essay were first published as Vondey, "Théologie pentecôtiste," 369–87. See also Vondey, *Pentecostalism*, 1–8.

2. See Vondey, *Pentecostalism*, 9–27.

charismatic movements in the established Roman Catholic, Protestant, and Eastern Orthodox churches that surfaced in North America during the 1960s, and so-called neocharismatic or neo-Pentecostal groups, "a catch-all category that comprises 18,810 independent, indigenous, post-denominational denominations and groups that cannot be classified as either Pentecostal or charismatic but share a common emphasis on the Holy Spirit, spiritual gifts, Pentecostal-like experiences (*not* Pentecostal terminology), signs and wonders, and power encounters."[3] The diversity of the movement and its transition from a localized and marginal phenomenon to worldwide proportions have made it difficult to identify and to situate Pentecostalism in the ecumenical landscape.

Pentecostals and non-Pentecostals alike have raised significant concerns about the unity of Pentecostal theology, the relationship of Pentecostal theology to the ecumenical traditions, and the integration of Pentecostal theology in broader Christian commitments to social justice, peace, and the conservation of creation. This chapter highlights the central efforts in these areas among Pentecostals and attempts to portray a realistic image of Pentecostal theology in the place of homogenous and romanticized pictures or false stereotypes. The primary purpose of this essay is to offer no more than an introduction to pertinent issues. In addition, this introduction is limited in scope and perspective in order to address primarily the Western ecumenical world. While this focus is not fully representative of global Pentecostalism, it allows the Western reader to identify more readily familiar theological issues and convergences. An introduction to global issues depends only partly on the same concerns and should be carried out as a distinct effort not necessarily informed by Western Pentecostal and ecumenical concerns. In order to address these differences, the chapter begins with an introduction to the global and local dimensions of Pentecostalism. The essay then offers an assessment of the unity of Pentecostal theology in the West that focuses on the form, concept, content, and core convictions of Pentecostal thought. The second part examines the shape of Pentecostal ecclesiology in its efforts toward the unity of Christians. The focus is on the origins, the transitions, concrete formulations, and the future of Pentecostal ecclesiology. The final part addresses the practical applications of Pentecostal theology. The focus here is on the Pentecostal commitment to the unity of the Christian life, social justice, and transformation. I argue that these realms represent

---

3. Burgess and van der Maas, *New International Dictionary*, xx.

a connecting point between Pentecostalism in the West and the global Pentecostal movement. This brief overview suggests that Pentecostal theology from an ecumenical perspective shows an inherent struggle for both self-realization as well as unity and integration. Pentecostal theology is in transition toward becoming a diversified contributor to the shape of global Christianity and the renewal of the theological agenda.[4]

PENTECOSTAL THEOLOGY BETWEEN THE GLOBAL AND THE LOCAL

Modern-day Pentecostalism readily suggests a "global" perspective in its staggering numbers and worldwide representation. Surveys and statistics including Pentecostals today quickly give the impression of a worldwide religious movement.[5] The sizable number of Pentecostals often serves to emphasize the homogeneity of Pentecostal beliefs and practices across the world and to allow for interpretations of the movement that are not bound to isolated phenomena. By adding the word "global" to the Pentecostal movement, we anticipate a certain redundancy in observing Pentecostalism worldwide in order to arrive at a definition of the term "Pentecostal" that applies as a common denominator to all variations of the movement. At the same time, Pentecostalism cannot simply be described from the outset as a global movement without dismissing the frequent emphasis that Pentecostalism is a thoroughly local phenomenon. For an ecumenical approach to Pentecostalism, neither the micro- nor the macro-vision is a realistic perspective of the Pentecostal world if maintained exclusively in the long run. In the contexts of the local and the global, Pentecostalism exhibits qualities of both sides.[6] In other words, what characterizes the identity of the Pentecostal movement is both its local roots and global temperament. We might say that Pentecostalism is "a religion made to travel"[7] between the local and the global. The most dominant theory to explain these interdependencies is the idea of globalization.

---

4. See Vondey, *Beyond Pentecostalism*, 1–15.

5. See Pew Research Center, "Spirit and Power"; Johnson et al., "Christianity 2010," 29–36; Johnstone and Mandryk, *Operation World*, 3. Relevant data can also be found at worldreligiondatabase.org and worldchristiandatabase.org.

6. See Robeck, "Global and Local," 34.

7. See Dempster et al., *Globalization of Pentecostalism*, 1.

Globalization explains Pentecostalism as a movement in transition from the local to the global.[8] Two dominant interpretations have emerged from this broad perspective, one that emphasizes the homogeneity and another that points to the heterogeneous nature of the development. The emphasis on a homogeneous globalization frequently ties together Pentecostalism and modernity and understands globalization as an inherent tendency of modern-day religious movements. In contrast, the other side resists the application of the term "Pentecostalism" to the movement as a generic global identifier. The emphasis on heterogeneity describes Pentecostalism in reverse terms and understands the movement as a global phenomenon that exists as always adapting local variations.[9] This perspective emphasizes significant differences in religiosity, spirituality, morality, social engagement, as well as political and economic participation among Pentecostals in East and West, the Northern and Southern Hemispheres, and Europe and the USA.[10] To this may be added the racial, social, and linguistic diversities of Pentecostal groups even on the regional level. If we adopt a heterogeneous interpretation, global Pentecostalism refers to cultural discontinuities and contradictions, including irreconcilable differences in theology and worship. The ecumenical community therefore does not have the luxury to expect conversations with global Pentecostalism, even if global representations among Pentecostals and the ecumenical community have become more visible.[11] The following introduction consequently reflects only the dominant Western Pentecostal and ecumenical perspectives without the claim that these perspectives are representative of Pentecostalism worldwide.

A more globally oriented introduction would necessitate a theory that can explain the relationship between local and global Pentecostalism without reverting exclusively to one side or the other. The range of Pentecostal and communities and their diversities worldwide can indeed be described with the term "glocalization"—the dismissal of "distance" between the local and the global that ultimately finds the global *in* the local and vice versa.[12] Instead of assuming the globalization *of* local Pentecostalism and thereby juxtaposing the global *against* the local, the understanding of Pentecostalism as a glocal phenomenon embraces the

8. See Robertson, *Globalization*, 49–60.
9. Poewe, *Charismatic Christianity*, 17.
10. See Plüss, "Globalization of Pentecostalism," 170–82.
11. For example, see the Global Christian Forum.
12. Robertson, "Glocalization," 25–44.

relationship between the local and the global because Pentecostalism as a whole depends on both dimensions. The following introduction attempts to illustrate this interdependence in the case of Pentecostalism from the ecumenical perspective of the West and by suggesting that there exists a point of convergence between Western and global Pentecostalism in the social activism of the movement.

Glocalization applied to Pentecostalism rejects a simplistic theory that equates the dynamics of Pentecostalism with either those of a globalizing modernity or its postmodern counterpart.[13] There is no global mass-culture that can be labeled "Pentecostalism" without identifying simultaneously the local roots or localized representations of what we term "Pentecostal." On the contrary, the globalization of Pentecostalism consists of the production and reproduction of the local in the global and the global in the local, the mediation, or more precisely, the encoding and decoding of local distinctiveness and global generality.[14] The dialectic process of localization and delocalization, globalization and deglobalization is accompanied by tensions and conflicts that do not lie either in the local *or* the global but in the fusion of both dimensions.[15] Consequently, it is the combination of the tensions inherent in a dedication to both the local and the global that forms the heart of Pentecostalism.[16] What is taking place among Pentecostals worldwide is an ongoing "reconfiguration of Pentecost"[17] that involves the simultaneity and interpenetration of the local and the global, sometimes in response to the other, sometimes in opposition, but never with the ability to escape either dimension. This perspective has significant implications for the actual reality we call "Pentecostalism" and for the way we seek to understand the unity and diversity of Pentecostal theology. Global Pentecostalism and Pentecostalism in the West are intertwined in a significant theological and ecumenical manner.

---

13. Meyer, "Pentecostalism and Globalization," 113–30.
14. Kalu, "Changing Tides," 3–23.
15. Bergunder, "Pfingstbewegung, Globalisierung, und Migration," 155–69.
16. See Martin, *Tongues of Fire*, 122.
17. Poloma, "Reconfiguration of Pentecost," 123–25.

THE UNITY AND DIVERSITY OF PENTECOSTAL THEOLOGY IN THE WEST

Pentecostal theology is born out of the need to narrate the experiences of the salvific work of God in Christ and the Holy Spirit and to do so in terms that do justice to their experiences rather than to official formulations of doctrine.[18] However, Pentecostal groups exhibit a broad variety of beliefs that are not always readily summed up in doctrinal statements. Western Pentecostals are reluctant to formulate extensive systems of official doctrines. The statements of faith and doctrinal teachings issued by particular Pentecostal groups do not easily apply to the entire movement. Some Pentecostal teachings stand in rather sharp contrast to orthodox Christian formulations and are considered heretical by many Pentecostal and non-Pentecostal groups. Pentecostals have found it difficult to present their own doctrinal formulations without adopting them from other traditions and without thereby sacrificing the distinctive experiences that identify them in distinction to those traditions. The charismatic movement in the mainline churches has had its own challenges of remaining an integral part of their traditions without giving the impression of simply adding to it a doctrine of the Spirit. Neo-Pentecostal groups have added little significant texture to the actual formulation of Pentecostal doctrine, primarily because there is no magisterial theological guidance or official authoritative teaching for all groups. Oneness Pentecostal theology presents a particular challenge within these groups due to its rejection of the Trinitarian tradition of the faith. The unity of Pentecostal theology is based less upon a particular content than a particular form of theological discourse and concept of doctrine rooted in Pentecostal spirituality.[19]

The *form* of theological discourse dominant among Pentecostals results from a strong reliance on Scripture as the foundational path to doctrinal formulations that support and direct Pentecostal experiences.[20] In Scripture, Pentecostals find a common emphasis on dreams, visions, prophecies, prayer, and worship that provide the foundation for articulating their own story. This articulation generally proceeds orally among Pentecostals, usually expressed in sermons, testimonies, and songs, and rarely in classical formulations of doctrine.[21] In trying

---

18. A prominent example is Yong, *Spirit Poured Out*, 81–120.
19. See Vondey, *Pentecostalism*, 69–88.
20. See Clifton, "Spirit and Doctrinal Development," 5–23.
21. See Guthrie, "Pentecostal Hymnody," 29–88.

to articulate their experiences, song, poetry, testimony, prophecy, and prayer seem the more appropriate media to Pentecostals than creedal formulations and doctrinal propositions. For classical Pentecostals, theology is identified not primarily with creeds and doctrines but with a worshipful response to God's saving activity.[22]

In their *concept* of doctrine, western Pentecostals stand closer to the Roman Catholic idea of the development of doctrine than to the Protestant understanding of doctrines as the unchangeable deposit of faith.[23] Formative in this understanding is the link between the authority of spirituality and the authority of doctrine (*lex orandi, lex credendi*).[24] For these Pentecostals, spirituality *is* doctrine since the starting point for all doctrine is the response to God by the human spirit. The response in immediate testimonies, visions, songs, tongues, or prayers is initially pre-cognitive, affective, and behavioral, or to put it differently, therapeutic and prophetic.[25] From there, a more articulate, scrutinized, and deliberative formulation of doctrine, such as creeds, dogmas, and official teachings are generally not attempted by Pentecostals. Nonetheless, most Pentecostals readily embrace formal articulations of doctrine from other traditions if these reflect their own spirituality and experiences.

In terms of *content*, the most immediate link between Pentecostal spirituality and doctrine is formed by soteriology. Formulations of Pentecostal doctrine, not only in the West, are ultimately rooted in the multidimensional character of salvation as it is observed and formulated among the Christian traditions.[26] This means that for Pentecostals all doctrine must remain verifiable in the concrete personal and communal experiences of God's redemptive activity. Salvation represents an epistemic and experiential commonality that informs all Pentecostal practices. This emphasis is clearly visible in the articulation of the so-called full gospel—a theological formulation among classical Pentecostals that mediates between narrative account and formulaic expression. Two different theological accounts are in circulation among Pentecostals in North America that nonetheless communicate very similar theological emphases: the four-fold gospel of Jesus as savior, Spirit baptizer, healer,

22. See Land, *Pentecostal Spirituality*, 32–47.
23. See Chan, "Church," 57–77.
24. See Stephenson, "Rule of Spirituality," 83–105.
25. See Plüss, *Therapeutic and Prophetic Narratives*, 1–25.
26. See Yong, *Spirit Poured Out*, 91–98.

and coming king, and the five-fold gospel that adds to this account the image of Jesus as sanctifier.[27]

Despite their first appearance, the *core convictions* of most Pentecostals are not simply identifiable as salvation, Spirit baptism, healing, sanctification, and a strong eschatological orientation. Rather, it is the biblical picture of Jesus that dominates these theological formulations. Salvation, sanctification, Spirit baptism, and other beliefs of Pentecostals are more than mere convictions of conversion, holiness, healing, or empowerment; they are seen as moments of the historical reality of Jesus in which Pentecostals continue to participate. In the person of Jesus Christ, spirituality and doctrine meet. The central confession of Christ dominates doctrinal narratives among Pentecostals. Or in other words, Pentecostal doctrine always expresses at heart a Christology.

However, the *starting point* for formulating Pentecostal doctrine is a distinctive spirituality that focuses on the presence, manifestations, and power of the Holy Spirit. Only by the Spirit is Christ present to the believer, and only the spiritually responsive person is able to enter into this presence of God.[28] As Calvary represents the window for Christ to the salvation of the world, Pentecost is seen as the door for Christians to enter the anointed presence of Christ. For Pentecostals, the Spirit is "God with us"[29] in palpable manifestations and personal experiences that always remain intimately related to the person of Jesus. From a Western ecumenical perspective, Pentecostal doctrine and spirituality are never exclusively directed toward Christ or the Spirit; they always form a Spirit-Christology.[30]

The *central expression* of Pentecostal theology is arguably the doctrine of Spirit baptism, which features at heart God's bestowal of the Holy Spirit on the human person. The majority of Pentecostals would agree that "Spirit baptism brings the reign of the Father, the reign of the crucified and risen Christ, and the reign of the divine life to all creation through the indwelling of the Spirit."[31] Pentecostals readily find in the biblical texts the unrestrained bestowal of the Spirit by the Father on the Son, documented in the anointed life of Christ, and the outpouring of the Spirit on all flesh on the day of Pentecost, documented in the

27. See Dayton, *Theological Roots of Pentecostalism*, 19–23.
28. Land, *Pentecostal Spirituality*, 59–60.
29. Land, *Pentecostal Spirituality*, 32.
30. See Del Colle, "Spirit-Christology," 91–112.
31. Macchia, *Baptized in the Spirit*, 89.

Spirit-filled life of believers. While formulations of this doctrine rarely depend on particular visions of the inner life of the triune God, the outpouring of the Holy Spirit is tied closely to the person of Jesus as the one who baptizes and is baptized with the Spirit of God. These confessions speak less of the Father or creation and more of the Word and the Spirit or regeneration and charismatic empowerment, often distinguishing between the work of the Spirit as the one who baptizes us into Christ and the work of Christ as the one who baptizes us in the Spirit.[32] This reciprocal emphasis contrasts with the frequent neglect of pneumatology in Western formulations of the doctrine of God. The Spirit-Christology eminent among Pentecostals favors a dynamic perspective of the person of Jesus that has only recently emerged among other Christian traditions.[33] Nonetheless, few of these considerations make their way into formal articulations of doctrine. Above all, the close connection between the doctrine of God and the various moments of the Spirit-filled life in the Pentecostal worldview suggests that the Pentecostal doctrine of God remains at heart always a doxology.

Challenges to the articulation of doctrine have come within Pentecostalism in particular from Oneness Pentecostals, a group of classical and neo-Pentecostals who reject classical Trinitarian formulations of the doctrine of God. Although the tensions originated in disputes over the correct administration of water baptism, the disagreements have mutated to proportions that currently represent the most significant challenges to a unified Pentecostal theology, particularly in the West. Doctrinal disagreements are concentrated in the acceptance and application of the creeds. David Bernard, senior theologian of the United Pentecostal Church International, the largest Oneness Pentecostal organization, emphasizes the lack of explicit Trinitarian language until the fourth century and sees the primary reason for the dominance of Trinitarian articulations in the necessary response to heresy.[34] Bernard faults the Nicene Creed for failing to provide a Trinitarian vocabulary, depending too strongly on a division of the confession of faith instead of its unity, and neglecting the notion of divine personhood.[35] For Oneness Pentecostals, the doctrine of God can be formulated apart from the traditional language of the creeds.

---

32. Macchia, *Baptized in the Spirit*, 113–29.
33. Prominent examples are Coffey, *Deus Trinitas*; Del Colle, *Christ and the Spirit*.
34. Bernard, *Oneness and Trinity*, 165–74.
35. Bernard, *Trinitarian Controversy*, 9–23.

Oneness Pentecostals view the Nicene-Constantinopolitan Creed as the result of an inadmissible amalgamation of the radical monotheism of the Old Testament and the redemptive manifestations of the Father, Son, and Holy Spirit in the New Testament.[36] Held responsible for this confusion is a departure from the biblical revelation and subjection of Scripture to philosophical reasoning. While the biblical witness affirms the unity and diversity of the Father, Son, and Holy Spirit in the work of salvation, Oneness Pentecostals see neither a threefold division of works nor a threefold division of persons in the doctrine of God. In contrast to the creedal texts, Oneness Pentecostals attribute the idea of personhood only to Jesus Christ.[37]

The emphasis on the single name of Jesus has earned Oneness Pentecostals the misleading characterization of being a "Jesus-only" movement. Although the singular emphasis on Jesus is typical for the group, it should be understood as an emphasis on the "name" that replaces the traditional emphasis on the divine persons.[38] Simply put, for Oneness Pentecostals, in God "the name and the person are synonymous."[39] This identification avoids the univocal use of the term "person" for the Father, Son, and Holy Spirit. Oneness Pentecostal doctrine replaces the idea of three "persons" with the concept of the single "name" of God as it is revealed in the person of Jesus Christ. In other words: the person of Jesus *is* the name of God. This central confession is actualized through water baptism "in Jesus' name" so that practically and theologically Jesus Christ is proclaimed as the only personification of God.

The *central tensions* in Pentecostal theology exist in the different use of biblical designations for God. When Trinitarian Pentecostals speak of God as "Father," "Son," and "Spirit," they highlight the necessary and coexistent redemptive roles of God in the work of salvation. In Oneness Pentecostal doctrine, these functions of God are expressed in the terms of "creator," "savior," and "sanctifier" in order to characterize the essential unity of God's being. The biblical terms "Father," "Son," and "Spirit" are instead taken as redemptive titles indicative of the closeness of relationship between God and humanity. The title of "Father" indicates the transcendence of God, the title of "Son" the incarnation, and the title of "Spirit" the indwelling of God in the believer. For Oneness Pentecostals, all of these

---

36. See Chalfant, "Fall," 351–85.
37. See Bernard, *Oneness View*, 5–19.
38. Reed, *"In Jesus' Name,"* 227–306.
39. Butler, *Oneness Pentecostalism*, 89–90.

roles are manifestations of the person of Jesus Christ. Hence, Oneness Pentecostals "do not experience three personalities when they worship, nor do they receive three spirits, but they are in relationship with one personal spirit being."[40] This Spirit-oriented perspective on the redemptive manifestations of God illustrates the important feature of Oneness Pentecostal doctrine to speak of the Father, Son, and Holy Spirit as simultaneous rather than successive manifestations. In practice, the experience of the Spirit is the experience of the Son and the experience of the Father who are all simultaneous manifestations of the one being of God and ultimately reveal the one person of Jesus Christ. For Oneness Pentecostals, the person of Jesus remains the revelation of the single being of God who encompasses and supersedes the redemptive manifestations of the Father, Son, and Holy Spirit as the eternal Lord of glory.

The *reconciliation* between Oneness and Trinitarian Pentecostal theology has proven difficult. No conversations have taken place between the two groups outside of the West. Even there, the Oneness–Trinitarian Pentecostal dialogue (2002–2007), while received with much optimism, reveals little alteration in either group's theological position.[41] Although the vocabulary of "orthodox" and "heretical" has subsided and the conversation has become impartial and respectful, it is unlikely that the two opposing views on the doctrine of God will ever coalesce. Nonetheless, while each side continues to uphold the biblical support for their respective position, theologically both sides significantly overlap.[42] Oneness Pentecostals exhibit an unexpected triadic element in their understanding of God, while Trinitarian Pentecostals tend to collapse the experiential reality of the three divine persons into a central experience of Christ or the Holy Spirit. For both sides, it is the authority of spirituality that dictates the theological position. The lack of concurrent experience of all three divine persons, or to put it positively, the particular elevation of one person in worship and encounter suggests significant theological agreements among Pentecostals.[43] The

40. "Oneness–Trinitarian Pentecostal Final Report," 203–24 (no. 40).

41. See Vondey, "Oneness and Trinitarian Pentecostalism," 86–102. See also the responses to the report: Johnson, "Brief Oneness Pentecostal Response"; Haney, "Brief Oneness Pentecostal Response"; Wood, "Trinitarian Pentecostal Response"; Menzies, "Trinitarian Pentecostal Response"; Segraves, "Oneness Pentecostal Response"; Shaka, "Trinitarian Pentecostal Response"; Ramírez, "Historian's Response"; Del Colle, "Catholic Response"; and Reed, "Anglican Response."

42. See "Oneness–Trinitarian Pentecostal Final Report," 206–7.

43. See Vondey, *Beyond Pentecostalism*, 98–108.

unity of Pentecostal theology in the West faces confrontation only in specific doctrinal formulations or practical applications.

PENTECOSTAL ECCLESIOLOGY AND CHRISTIAN UNITY

Pentecostal ecclesiology, even if limited to the First World, is not easily placed among the Christian traditions. Pentecostals are participating in a variety of ecumenical conversations, often on the grassroots level but also in regional, national, and international contexts.[44] Yet, the ecumenical mindset of Pentecostals is deeply restricted by the absence of a comprehensive Pentecostal ecclesiology. The movement has neither formulated a theology of the church nor situated itself consistently in any existing proposals.[45] The most persistent ecclesiological label for modern-day Pentecostalism is without doubt the description as a "movement." However, this designation bears significant consequences for both Pentecostal self-understanding and the possibility of ecumenical relations with Pentecostals. The self-designation as a "movement" used by Pentecostals is often a critical, even countercultural choice that expresses the contrast to what Pentecostals frequently describe as the "stagnation" and "institutionalism" of the so-called "old churches."[46] Pentecostals understand their ecclesial identity in often radical opposition to the historical consciousness of the established churches; many see in the existing use of the term "church" itself a sectarian designation. The distinction of Pentecostalism as a "movement" from the broader, established notion of "church" highlights the difficulty and resistance of fitting Pentecostal ecclesiology in established classifications.

The *basis of ecclesiological efforts* among Pentecostals in the West is supported by a deep-seated focus on eschatology and evangelization.[47] Pentecostal groups have understood themselves fundamentally as a missionary movement of the Holy Spirit. This self-designation derives from the biblical idea of the Great Commission understood as the central

---

44. See Vondey, "Pentecostals and Ecumenism," 318–30.

45. Recent examples include Lord, *Network Church*; Chan, *Pentecostal Ecclesiology*; Thomas, *Toward a Pentecostal Ecclesiology*.

46. See Vondey, "Denomination," 100–116.

47. See Vondey, *Pentecostalism*, 49–68.

motivation for the evangelistic and eschatological life of the church.[48] Pentecostals understand themselves as the realization of the biblical promise of the outpouring of the Holy Spirit on all flesh, a movement in and beyond the churches—but not a church in itself. As a result, Pentecostal ecclesiology often displays a sense for what the church is *not* rather than for what the church actually is. In its most basic form, the church remains essentially identical with the kingdom of God as an ideal yet to be reached but not a reality already attained.[49] Pentecostalism in this sense is a movement becoming the church, a transformation of existing traditions into one movement toward the church. This rejection of the designation "church" has made cooperation with Pentecostals difficult on many levels. A remedy for this dilemma is not simply found in a revision of Pentecostal doctrine or ecumenical practices.

The *dilemma of Pentecostal ecclesiology* is its transitional character. Western Pentecostals have shifted, expanded, and modified their self-understanding dramatically during the twentieth century, first in response to the critical attitude toward Pentecostals and the resulting ecumenical isolation, then in response to the worldwide expansion of the movement and the resulting exposure to different ecclesiastical traditions, also in response to the need to find structural and organizational stability, and eventually in response to Pentecostal engagement in ecumenical conversations. Initially, classical Pentecostals saw themselves as a movement of the Spirit that swept across the existing denominations and that would soon usher into the kingdom of God.

As the eschatological expectations failed to materialize, organizational instabilities, administrative weaknesses, and the absence of any clearly formulated theological understanding of the church soon caught up with the growth, stability, coherence, and unity of the movement.[50] For a theological resolve, Pentecostals turned to the existing visible structures of denominations surrounding them and adopted the title "church" as a means of self-designation.[51] The establishment of effective missionary structures initiated a widespread institutionalization and denominationalization among Pentecostal groups that promises growth, stability, and survival—yet still without formulating an accompanying ecclesiology. As a result, missionary and evangelistic activities among Pentecostals have

---

48. See Anderson, *Spreading Fires*, 46–72.
49. See Vondey, "Point de vue pentecôstiste," 23–26.
50. Faupel, *Everlasting Gospel*, 187–227.
51. See Synan, *Holiness-Pentecostal Movement*, 77–93.

become the formal endeavor of particular Pentecostal churches. The eschatological unity of the church is no longer the final realization of the Pentecostal movement, since the church is now already located within today's Pentecostalism or, perhaps more pragmatically, among the Pentecostal denominations.[52] This perspective has served as implicit justification for establishing and maintaining denominational structures without questioning if they are genuine to the Pentecostal ethos.

Denominations formed quickly and spread rapidly throughout Pentecostalism and virtually eliminated the original mindset of a movement. Instead, Pentecostal denominations, particularly in the West and the Northern Hemisphere, have entered a competitive ecclesiastical mindset among themselves and with others.[53] A closer look reveals that Pentecostal groups have frequently adopted the title "church" not only for the local assembly but also for the administrative group of churches that associate with one another on a regional or national level. Internal dissention and schisms hastened the process of institutionalization, including groups who continue to reject any denominational designation outright.[54] This shift to the realm of formal organization has complicated the use of the designation "church" and effectively shut the door to a more pronounced ecumenical theology and participation. The adoption of the traditional classification, "church," inevitably led to confrontation internally as well as with other churches and denominations. The Pentecostal self-understanding today allows for the existence of multiple churches and denominations, yet there has been no parallel development to advance the communication and cooperation of churches in and beyond the Pentecostal movement.

The *most celebrated self-description* among Pentecostals in the West is found in the ecumenical concept of "koinonia"—a New Testament idea of the fellowship of believers rooted in the Trinitarian communion of God.[55] Formulated in large part in conversations between classical Pentecostals and Roman Catholics, ecumenical perspectives on "koinonia" have become a widely accepted and fruitful basis for approaching a shared understanding of the church.[56] For Pentecostals, the church already exists in "koinonia" due to the divine action manifested in the

52. Vondey, *Beyond Pentecostalism*, 155–57.
53. See Anderson, *Vision of the Disinherited*, 192–94.
54. Anderson, *Vision of the Disinherited*, 194.
55. See Macchia, "Nature and Purpose," 243–55.
56. See "Perspectives on *Koinonia*," 133–58.

outpouring of the Holy Spirit. This pneumatological understanding of Christian unity implies for Pentecostals a shared life in the Spirit and a common manifestation of spiritual gifts that exists not merely in the abstract ideal but in the concrete historical reality of the Christian life.[57] The neglect of this emphasis in the churches catholic remains for many Pentecostals the strongest obstacle to ecumenical participation. The large majority of this sentiment stems from convictions generally uninformed by detailed ecumenical discussions. Pentecostals worldwide exhibit a rather weak ecumenical pedagogy, although they certainly are not alone in its tangible expressions.

The *experience of church* remains the most central contribution to formulations of Pentecostal ecclesiology. There exist a variety of experiences of "koinonia" among Pentecostals, even within the limited scope of this essay, that are often determined by the level of submission to ecclesial authority, institutional communication and cooperation, existing church structures and processes.[58] On a more pragmatic level, ecumenical participation often depends on the negative or positive influences that have shaped a person's self-understanding. Pentecostals allow for change and transition between different perspectives and ecumenical attitudes as part of arriving at their own self-understanding that is still emerging.[59] For the larger ecumenical community, this fluctuation is sometimes perceived as an inherent instability that prevents concrete achievements and long-lasting relationships. This perspective runs the risk of divorcing Pentecostalism from the common endeavor for Christian unity. Isolated from the ecumenical movement, Pentecostals will not arrive at a consensus on the global Pentecostal identity.

Formulations of Pentecostal ecclesiology remain an effort in transition. Most attempts to formulate a theology of the church are made from the perspective of the First World. Since Pentecostalism itself has not remained a defined ecclesiastical entity, efforts in Pentecostal ecclesiology are indebted to the diverse representations and streams of Pentecostal groups in the West (although global Pentecostalism exhibits similar characteristics). This movement of transition internal to Pentecostalism affects the self-understanding of Pentecostals externally among the churches. For example, among classical Pentecostals, the church traditionally stands for a self-governing, self-supporting, and

57. Macchia, "Nature and Purpose," 243–55.
58. See "Perspectives on *Koinonia*," 150–53.
59. See Vondey, "Pentecostal Perspectives," 55–68.

self-propagating body that proclaims an unchanging gospel to all cultures and contexts.[60] The expansion of classical Pentecostalism and the rise of new Pentecostal streams have turned the focus to the further contextualization of the church on the grassroots level in order to remain relevant and meaningful. In contrast, the ecclesiology of the charismatic movement is largely shaped by the mother church in which it is able to unfold. The ethos of Pentecostalism as a movement is upheld in these contexts by relating the charismatic revival to the historical life of the church rather than its abstract essence. Put differently, Pentecostalism is understood as a new movement in the church or the church in movement but not as the church itself.[61] The neo-Pentecostal movement has shifted Pentecostal ecclesiology again into quite opposite directions and much closer to a free church theology.[62] The notion of movement is here synonymous with a diachronic plurality of the churches in a framework of ecclesial interdependence where churches operate under a universal outpouring of the Holy Spirit that changes and varies from congregation to congregation and is more closely aligned with a personal confession of faith.[63] Global Pentecostalism does not propose one particular structure of movement but suggests that "church" is experienced in a diversity of rhythms, beliefs, and practices.

The *future of Pentecostal ecclesiology* faces at least two major challenges. First, there exists no consistent, historical definition of the term "church" among Pentecostals worldwide. Whereas the established Christian traditions possess long-standing accounts of the nature and purpose of the church, Pentecostals do not share a common idea and theology of the body of Christ.[64] Second, the diversity of Pentecostal perspectives on the church allows at best for multiple theologies of the church that reflect both the tensions within the Pentecostal movement and the challenges of ecumenical reconciliation. Pentecostals have entered a phase of ecumenical pragmatism—an intermediate stage on the way to more genuine Pentecostal forms of participation.[65] Contemporary approaches to ecumenism slowly move beyond Anglo-European dominance to broader international participation and ecumenical organization that address the

60. See Hodges, *Theology of the Church*, 40–67.
61. Mühlen, "Kirche in Bewegung," 22–25.
62. See Volf, *After Our Likeness*, 127–282.
63. Volf, *After Our Likeness*, 228–33.
64. See Kärkkäinen, *Introduction to Ecclesiology*, 68–78.
65. Vondey, "Presuppositions for Pentecostal Engagement," 344–58.

concerns of the broader Pentecostal community.⁶⁶ Reasons that this development is filled with tensions should not be sought in the pluralistic image of Pentecostal ecclesiology alone but rather in the absence of opportunities for Pentecostals to define themselves as Pentecostals among the churches. Doctrinal agreement and organizational unity are not in the immediate purview of the forum. Rather more modest goals exist to contribute to mutual understanding, to encourage communication, to overcome existing stereotypes, and to build up ecumenical communion. While Pentecostalism has from the outset been an ecumenical movement, the contours, organizational, and institutional shape of ecumenical fellowship with Pentecostals is still very much in development.

PENTECOSTAL THEOLOGY AND THE UNITY OF THE CHRISTIAN LIFE

In this final section, I suggest that there exists a point of convergence between the local and the global dimension of Pentecostalism in the social activism of the movement. For the sake of argument of the glocalization of Pentecostalism, the purview is expanded slightly beyond the West to the Southern Hemisphere. In this broader context, sociological studies suggest that Pentecostalism can be perceived as an active and participatory, voluntary, and transformative movement directed toward egalitarian ideals.⁶⁷ There exists among Pentecostals worldwide a large group that might be termed "progressive Pentecostals" oriented toward social transformation.⁶⁸ This emphasis is a direct result of the practical application of Pentecostal theology. The progressive groups often understand social engagement as a direct mandate from God, exemplified in the Scriptures, and a normative element of the Christian life. Although Pentecostalism can be seen as a mechanism associated with social change across the entire range of socioeconomic conditions, a significant characteristic of these groups is the personal experience of poverty, deprivation, oppression, and persecution.⁶⁹ Among the poor, Pentecostalism is seen as a form of religious participation in the sociocultural reality that affords new and effective means to cope with and to overcome economic

---

66. See Vondey, *Continuing and Building Relationships*, 1–26.
67. See Vondey, *Pentecostalism*, 89–131.
68. See Miller and Yamamori, *Global Pentecostalism*, 31–34.
69. Gerlach and Hine, *People, Power, Change*, xxii–xxiii.

and political oppression. In some cases, both elements together shape a highly activist, even revolutionary attitude against the status quo. More stable and traditional environments see Pentecostalism as a vehicle to address concerns of human development by those not immediately suffering from social, political, or economic oppression but identifying with a concern for the poor and the persecuted.

At least in principle, a combination of these mechanisms forms the seedbed for social engagement among progressive Pentecostal groups worldwide that have led to *explicit social engagement*. Consistent models include emergency services (response to earthquakes and floods), medical assistance (including medical response to disasters, preventive care, drug rehabilitation programs, psychological services, and establishing health and dental clinics), educational programs (especially schools and day care), economic development (including job training, housing development, urban development programs, youth programs, and microenterprise loans), mercy ministries (such as homeless shelters, food banks, clothing services, and services to the elderly), counseling services (assisting cases of addiction, pregnancy, divorce, depression, or prison ministries), policy change (with focus on monitoring elections, opposing corruption, or advocating a living wage), and services in the arts (with training in music, drama, and dance).[70] Nonetheless, a consistent theological foundation for these social engagements among progressive Pentecostals has yet to be formulated. Such a basis could provide a central connection between Pentecostals in the West and non-Western perspectives and therefore allow for an expansion of Western ecumenical perspectives to Pentecostalism worldwide.

From a Western *theological perspective*, Pentecostal commitment to the unity of the Christian life is derived from the self-understanding of Pentecostals as an eschatological movement of the Holy Spirit. The outpouring of the Holy Spirit without partiality is interpreted as both gift and mandate. As a gift from God, Pentecostals are convinced that the modern-day Pentecost marks the beginning of the end time, an eschatological signpost for the imminent return of Christ, the judgment of the world, and the new creation.[71] The universal gift of the Spirit is the final invitation to a dying world to receive salvation, sanctification, empowerment, and healing in the last days. For Pentecostals, the outpouring of

---

70. Miller and Yamamori, *Global Pentecostalism*, 41–43.
71. See Faupel, *Everlasting Gospel*, 187–227.

the Spirit penetrates the last dominion of Satan, demonic strongholds throughout the world including governments, political structures, destructive public and social organizations, false religions, oppression, poverty, and persecution. No places, publics, or persons are excluded from the fulfillment of the promises of God heralded by the coming of the Holy Spirit. As social mandate, Pentecostals see themselves as harbingers of the outpouring of the Spirit to the ends of the earth. The baptism of the Spirit is seen as the source of divine power available to everyone for the sanctification, conversion, and salvation of the whole world.[72] In turn, the outpouring of the Spirit is the sign that this mandate had been received around the globe. This mandate to share the universal availability of the Holy Spirit with the world marks the heartbeat of Pentecostal theology worldwide. Since the Spirit has been poured out on all, the mandate is service to all—ministry to the children and youth, adults, and the elderly, men and women, the sick, the dying, the homeless, natives, immigrants, businesses, schools, hospitals, the unevangelized, and those who have heard the gospel but know nothing of the power of the Spirit.[73] The conviction of the outpouring of the Spirit on all flesh inspires, at least in expectation and enthusiasm, an environment of democratic, egalitarian ideals. In its outward manifestation, the ideal of the outpouring of the Spirit on "all flesh" is seen as bursting open the chains of social, economic, political, and religious segregation.

The application of Pentecostal theology to the Christian life follows the propagation of egalitarian ideals and the struggle with their contradictions. Put negatively, for Pentecostals, the promise of the Spirit is given not exclusively to one society or nation; it is not limited to the political, economic, cultural, or religious elite, the church or the believer, the priest or the clergy, the educated, the adult, man or woman. Put positively, the outpouring of the Spirit makes possible the engagement of all creation and therefore its ultimate reconciliation with God.[74] Pentecostals understand themselves as a prophetic voice announcing the final transformation in the relationship of God and the world in which the whole of creation is subject to the presence and activity of God's Spirit. "Pentecost" in this sense becomes a watchword for the transformation of creation, its conversion and empowerment to participate in the Spirit's

---

72. McGee, *Miracles, Missions*, 101–18.
73. See Miller and Yamamori, *Global Pentecostalism*, 39–128.
74. Yong, *Spirit Poured Out*, 292–301.

redemption. At least theologically, the participation of creation in this redemptive process knows no boundaries.

The *central notion* underlying the theological commitment to social action is the prophethood of all believers, an idea similar to the Protestant emphasis on the priesthood of the faithful but with expanded focus on the mobilization of all people for the preaching of the gospel, mission, evangelization, the healing of the sick, prophecy, exorcism, and the exercise of other spiritual gifts. The prophethood of all believers emphasizes the charismatic functions of anyone who is subject to the anointing of the Holy Spirit regardless of social, economic, religious, or cultural status. Gender, age, race, ethnicity, or education are not indicative of the anointing of the Spirit and therefore do not imply a measure of authority, vocation, or position. At least from a Western perspective, the prophethood of all believers functions in an original "protestant" sense as a countercultural critique that exposes existing ecclesiastical structures as restricting the full participation of all believers in the body of Christ.[75] The universal outpouring of the Spirit, captured in the image of Spirit baptism, inspires a reinterpretation and reconstruction of the world, frequently offering a critical, biblical, political, theological, and ethical alternative to the established institutional patterns of the orthodox establishment that favor more restrictive forms of participation and authority. The prophetic function of the underprivileged, particularly the ministry of women as well as those with no formal clerical training or those who previously held priestly functions in non-Christian religions, has posed severe challenges to the established institutions.[76] The challenges pertain not only to the integration of charismatic manifestations in all churches but to the role and extent of participation in the church's service and ministry by those who manifest such gifts regardless of the dictates of class, society, history, tradition, and culture. In other words, the realization of Pentecostal egalitarian ideals requires their tangible manifestation as practices of equality among all believers in the body of Christ.

The concrete realization of Pentecostal ideals has encountered *significant challenges* and resistance not only among Pentecostal groups worldwide. The demand to put into practice the breadth of equality, impartiality, and democracy demanded by Pentecostal theology has met considerable difficulties. The Pentecostal movement in North America,

---

75. See Macchia, "Tongues as a Sign," 61–76.
76. See Barfoot and Sheppard, "Prophetic vs. Priestly Religion," 2–17.

for example, has significantly changed its attitude during the twentieth century from a dominant pacifism to the support of war.[77] While these positions are more clearly defined, there exist few Pentecostal positions on the care for the creation.[78] Whatever the state of involvement, opportunities to become a pioneer for issues of social justice were squandered, and the movement is torn between its idealistic intentions and the reality of complicity, among other things, in racial segregation, gender discrimination, nationalism, consumerism, and triumphalism.[79] Failure to reconcile intentions and practices of reconciliation has further contributed to critical questions of the movement's overall concern for issues of social justice, especially in the West.[80] In the First World, the perplexity of this situation is best explained by shifting attention to the factors that contribute to the coexistence of egalitarian ideals and their practical counterparts in Pentecostal communities. The result is a great deal of ambivalence spread throughout the Pentecostal movement.

Contemporary Pentecostalism in the West displays an ambivalent *social consciousness*. Any attempt to construct a homogeneous theology of Pentecostal social ethics inevitably results in the misleading assumption that either egalitarianism or triumphalism is dominant or that the tensions between both sides are negligible. The local and particular forms of the movement typically contain Pentecostals that are rather indifferent toward social justice, peace, and the conservation of creation. What we find among Pentecostals is not only a wide range of attitudes toward social engagement but also a social consciousness in transition that has become characteristic of the state of affairs of the young movement worldwide. A proper assessment of Pentecostal theology therefore must take into account the dominant extremes as well as the position of ambivalence, ignorance, and shifting allegiances. The engagement of Pentecostal theology with social, economic, and political issues is not static; it is highly dependent on existing conditions, dominant cultural perspectives, economic developments, political leadership, religious examples and the corresponding desires for acceptance and effectiveness or reformation and

---

77. See Alexander, *Peace to War*, 293–328.

78. See Yong, *Spirit Renews*, xi–xxiii.

79. See Vondey, *Pentecostalism*, 119–24; Horn, "From Human Rights," 213–27; Martin, "Pentecostal Gender Paradox," 52–66; Poewe-Hexham and Hexham, "Charismatic Churches and Apartheid," 73–83; MacRobert, *Black Roots*, 60–76.

80. Kärkkäinen, "Are Pentecostals Oblivious," 387–404.

change. Hence, Pentecostal groups exhibit sometimes a radical break and at other times a gradual shift in social involvement.

Pentecostal involvement in social, economic, and political issues of the Christian life can be stereotyped as active or passive, progressive or regressive, accommodative or counter-cultural.[81] A one-sided perspective of the movement's social engagement will likely capture a large portion of the Pentecostal social ethos. However, neglect of the tangible differences and shifts in the movement's social consciousness fail to account for both the oppositional forces present among Pentecostals as well as the diverse range of socioeconomic and political modalities among Pentecostals worldwide. A view inclusive of the tensions does not have the luxury to speak of a single Pentecostal social ethics but instead of a Pentecostal view of the Christian life that is multifarious, ambiguous, and, at times, contradictory.

If these characterizations are correct, then the *transitional nature* of the social consciousness and behavior of modern-day Pentecostalism is not temporary but here to stay. Even when there is evidence that Pentecostal social ethics are solidifying under pressure of socialization, institutionalization, and secularization (especially in the West), the resulting expressions cannot be seen as normative for the theology of the entire movement.[82] This pluralistic identity should not be understood as relativism, that is, an intentional lack of direction and decision-making. It is perhaps more adequately identified as a form of "prophetic activism" that has come to include progressive and conservative means of Christian social engagement.[83] As prophetic, Pentecostal social activism takes place in the "borderlands" of globalization, internationalization, urbanization, and industrialization.[84] In these places, the forms of social engagement are as varied as the challenges. Pentecostalism is still in the process of finding an ethical methodology that is genuine to the different faces of the movement and enables them to respond to the reality and crisis of pluralism characteristic of the twenty-first-century world.[85] The worldwide economic downturn and various dramatic socioeconomic and political changes since the end of the twentieth century have contributed to a widening of these borderlands across the globe. The

81. See Yong, *Days of Caesar*, 3–38.
82. See Vondey, *Beyond Pentecostalism*, 182–91.
83. See Slessarev-Jamir, *Prophetic Activism*, 1–34.
84. Slessarev-Jamir, *Prophetic Activism*, 22–26.
85. See Wariboko, *Pentecostal Principle*, 161–95.

corresponding need to face the various social struggles in these transitional contexts anticipates the further spread of Pentecostalism in its diverse range from social activism to triumphalism.

CONCLUSION

This brief survey of the unity and coherence of Pentecostal theology in the West offers a simplified but nonetheless suggestive image of the character of Pentecostal thought on a larger scale. Contemporary theology among Pentecostals is in transition, and its manifold expressions cannot be easily applied to the entire movement or seen as normative for the manner and expression of Pentecostal thought. Nonetheless, if the preceding survey is suggestive of traits in the larger Pentecostal movement worldwide, these qualities will undoubtedly surface in the local and the global dimensions of Pentecostal theology during the twenty-first century. From a worldwide ecumenical perspective, Pentecostal theology may be characterized with the helpful metaphor of play.[86] On one level, this metaphor suggests that Pentecostal thought is spontaneous, improvisational, and playful. Worship and witness are more important to Pentecostals than propositional statements and formal doctrine. On another level, the metaphor of play indicates the distinction of Pentecostal thought from traditional theological forms. There exists a certain unwillingness among Pentecostals to engage in the use of terms, concepts, and authoritative statements that dictate the formulation of their proposals and experiences. On a third level, play suggests that Pentecostals try to imagine anew traditional theological categories in ways that describe creatively and effectively their own experiences and convictions. Pentecostal theology is still very much searching for the form and method that are true to the Pentecostal ethos in general. Existing theological efforts are provisional and programmatic, albeit consistent with central themes that mark the Pentecostal identity. Finally, the metaphor of play also expresses a substantial unity of Pentecostal thought and method. This unity, although characterized by a diversity of voices, allows us to speak of Pentecostal theology as a singular and unified phenomenon that can be recognized and engaged in ecumenical conversation. Pentecostals seek this conversation with substantial and often seemingly provocative proposals. At this point,

---

86. See Vondey, *Beyond Pentecostalism*, 171–201.

it may be helpful to interpret Pentecostal theology as an *invitation* to engage in the joyful and mysterious sharing of theological gifts that are manifested in different ways among the ecumenical community. How this invitation is shaped by the global Pentecostal communities remains to be seen. Although the influence of Western Pentecostalism is great, worldwide Pentecostalism exhibits different varieties and often sharper distinctions in theology and praxis that are more difficult to reconcile with one another and with the ecumenical world. The particular gift of Pentecostal theology may still need to be named, but it is apparent that Pentecostals wish to contribute to the ecumenical world in a manner that appreciates, challenges, and expands the theological horizon of the body of Christ through the voice of the Holy Spirit.

2

The Hierarchy of Truths and Pentecostal Identity

AMNESIA IS THE TOTAL or partial loss of memory.[1] Questions such as where you come from, where you belong, or what your purpose is no longer create an immediate reality and recognizable identity. Postmodernism[2] has created a somewhat universal amnesia. The postmodern worldview, with its narcissistic individualism, pluralism, deconstructionism, and loss of common consciousness, has gradually reduced the essential means by which we have identified ourselves in the past. The lack of common "identifiers" has often found an expression in the now global question, "Who in the world am I?"

In this context of global uncertainties one group has provided the world with elements of stability: stable growth, growing significance, significant change—the Pentecostal movement. But Pentecostalism is plagued by the same problems. As the eighteenth Pentecostal World Conference in Seoul (1998) acknowledged, at the beginning of the

---

1. This essay was presented at the twenty-ninth meeting of the Society for Pentecostal Studies, Kirkland, Washington, March 18, 2000. I am particularly referring to the concept of "cultural memory," defined by Assmann, *Kulturelle Gedächtnis*, 22–45, 77. See now, Assmann, *Cultural Memory*.

2. I use the term "postmodern" as an expression of the sociological, philosophical, and aesthetical transformation beginning in the last part of the nineteenth century.

twenty-first century the question "Who in the world are Pentecostals?"[3] has become one of the most significant issues. That this realization comes from Asia should not surprise us. A concept has developed at the end of the twentieth century that too easily divided the religious world of Pentecostals, among others into North American Pentecostalism, European Pentecostalism, and Asian Pentecostalism. Yet, particularly in Asia, the expression of Pentecostalism can differ greatly from one country to another as the result of a different cultural and historical development of Pentecostal churches and leadership and the subsequent formulation of a congruent Pentecostal theology. The situation in Asia is paradigmatic for the worldwide situation of Pentecostalism. It expresses the most urgent question Pentecostals are facing today: What is the global identity of the Pentecostal movement?

Attaining answers to these questions has become increasingly difficult. In addition to the question of global Pentecostal self-consciousness, there is also a growing awareness of a lack of terminology in order to adequately express the distinctive impressions and experiences of Pentecostalism to those outside of the movement.[4] As a consequence, the distinctive elements of the movement are often misrepresented, its theological message misinterpreted, and its significance misjudged. A solution to the problems is not located in Asia, North America, or Europe alone. Pentecostals need to learn about themselves together in a global context. They may find that behind their different expressions lies a common foundation for a global Pentecostal identity. I want to suggest that the postmodern problem of Pentecostalism is one of memory. The "identifiers" of the past are no longer sufficient to adequately establish and preserve Pentecostal identity in the present. Pentecostals need an appropriate "system" that will allow them to determine and describe their global and ecumenical existence. I submit that the notion of the "hierarchy of truths" is helpful in this endeavor. Thus, I will first introduce the concept and evaluate it in regard to its usefulness as an ecumenical tool and for approaching Pentecostal identity. I will then apply the concept to distinctive themes of Pentecostalism and, in a final

---

3. Menzies listed this question among the most significant issues in "Frontiers in Theology." Robeck Jr. focused on the problem in "Making Sense of Pentecostalism." See also Johns, "Adolescence of Pentecostalism," 3–18.

4. The lack of theological expression has been recognized by many Pentecostal and non-Pentecostal scholars. Some who voiced this critique are Jürgen Moltmann, Michael Welker, Miroslav Volf, and others mentioned in this study.

step, suggest how this is valuable for the preservation and communication of the Pentecostal tradition.

A HERMENEUTIC OF THE "HIERARCHY OF TRUTHS"

In 1990, a study document of the Joint Working Group (JWG) of the World Council of Churches and the Roman Catholic Church took up the notion of the "hierarchy of truths" (*hierarchia veritatum*), as it had been introduced in the Second Vatican's Council's *Decree on Ecumenism* (1964).[5] The concept was received by many with high hopes for its implications in ecumenical dialogue. Several books and over forty articles and essays have appeared devoted to the issue; some even considered it "the most revolutionary to be found."[6] The concept is understood as an instrument of common discernment that assists the ecumenical endeavor by "more adequately assessing expressions of the truth of revelation, their interrelation, their necessity, and the possible diversity of formulations."[7] This suggests ecumenical dialogue "based upon a communion in the 'foundation' that already exists and will point the way to that ordering of priorities that makes possible gradual growth into full [visible] communion."[8] If understood this way, the *hierarchia veritatum* is indeed valuable not only for an ecumenical appreciation of Pentecostal identity but also for an evaluation of distinctive Pentecostal themes as part of that identity. A common understanding of the concept appears to be one of its primary presuppositions. The post-conciliar literature suggests, however, that the ecumenical use of the concept must begin with a proper hermeneutic of its terms.

The study document of the JWG points to the history of the church as evidence for the existence of a certain hierarchical understanding of truths.[9] The foundation of this hierarchy is the "mystery of Jesus Christ"[10]

---

5. "Notion of Hierarchy," 561–62.

6. Cullmann, "Comments on the Decree," 93–94; also Schlink, "Hierarchie der Wahrheiten," 36–48.

7. "Notion of Hierarchy," 569.

8. "Notion of Hierarchy," 568.

9. This has been confirmed in Valeske, *Hierarchia Veritatum*, 69–187. Several studies have pointed out historical precedents in Scripture and the history of Christian theology; see the overview by Henn, "Hierarchy of Truths," 439–71.

10. Suggestions to express the mystery have been the *Kyrios Christos* or early creeds

as the fundamental truth to which all other elements of the hierarchy are related in different ways.[11] This indicates "an order of importance ... according to the greater or lesser proximity"[12] that doctrines have to that foundation. It will be imperative to begin with a clarification of the terminology employed, particularly of the central terms "hierarchy" and "truth," in order to facilitate the use of the concept for Pentecostalism.

A systematic treatise of the concept of "truth" as it relates to the understanding of truth in general and the relation of revelation, faith, dogma, and doctrine has yet to be produced.[13] In a postmodern context, it will be increasingly difficult to work out a common, universal apparatus with which the concept of "truth" is ecumenically approached. Nevertheless, there seems to exist a certain agreement among scholars that not all truth is of the same significance.[14] Andrea Pangrazio, who introduced the concept at Vatican II, distinguished between truths that belong to the order of the end and those that belong to the order of the means of salvation.[15] Oscar Cullmann distinguished between pure and impure truths,[16] Yves Congar between truths of explicit faith and truths of implicit agreement,[17] Karl Rahner between truths necessary for and others not necessary for salvation,[18] Patrick O'Connell between an ontological reality and an epistemological order of truths,[19] Wolfgang Dietzfelbinger between central and marginal truths,[20] and Edmund Schlink between eternal truth and the historical expressions of truth.[21]

---

of Scripture (1 Cor 15:3–8; Phil 2:5–11), the Apostolic Creed, the Nicene-Constantinopolitan Creed, and others.

11. "Notion of Hierarchy," 564.

12. "Notion of Hierarchy," 564–65.

13. Lowery approached the relation of doctrine and dogma as part of the concept in "Hierarchy of Truths."

14. Cardona, "'Jerarchia de las verdades,'" 150–59, emphasizes that all truths are true regardless of their hierarchical position, that they are further interrelated to such an extent that a hierarchical order may become a "suicidal vivisection" (*vivisección suicida*).

15. Pangrazio, "Mystery," 188–92. Pangrazio was criticized later for placing the ecclesiology on a different level than Christology and the doctrine of the Trinity; see Houtepen, "*Hierarchia Veritatum* and Orthodoxy," 39–52.

16. Cullmann, "Einheit in der Vielfalt," 363–64.

17. Congar, "Articles fondamentaux," 868–82.

18. Rahner uses the term "heilsnotwendig" in "Dogma," 439–40.

19. O'Connell, "Hierarchy of Truths," 86.

20. Dietzfelbinger, "Hierarchie der Wahrheiten," 619–24; also Schoonenberg, "Historiciteit en interpretatie," 293–98.

21. Schlink, "Hierarchie der Wahrheiten," 1–12.

Several things are noteworthy in this debate. First, not all truths are considered as of the same "weight."[22] Second, the hierarchy of truths is a hermeneutical tool for the qualitative assessment of that "weight" including the reevaluation of particular doctrines.[23] Third, there is a common search for a possible "objective" rationale for the ordering of truths[24] depending on their relation to a central and fundamental truth.[25] Fourth, an adequate ordering of truths must also consider the importance of the church's ongoing penetration into the revealed mystery.[26] Finally, no element of truth must be excluded from the whole of the hierarchy.[27]

"Hierarchy today is widely under attack," as Terrence L. Nichols noted recently.[28] However, the "crucial question is not: should there be hierarchy? Rather it is: what kind of hierarchy should there be, and how should it be structured?"[29] "Hierarchy" implies both relationship and order among truths. This relationship is governed by a certain "foundation" in relation to which all other doctrines are ordered. Even though all "those elements which make up the Church must be kept with equal fidelity not all of them are of equal importance."[30] The *Decree on Ecumenism* employed two terms as aids for conceptualizing this hierarchical relationship of truths: the term "foundation" and the term "link" (*nexus*).

Any description of the foundation on a conceptual level, so the recommendation of the JWG, "should refer to the person and mystery of Jesus Christ."[31] This endeavor, however, is limited because "no one formula can fully grasp or express its reality."[32] As a result, there is no ecumenical

---

22. Lowery distinguished four views of modern scholarship that: (1) doctrines are unrelated to revealed truth; (2) doctrines are equal to revealed truths; (3) there are essential and non-essential truths; and (4) there are foundational and nonfoundational truths. See Lowery, "Hierarchy of Truths," 3–14.

23. See Schoonenberg, "Historiciteit," 296–98. Schützeichel, "Hierarchische Denken," 97, even considered it a principle of form (*Gestaltungsprinzip*) for all of theology.

24. A transcendental, objective rationale not based on the content of truths, suggested Mühlen, "Lehre des Vaticanum II," 303–35.

25. See Froitzheim, "Logische Vorüberlegungen zum Thema," 456.

26. See Jelly, "Marian Dogmas," 19–40.

27. See Jelly, "St. Thomas' Theological Interpretation," 226.

28. Nichols, *All May Be One*, 5.

29. Nichols, *All May Be One*, 7.

30. Pangrazio, "Mystery," 191.

31. "Notion of Hierarchy," 566.

32. "Notion of Hierarchy," 565–66.

consensus as to what precisely should be identified as that foundation,[33] and it will be one of the foremost ecumenical tasks of the coming decades to move beyond a silent agreement to an adequately voiced description. For the purpose of this study, I suggest the following description: Jesus of Nazareth, born, crucified and raised for the church, in his inseparable and coequal relation with the Father and the Holy Spirit.[34]

Another question which also has not been adequately explored is how other elements of Christian faith are then related to that foundation in Christ and to each another. This lack of definition suggests that various principles of evaluating and ordering truths are, in fact, permissible.[35] Such an understanding seems consistent with the Roman Catholic view that "almost everyone, *though in different ways*, longs for the one visible church of God."[36] The question is, however, whether there is not one particular direction from which one can best approach the concept.

This question of *directionality* seems to be most important in the discussion of the relationship of truths. The literature on the hierarchy of truths shows this common agreement: that truths are ordered in their relation to the foundation and not vice versa. This does not deny a mutual relation between that foundation and other truths; however, this agreement underlines that it is in the nature of the mystery that it cannot be grasped in its entirety, its temporality, and relationality. Any communal[37] approach to a Pentecostal "hierarchy of truths" should therefore begin not with the foundation but the elements distinctive of the Pentecostal tradition.

---

33. Some suggest to order doctrines on the basis of the degree of their explicitness in Scripture, others based on their necessity for salvation, and again others on the basis of their psychological or sociological functioning in a person's belief system; see Tavard, "Hierarchia Veritatum," 439–71.

34. This definition aims to include Trinitarian, ecclesiological, and soteriological aspects; see these aspects in *Dei Verbum* 2, 4, 7, 15; Rahner, "Geheimnis," 596; Mühlen, "Bedeutung der Differenz," 200–205; Schützeichel, "Hierarchische Denken," 101–3; also Aquinas, *Summa Theologica*, II-II, q. 1, art. 6 ad. 1 and II, q. 1, art. 8, c, as well as the Nicene-Constantinopolitan Creed.

35. Among the various criteria suggested are Scripture, tradition, creeds, the church fathers, the liturgy, the official teaching of the church, and the *sensus fidelium*; see Thils, "Colloque sur le thème," 247–48.

36. *Decree on Ecumenism*, 1 (emphasis added). Translation taken from Flannery, *Vatican Council II*, 499–523.

37. Balthasar has warned that it must never be an individual who determines "what is central and what is peripheral," in *Truth Is Symphonic*, 76.

EVALUATION OF THE CONCEPT *HIERARCHIA VERITATUM*

Inadequate and inconsistent use of terminology is largely responsible for the ecumenical neglect of the otherwise valuable concept of a *hierarchia veritatum*. The term "hierarchy" involves several problematic issues that are, in fact, inimical to the ecumenical spirit of the overall concept. First, "hierarchy" designates a strict and fixed system or systems of order[38] in which the inferior are subject to the superior in their relation to the highest—not the lowest or the central—element; the term "foundation" therefore seems inadequate. Second, a hierarchy allows for an open, indefinite continuum to the lowest but only for a limited, definite continuum to the highest element. This does not explicitly rule out the exclusion of some elements from the "fundamental" order or even the dispensability of others from the whole system. Further, the consistent use of the hierarchical concept may lead to the application of the principle of subordination also at the very top of the structure, that is, at the "fundamental" truth. The result of this can be a hardening of the hierarchical structure to the point of ecumenical incompatibility. Third, hierarchy explains the interrelatedness of elements only in terms of their subordination but not in regard to their overall function as part of the whole. Yet scholars who referred to the fundamental truth as the ordering principle have repeatedly called for another, second principle of interrelatedness.[39] Finally, the concept suggests a relation of different hierarchies at the top but allows for a relation of the whole only in terms of either non-integrating tolerance[40] or the complete integration, and thus disintegration, of one hierarchy into another.[41] These shortcomings suggest that the term "hierarchy" is

---

38. Henn suggested several spatial images of which only the linear (the high point in a continuum) but not a circular, organic, or structural correspond to the historical and etymological reality of the term. See Henn, "Hierarchy of Truths," 440. Several other authors have employed the latter images and preferred a redefinition of hierarchy rather than a change of terminology. Nichols suggests a "participatory model" similar to my suggestion of a *corpus*; Nichols, *All May Be One*, 14–20.

39. Witte, *Alnaargelang hun band*, 222, sees a significant move away from a single principle in *Mysterium ecclesiae*. Congar established a perspective of subjective and objective truth in *Diversity and Communion*, 126–33, 212–16. Cullmann places the hierarchy in a larger concept of the diversity and plurality of charisms in "Einheit in der Vielfalt," 356–64.

40. Often under use of the euphemism "unity in (reconciled) diversity."

41. See the ecumenical terminology "organic union" and "corporate union" quoted in Rusch and Gros, *Deepening Communion*, 20–24, which they draw from

inadequate as an expression of the overall idea. In order to protect the general concept, I suggest instead the use of the term "body" (*corpus*)[42] as it embraces the ecumenical understanding of the concept both in Scripture and throughout Christian history.

The term *corpus veritatum* protects the general concept and offers several advantages. First, it implies an organic,[43] variable system over against a strict, hierarchical one. Second, the use of the terms "foundation," "core," and "center" are adequate here in that they point to the main truth as the central and foundational, that is, life-giving and sustaining element: the mystery of Christ. Third, *corpus* underlines the indispensability of all elements of the body. The use of the term in 1 Cor 12 further suggests that the ordering of truths may happen on a fluctuating scale that weighs expressions of truths according to their relative function at a given moment in order "that there should be no schism in the body, but that the members should have the same care for one another."[44] The term "body" allows for this kind of evaluation. Fourth, *corpus* implies a particular relationship of individual truths to both the life-giving center as well as to other elements. Finally, the scriptural ideals of marriage and koinonia, stressed often by Pentecostals, invite the idea of ecumenical union of different bodies of truths. With this re-formulation of the terminology involved, the basic understanding of the original concept has been preserved and purified, and it can now be applied to the question of Pentecostal identity.

TOWARD A PENTECOSTAL *CORPUS VERITATUM*

Since the rise of modern classical Pentecostalism in the early twentieth century,[45] the majority of approaches to the identity of the movement in North America have focused on its most distinctive feature: the practice

---

the commissioned dialogue documents collected in *Facing Unity: Models, Forms, and Phases of Catholic–Lutheran Church Fellowship*.

42. Of course, we may consider the body as a form of hierarchy: see the following for a hierarchical view of organism: Nichols, *All May Be One*, 14–20; Polanyi, *Knowing and Being*; Weiss, "Living Systems," 3–55; Sheldrake, *Presence of the Past*, 95.

43. See Congar, *Diversity and Communion*, 151.

44. 1 Cor 12:25.

45. Following Synan's entry on "Classical Pentecostalism" in *New International Dictionary*, 219–22, the term is used to distinguish early Pentecostal churches from later "neo" and "charismatic" Pentecostalism.

of speaking in tongues.[46] Efforts to assert a more characteristic identity and to contextualize the movement, however, are largely the late result of the growing charismatic movement in the 1960s, which forced classical Pentecostalism to deal with its own identity.[47] The visible outcome is a large amount of literature dealing with the theological, historical, or sociological themes distinctive to the movement.[48] A unifying and ordering principle of identity, however, is still missing. Pentecostal scholars recognized the need for an ordering principle only in the 1980s.[49] As one of the first, William Faupel approached the issue by using the theory of "complementary models."[50] He suggested that models "are symbolic representations of aspects of reality that are not directly observable to us."[51] He understood them as provisional yet helpful for providing a "more whole understanding of reality."[52] In other words, Faupel was looking for a principle that related Pentecostal doctrines to the central mystery.[53] He identified four motifs: the Full Gospel, the Latter Rain, the Apostolic Faith, and Pentecostal[54]—with particular emphasis on such distinctive themes as divine healing, miracles, Spirit baptism, and the second coming of Christ. Faupel's search for "a symbolic representation" of the mystery contained, unintentionally as it may have been, sacramental undertones that remained unrecognized.

In 1987, Donald W. Dayton pointed to a similar pattern to illuminate the theological roots of Pentecostalism: salvation, baptism in the

46. This was observed already by Dayton, "Theological Roots of Pentecostalism," 3.

47. The charismatic movement produced a large amount of literature; classical Pentecostalism began only subsequently to deal with the question of its own identity.

48. E.g., Dayton, *Theological Roots of Pentecostalism*; Land, *Pentecostal Spirituality*; Miller, "Social Movement," 97–114; Solivan, *Spirit, Pathos, and Liberation*.

49. The 1980s brought a shift in understanding that perceived the early years of modern Pentecostalism no longer as the infancy but the heart of the movement. With this agree Land, *Pentecostal Spirituality*, 26; Hollenweger, "Critical Tradition of Pentecostalism," 7–17; Faupel, *Everlasting Gospel*, 309; and Dempster, "Search for Pentecostal Identity," 1–8.

50. Faupel, "Function of 'Models,'" 51–71.

51. Faupel, "Function of 'Models,'" 70.

52. Faupel, "Function of 'Models,'" 70.

53. Others have followed. Harvey Cox suggested a re-formulation of the terms "experience" and "Spirit"; see Cox, *Fire from Heaven*, 300–321. Solivan recently suggested the concept of *orthopathos* as the ordering principle to relate orthodoxy and orthopraxy; see Solivan, *Spirit, Pathos, and Liberation*, 70–92.

54. These are the titles applied to the movement by early Pentecostals; Faupel, "Function of 'Models,'" 52.

Holy Spirit, divine healing, and the return of Christ.[55] Anti-Pentecostal literature[56] seems to confirm the weight of these four themes. More recently, similar Pentecostal themes were even classified as an ecumenical challenge.[57] Dayton suggests that these "themes are well-nigh universal within the movement, appearing . . . in all branches and varieties of Pentecostalism" and "could also be traced outside classical Pentecostalism in the Charismatic movement or 'neo-Pentecostalism' and perhaps in third-world manifestations."[58] What is the place of these themes in a Pentecostal *corpus veritatum*? The attempt to evaluate these themes merely with the category of religious experience will at this time allow only for a limited understanding of their significance. However, if we also examine the position they occupy in Pentecostal teaching and worship, we will be able to more fully appreciate the role of these themes within a Pentecostal body of truths.

The four themes must be understood as only representative of a much wider and more complex system of Pentecostal doctrines. Dayton's emphasis was on the theological roots of the movement. Pentecostalism was subsequently forced to reassess its identity and other themes were emphasized in their own right.[59] Recently, Harvey Cox pointed out several interrelated positive and negative characteristics of the movement;[60] Lamar Vest has suggested eight distinctives;[61] Cheryl Bridges Johns has outlined five elements of a mature Pentecostalism;[62] Cecil Robeck suggested three features.[63] The answer to the question "Who in the world are Pentecostals?" seems to lie in a definition of these distinctive elements. However, Pentecostals must also consider

---

55. Dayton, *Theological Roots of Pentecostalism*, 21–22; see also Dayton, "Theological Roots of Pentecostalism," 4.

56. See Ward, "Anti-Pentecostal Argument," 99–122; and Bittlinger, *Papst und Pfingstler*, 10–16.

57. Moltmann and Kuschel, *Pentecostal Movements*, treat Spirit baptism, healing, tongues, prophecy, and praying in the Spirit, and a new congregationalism.

58. Dayton, *Theological Roots of Pentecostalism*, 21–22, 31.

59. See Faupel, *Everlasting Gospel*, 228–309. Additional themes were suggested by Frodsham, *With Signs Following*; see also Cox, *Fire from Heaven*, 81–160.

60. Cox, "Personal Reflections on Pentecostalism," 29–34.

61. Vest, *Spiritual Balance*, 35–36.

62. Johns, "Adolescence of Pentecostalism," 10–17.

63. Robeck, "Taking Stock of Pentecostalism," 35–60.

the question whether that which is *distinctive* to Pentecostalism is also *central* (life-giving) to the movement.[64]

The four-fold pattern allows us to approach Pentecostal identity on a substantial level. An early, clear expression of the Pentecostal themes is found in the writings of Aimee S. McPherson, who summarized them as follows: "Jesus saves us according to John 3:16. He baptizes us with the Holy Spirit according to Acts 2:4. He heals our bodies according to James 5:14–15. And Jesus is coming again to receive us unto Himself according to 1 Thessalonians 4:16–17."[65] This account places the four themes in a threefold order. First, the center is the person and work of Jesus of Nazareth. Second, the themes are placed distinct from this center at a certain distance. They are "not a goal to be reached . . . but a door [to] . . . a greater fullness of life in the Spirit."[66] Third, the themes are related to the center through a specific link: the gospel. Scripture occupies an intermediate position between the center and the four distinctive elements of Pentecostalism. The question is in what way the scriptures relate the four themes to the central mystery.

McPherson's summary suggests that the biblical scriptures relate the four elements of Pentecostal experience to the central mystery through the activity of the life-giving center; in other words, through the *subjectivity* of the mystery of Christ and the *objectivity* of the distinctive Pentecostal experiences. This means, for example, that divine healing receives its position in a Pentecostal *corpus veritatum* through the subjectivity of the mystery of Christ rather than its own, inherent and relative degree of power, effectiveness, or frequency. In other words, the *directionality* is from Christ to the Pentecostal themes and not vice versa. However, Pentecostals determine the significance of the four themes still generally by their manifestations, or modes of temporality, that is, their directionality to Christ.

In 1994 Ralph Del Colle explored this directionality. As one example of the fourfold pattern, he suggested that "Spirit-Baptism incorporates the various modes of temporality in the divine experience."[67] He further suggests a certain incongruity: "The eternality of God as timelessness . . . creates and incorporates in the divine life the variable

---

64. Dabney, "Saul's Armor," 115–46, suggests that not the fourfold theme but pneumatology as such is central to Pentecostalism.

65. Cox, *Four-Square Gospel*, 9.

66. The statement is taken from the unpublished report "Proposed Description," 38.

67. Del Colle, "Trinity and Temporality," 99–113.

possibilities of temporality in the created order," which, however, "we can . . . only partially realize."[68] In other words, the human experience is limited in its temporal perception of the divine; the directionality, I want to say, is opposite to that of a *corpus veritatum*. One result of this reversal is a certain disorder in the human perception and association of the divine mystery—a lack of "confirmation" of the divine order of truth in the temporality of human life, resulting in an ever-widening gap between the human experience of the divine temporality and the eternality of the divine mystery. The gap is particularly apparent to non-Pentecostals, that is, those who have not had a "Pentecostal experience." How then can Pentecostalism communicate its central themes? How can their meaningfulness be preserved for future generations, or in other words, how can we prevent a Pentecostal amnesia?

In 1993, Frank Macchia sought to establish the relation between human experience and the divine through a sacramental interpretation of *glossolalia*.[69] Like others before him,[70] Macchia tried to solve the problem by reinterpreting the temporal aspects of the Pentecostal experience and, so to speak, reversing the directionality in the *corpus veritatum*. Paul Tillich had emphasized that the relation between the human and the divine is realized from the divine initiative, not from the human.[71] In agreement with Karl Rahner, this meant that through sacramental signification, the divine presence is realized in the human temporality.[72] Thus, Macchia concludes that the "sacraments are understood now as contexts for a dynamic and personal divine/human encounter."[73] However, if sacramental expression is instrumental for this encounter, in which expression and how is encounter possible?[74] In other words, can we understand the sacraments as the ordering principle of a Pentecostal *corpus veritatum*?

Throughout the modern Pentecostal-Roman Catholic dialogue, we find agreement on the importance of the sacraments. Pentecostals

---

68. Del Colle, "Trinity and Temporality," 112.
69. Macchia, "Tongues as a Sign," 61–76.
70. E.g., Tugwell, "Speech-Giving Spirit, 151; Samarin, *Tongues of Men*, 232.
71. Tillich, *Protestant Era*, 94–112.
72. Rahner, *Later Writings*, 221–52.
73. Macchia, "Tongues as a Sign," 71.
74. Some suggestions were made by Johns and Johns, "Yielding to the Spirit," 109–32.

emphasize the role of the Eucharist[75] and of baptism[76] in the life of the church. Steve Land even speaks of the Eucharist as an occasion in worship to be converted, healed, sanctified, and filled with the Spirit,[77] that is, a manifestation of all four Pentecostal themes. Others have noted the importance of footwashing,[78] and the role of the laying on of hands in divine healing.[79] Sacraments are, in fact, a temporal manifestation of the very mystery[80] of Christ. For some Pentecostals they are a real sign "for a real journey with a real destination"[81]—a directionality from the human experience to the divine mystery. Many Pentecostals, however, are uncomfortable with controlled liturgical forms[82] and most do not derive their ecclesial identity from the celebration of the sacraments.[83] What then is their significance for Pentecostal identity?

The New Testament portrays sacramental rituals as an act of remembrance.[84] Christ instructs us, "Do this in remembrance of me." In the Old Testament we are reminded of the deeds of God in the earlier covenant.[85] The Jewish liturgy of the Passover even suggests that "in every generation each is obliged to see herself or himself as one who has come out of Egypt."[86] However,

> memory, as in biblical usage, is more than a recalling to mind of the past. It is the work of the Holy Spirit linking the past with

---

75. See the "Final Report of the Dialogue Between the Secretariat for Promoting Christian Unity of the Roman Catholic Church and Some Classical Pentecostals 1977–1982" in Vondey, *Pentecostalism*, 113–32.

76. "Perspectives on *Koinonia*," 101–12.

77. Land, *Pentecostal Spirituality*, 115–16.

78. See Thomas, *Footwashing in John 13*, 172–89.

79. Land, "Living Faith," 14–15.

80. The word "sacrament" is the Latin rendering of the Greek *mystērion*; see Eph 1:9; 3:2–3; Col 1:26; 1 Tim 3:16. See also Rusch and Gros, *Deepening Communion*, 283–320, quoting "The Word of Life: Methodist-Roman Catholic Dialogue, Sixth Series (1991–1996)," which states that "the sacraments of the church may be considered as particular instances of the divine mystery."

81. Land, "Living Faith," 10–11.

82. Hollenweger, *Enthusiastisches Christentum*, 434.

83. Lee, "Pneumatological Ecclesiology," 247. "For Pentecostals, the central element of worship is the preaching of the word . . . of secondary importance are participation in baptism and the Lord's Supper." See also Rusch and Gros, *Deepening Communion*, 416, who quote here "Perspectives on *Koinonia*."

84. See Luke 22:19; 1 Cor 11:24–25.

85. See Exod 13:8–10, 14–16; Deut 6:20–25; 29:9–14.

86. m. Pesah, 10:5.

the present and maintaining the memory of that on which everything depends. . . . Through the Spirit, therefore, the power of what is remembered is made present afresh, and succeeding generations appropriate the event commemorated.[87]

The past experience of the divine mystery becomes a present reality in the celebration of God's people. The past is not only remembered, it is kept alive and infused with new meaning.[88] The sacraments offer Pentecostals what they have called for: to regard the historical roots of the movement no longer as the infancy but as the heart of the movement. In celebrating the sacraments, Pentecostals can remember and relive the work of God as it is recorded in God's word and the history of the Pentecostal people.[89] The sacraments can provide structure, clarity, and expression to the central themes of Pentecostalism.[90] This leads to my initial conclusion.

CONCLUSION

The concept of a *corpus veritatum* makes several important contributions to Pentecostal identity. First, it calls on Pentecostals to work out more precisely the distinctive features of the movement in order to more clearly express and present Pentecostalism. Second, the distinctive themes of Pentecostalism are essential for the life of the movement, yet Pentecostal identity reaches beyond the mere Pentecostal experience; the themes must be expressed and preserved in their right relationship to the foundation of Christian faith. Third, Pentecostal identity does not have to be created; it already exists. Pentecostals need no reinterpretation of the past but a re-evaluation of the present in light of the past. This

---

87. Rusch and Gros, *Deepening Communion*, 323–39, quoting "The Church as Communion in Christ: Second Report from the International Commission for Dialogue Between the Disciples of Christ and the Roman Catholic Church."

88. For the sacraments as instituting mediation of identity, see Chauvet, *Symbol and Sacrament*, 409–46.

89. This concerns less the locutionary dimension—their objectivity—than the illocutionary dimension—it makes possible "Pentecostal" acts that are carried on by sons and daughters. See Vondey, "Pentecostal Identity." The same language is also employed with regard to sacramental theology by Chauvet, *Symbole et Sacrament*, 132–35.

90. Editorial note: since the original publication of this essay, several publications have emphasized this theme, e.g., Tomberlin, *Pentecostal Sacraments*; Augustine, "Spirit in Word"; Kärkkäinen, "Prayer, Liturgy, and Sacramentality."

re-evaluation is an act of remembrance (*anamnēsis*)[91] that necessitates a *corpus sacramentorum* corresponding to the *corpus veritatum*. Pentecostals will have to re-evaluate the instrumental role of sacraments for a theological expression of Pentecostal identity. Sacraments, by the power of the Holy Spirit, "bring into our lives the lifegiving action"[92] of the mystery of Christ, and provide Pentecostals with the means to establish and preserve the Pentecostal essence and thus to theologically formulate and strengthen a global Pentecostal identity. The Spirit makes God visible and audible in the memorial of the past of the community where this memory is kept alive. The present, then, will be no longer only a reliving of the past—it will be the beginning of everything.

---

91. This understanding can be found in the 1982 document of the Joint International Commission Between the Roman Catholic Church and the Eastern Orthodox Church, "Mystery of the Church," 188–97.

92. For this phrase, see "Towards a Statement of the Church: Methodist–Roman Catholic Dialogue, Fourth Series (1982–1986)" quoted in Rusch and Gros, *Deepening Communion*, 235–539.

3

Pentecostalism as a Theological Tradition

THERE EXISTS A PERSISTENT and widespread ignorance and confusion among Pentecostals and the wider Christian community about Pentecostalism as a theological tradition. Identified in contrast to the ecclesiastical establishment, Pentecostal theology seems to offer no more than a sporadic collection of additional doctrines derived from the spurious invention of beliefs and practices exaggerated to maintain the longevity of a revival movement. Shaped by influential micro and macro dynamics that both assert and question the idea of a global tradition while insisting on the endurance of particularity, the movement has begun to solidify its religious presence worldwide without asserting its theological identity. The tendency to define anything as "Pentecostal" that does not fit other traditions seems to have become commonplace. Amid the countless competing options and pressures from other more readily identifiable traditions, Pentecostalism risks that a diversification of too many tongues, doctrines, and practices will diminish the movement in the theological worldview of the Christian confessions.

Far from an internal debate, the pursuit of a theological tradition among Pentecostals responds to pressing questions of the recognition, invention, and rejection of tradition in the late-modern world. Tradition, to put it succinctly, is a concern not for the past but for the future of

Pentecostalism. This essay critically examines the challenges of designating Pentecostal theology as a global tradition by asking (1) What theological elements constitute Pentecostalism as a tradition; (2) what the dominant theological patterns of its reenactment are; and (3) how these constructs aid or resist the formation of Pentecostal theology in the future. What is at stake for Pentecostalism as a theological tradition is not so much *what* Pentecostals believe but *how* they believe, because the patterns that guide the reenactment of their tradition in a cosmopolitan conversation determine not only the identity of what we recognize as Pentecostal but also its endurance as a global movement. I begin with a definition of tradition amid a discussion of Pentecostal anti-traditionalism before offering a critical assessment of the dominant elements that constitute Pentecostal theology as a developing and emerging tradition.

A MOVEMENT BETWEEN TRADITION AND ANTI-TRADITIONALISM

Although rarely articulated, Pentecostals typically follow the most elementary definition of tradition as "anything which is transmitted or handed down from the past to the present."[1] Tradition is the quality of that "which is believed to have existed or to have been performed or believed in the past."[2] More precisely, the reenactment of the past "is not the tradition; the tradition is the pattern which guides the reenactment."[3] In this sense, to speak of a Pentecostal tradition refers to the patterns of Pentecostal theology developing in a multiplicity of contexts that seemingly resist singular proposals of Pentecostal identity. The global diversity of the movement has led some to claim that "it is inaccurate to refer to Pentecostalism as a Christian 'tradition.'"[4] Anthony Giddens, known for his contributions to the study of globalization, similarly suggests that the "experimental" character of modernity contradicts the very idea of tradition because a unified global identity can arise only at the cost of forsaking the diversified traditional contexts.[5] Undeniably, global Pentecostalism

---

1. Shils, *Tradition*, 12. See Friesen, "Pentecostal Antitraditionalism," 191–215; Chan, *Pentecostal Theology*.
2. Shils, *Tradition*, 13.
3. Shils, *Tradition*, 31.
4. Anderson, *Ends of the Earth*, 5.
5. Giddens, "Post-Traditional Society," 59, 96.

has developed amid a variety of changing contexts including the suppression, creation, and legitimization of a myriad of Pentecostal, charismatic, and Pentecostal-like reenactments of the past. Giddens has suggested five essential patterns of tradition challenged by this global trajectory: (1) collective memory; (2) ritual expression; (3) a formulaic conception of truth; (4) guardians of the tradition; and (5) its normative content.[6] These patterns are significant because they identify a tradition by delineating its greatest challenges. The demands overlap in almost narrative fashion, and applying these elements to Pentecostalism can chart the territory for recognizing the existential questions the movement faces in its struggle for a genuine theological identity.

However, the entire endeavor is threatened by a persistent but vague "anti-traditionalism" among Pentecostals that holds to the idea of tradition but rejects a particular reenactment of the past.[7] Pentecostals harbor an ideological anti-traditionalism reflective of the modern age that principally questions the validity of the dominant confessional traditions. This ideological critique surfaces primarily as the dismissal of the validity of a collective historical consciousness.[8] Christian history is associated with reaching "a broad consensus of what elements are fundamental to the Christian faith," and Pentecostals are reluctant "to give this consensus a status of tradition."[9] To prevent applying this critique also to their own history, this skepticism manifests itself mostly as a criticism of the institutional practices and ecclesiastical creeds of Christendom and interprets Pentecostal theology instead as functioning through alternative means.[10] Hence, Pentecostals can affirm doctrines that have shaped their own particular history, as part of a larger restorationism with focus on the apostolic tradition, yet are unable to agree whether to embrace or reject historical dogmas that form the indisputable heart of the established Christian confessions.[11]

In what follows, I want to show the consequences of this ideological, historical, and institutional critique by offering a classification and interpretation of the challenges we find in Pentecostalism as a global theological tradition. In the Pentecostal world, to appropriate Giddens's

6. Giddens, "Post-Traditional Society," 63.
7. Friesen, "Pentecostal Antitraditionalism," 202–6.
8. Friesen, "Pentecostal Antitraditionalism," 207–12.
9. See the record in Vondey, *Pentecostalism*, 113–32.
10. See Vondey, *Beyond Pentecostalism*, 78–170.
11. For a discussion of disagreements see Vondey, *Pentecostalism*.

typology, the theological identity of the movement will have to be negotiated in discursive action or risk stagnation and further segmentation.[12] Even if we challenge the ambiguous Pentecostal anti-traditionalism and Giddens's own assertion of a post-traditional global modernity, the task ahead is to identify the authenticity of Pentecostalism as a tradition amid a worldwide dynamic that proceeds in no obvious direction. The most immediate challenge to the identity as a tradition is how Pentecostals organize the reenactment of their past without falling prey to their own anti-traditionalism.

COLLECTIVE MEMORY AND PENTECOSTAL ANAMNESIS

Memory is of indisputable importance for the community that recalls God's actions in the past, preserves this remembrance in the present, and projects it onto the future (see chapter 2). "Tradition," says Giddens, "is an *organizing medium of collective memory*."[13] Giddens is not pointing merely to an actual, shared history (which admittedly is shorter for the young Pentecostal movement than for other traditions) but to the mechanisms which tie a community to the roots of the convictions and ideas that mark their existential identity. For Christians, and the central importance of the gospel, the anamnesis of the Last Supper presents undoubtedly the most decisive mnemonic device of this collective memory.[14] In the church's eucharistic tradition, anamnesis proceeds "as the ceremonial re-presentation of a salutary event of the past, in order that the event may lay hold of the situation of the celebrant."[15] The collective memory is fully embedded in a sacramental system of liturgical celebration in which not only the past but all time is made "eschatologically transparent."[16] The memory of Christ illuminates the entire life of the Christian community so that what the church remembers becomes present again, not as past event but as re-presented reality in a present that points to the future.

Yet, eucharistic anamnesis is only marginally important to the Pentecostal world where eucharistic practices are scarce, and a global

12. Giddens, "Post-Traditional Society," 105.
13. Giddens, "Post-Traditional Society," 64 (emphasis original).
14. Dahl, *Jesus in the Memory*.
15. Rahner and Vorgrimler, "Anamnesis," 10.
16. Schmemann, *Introduction to Liturgical Theology*, 71.

sacramental theology is virtually nonexistent. Pentecostals reject neither sacramentality nor eucharistic celebration.[17] However, a eucharistic anamnesis has not proven effective for commemorating the core memory of what Pentecostals find essential to their identity. Instead, if communal anamnesis is indispensable for the Christian tradition, an alternative must be found, which incorporates eucharistic sacramentality into a memory in which Pentecostals can identify themselves collectively.[18] It is not a novel argument to suggest that the Pentecostal tradition is deeply rooted in the day of Pentecost. Yet, if the Pentecostal memory prefers Pentecost over the Last Supper, does this "Pentecostal" anamnesis proceed analogous to a eucharistic remembrance?

Pentecostal anamnesis is not located in the past (at Pentecost) but in the community that has been transformed by Pentecost in the present. The memory of Pentecost is a specific construct and representation of the original Pentecost that interrupts and intensifies, challenges and critiques the present community in light of Pentecost's eschatological transparency. Eucharistic anamnesis is perhaps not "transparent" enough to signify Pentecost as "an event that 'makes the church.'"[19] Concerns about "the linkage between sacraments and the Spirit,"[20] the unity "between the formal structure of the eucharistic celebration and the spontaneity of the charismatic gifts,"[21] and an overdeveloped sacramental theology[22] have kept Pentecostals from developing a specifically eucharistic anamnesis. However, even if a Pentecostal memory is not strictly bound to the Last Supper, the preference for Pentecost does not disqualify a sacramental theology and its ritual (eucharistic) enactment.[23] Instead, if the Last Supper is contained in the memory of Pentecost, the challenge for Pentecostal anamnesis is precisely in identifying the organizing medium for this comprehensive memory. The rise of Pentecostalism as a global movement urges the forsaking of any claims that Pentecostal anti-traditionalism is rooted in an anti-liturgical, anti-ritual, and anti-sacramental praxis.

---

17. Green, *Toward a Pentecostal Theology*, 74–181.

18. Although Oneness Pentecostals focus on water baptism, they have not articulated its significance for their collective identity.

19. Macchia, "Nature and Purpose," 244.

20. See the record in Vondey, *Pentecostalism*, 135.

21. See the record in Vondey, *Pentecostalism*, 101–12.

22. See the record in Vondey, *Pentecostalism*, 122.

23. See Augustine, *Common Good*, 121–59.

DANGEROUS RITUALS AND ORAL SACRAMENTALITY

Ritual is important for Giddens because its deep involvement in practice confers integrity upon the tradition.[24] Rituals provide collective memory with recognizable forms in a productive (and reproductive) framework that allows for not only identification of but also participation in the tradition. Yet, the rejection of strict ritual practices is a significant part of Pentecostal anti-traditionalism and its insistence that Pentecost, for all its continuity with the past, marks a decisive new and transformative event for the church. Pentecostals are concerned that ritualizing a Pentecostal anamnesis suppresses the vibrancy and spontaneity of their response to the Holy Spirit. Helpful here is the insight of Johann Baptist Metz that anamnesis always consists of "dangerous memories . . . which make demands on us" because "they break through the canon of the prevailing structures of plausibility and have certain subversive features."[25] Appropriating Metz for Pentecostal anamnesis, the memory of Pentecost is dangerous because of its "apocalyptic consciousness" that allows the experience of the Spirit of the ascended Christ to be transformed by "a future that is still outstanding."[26] The subversive power of this memory resides in being "made explicit in narrative form"[27] in the gospel of a church that articulates its collective anamnesis to prevent that its "dangerous quality is extinguished by the mechanisms of its institutional mediation."[28] Pentecostals must come to terms with the subversive forms of their own memory bound to their particular narrative expressions of the gospel. Collective memory cannot function without an indigenous articulation and communication: the form of remembering Pentecost must be located in the memory of Pentecost itself. Put differently, authentic rituals originate from the memory they transmit, and for an anamnesis of Pentecost, the primary ritual medium is orality.

Walter Hollenweger has highlighted the "oral roots" and "oral liturgy" of global Pentecostalism.[29] The preference for oral transmission of a tradition is sometimes called "oral culture" to denote that there is more

---

24. Giddens, "Post-Traditional Society," 64.
25. Metz, *Faith in History*, 109-10. See Morrill, *Anamnesis*, 19-72.
26. Metz, *Faith in History*, 185, 200.
27. Metz, *Faith in History*, 196.
28. Metz, *Faith in History*, 202.
29. Hollenweger, *Pentecostalism*, 99-105, 269-87.

to orality than a simple contrast to literacy.[30] Oral cultures depend on memory to preserve the permanence of their tradition.[31] For Pentecostals, orality is itself a form of anamnesis: the memory of the word of God spoken and heard, the Spirit poured out and received, and the human response in prophetic witness, tongues, testimonies, preaching, poems, prayers, and songs.[32] Pentecostal orality is not simply a mode of witness to the gospel familiar to the speaker; it is dangerous because it proceeds "in *other* languages" (Acts 2:4; emphasis added) and in the "native language" (v. 8) of those who hear and understand (v. 11) even when this exceeds the mode of speaking (and understanding) of the speaker. In the multiplicity of languages at Pentecost, theological orality escapes pure subjectivity and becomes the cradle of a global tradition.

The global orality of Pentecost emerges from a theological epistemology that is born with the outpouring of the Holy Spirit and its manifestation in many sounds, languages, and tongues. Pentecostal orality emerges from the voice of the Spirit embodied by the community in worship and witness to the world.[33] What this pneumatic orality communicates is the immediate and volatile nature—the dangerous memory—of the outpouring of God's Spirit "on all flesh" and that those who have received the Spirit cannot but speak, even if their flesh neither commands nor understands what is pronounced. Orality as ritual medium refers to the entire array of embodied functions needed to articulate and communicate the encounter with God facilitated by the Spirit. Where, in principle, the proclamation that "the Word of God became flesh" indicates that the oral embodiment of God proceeds along the full range from the spoken to the incarnate Word, experienced at Pentecost in the outpouring of the Holy Spirit, Pentecostal orality refers to the whole range of human embodied proclamation: tongues, lips, hands, feet, head, chests, lungs, and heart—all of the body participates in the encounter to facilitate its mystery. In the terms of a eucharistic anamnesis, orality is a sacramental embodiment of the Pentecostal memory because it has the capacity to manifest God's presence as an outward sign to humanity.

It is therefore more accurate to speak of an oral sacramentality among Pentecostals, an anamnesis that is focused not only on the word but on the entirety of embodied rituals. Pentecost (as reception of the

30. Ong, *Orality and Literacy*.
31. Camery-Hogatt, "Word of God," 225–55.
32. Vondey, *Beyond Pentecostalism*, 61.
33. Hollingsworth, "Spirit and Voice," 189–213.

Spirit)—analogous to the Eucharist (as reception of Christ)—is an event within language *and* the body as the site of the encounter with God. Symbols, larger than words, are the medium of orality and, as Paul Tillich suggests, it is precisely the "symbolic material" that determines the dangerous potential of religious memory.[34] Pentecostals may respond to Tillich that the dangerous potential of sacramental rituals lies not merely in their capacity but in their actualization of a personal, transformative encounter with God. Pentecostal sacramentality is oral (and dangerous) because it affirms the orality of a common humanity that embraces all the signs and symbols that communicate the material, embodied, spiritual, and mystical manifestations not only of God's presence but of God's power.

Yet, many Pentecostals, especially in the West and the Northern Hemisphere, have domesticated their orality and the range of its symbolic reach. The effects of industrialization, urbanization, globalization, and the digital revolution have challenged oral tradition and hindered the development of a comprehensive Pentecostal hermeneutic that pays tribute to its oral cultures.[35] Suppressed by the politics of language, the subversive nature of Pentecostal orality has been smothered by concerns for exegetical, empirical, psychological, and sociolinguistic analysis,[36] which offer little focus on the tradition. A preference for the supernatural has ignored the incarnational principle at the root of sacramental convictions about how the natural world can function as media for the outpouring of God's presence and power. In turn, the lack of a sacramental aesthetic of resistance has downplayed the dangerous potential of the tradition. The primary challenge of this semantically reduced orality is not the authenticity of its rituals, for non-authentic rituals can still function as mnemonic devices, but the truth of its sacramental symbols and the degree to which these embody Pentecost. Despite their cosmopolitan roots and global languages, Pentecostals must first remember *how* to speak as an oral tradition to a world unaccustomed to the language of the Spirit.

---

34. Tillich, "Meaning and Justification," 165–71.
35. Medina, "Orality and Context," 97–123.
36. Tupamahu, "Tongues as a Site," 294–311.

FORMULAIC TRUTH AND THE LANGUAGE OF PENTECOST

Ritual language is important, Giddens insists, because it conveys "certain *communicative events*"[37] that identify the truth of a tradition. While the life, death, and resurrection of Christ clearly delineate the communicative events of the eucharistic anamnesis, Pentecostals struggle to identify the events at the core of their collective memory and its corresponding oral expression. That orality is a problem in the life of the tradition is particularly apparent in the manifestation of glossolalia, the language of Pentecost but notably absent from the language of Pentecostal theology. There is very little "residual orality"[38] in Pentecostal formulations of doctrine despite the origins of their sacramental orality in worship and witness. Pentecostals tend to articulate the meaning of tongues almost exclusively in terms of function, primarily as evidence of the baptism in the Spirit.[39] In the terms of a eucharistic tradition, Pentecostals celebrate that glossolalia signify Spirit baptism "by the power of performing the act" (*ex opere operanto*) without asking how this ritual can achieve its end "through the power of the one performing the work" (*ex opere operantis*). The ideology of an embodied literalism interprets the function of glossolalia in predominantly causal and evidential language at the cost of neglecting the symbolic reach and existential material of the communicative event. Significant for the concerns of its theological tradition is that the formulaic language of tongues as the "initial physical evidence" of Spirit baptism denies glossolalia its enduring iconic (and iconoclastic), (broken) symbolic, and (dangerous) sacramental power.[40] The truth of glossolalia has encountered a global crisis of signification: Pentecostals practice glossolalia (formally and ritually) without any consensus on its meaning for the tradition.

It is noteworthy that for Giddens, formalized or ritualized language can convey truth even if the discourse itself constitutes an obstacle, because "formulaic truth is an attribution of causal efficacy to ritual . . . not to the propositional content of statements."[41] While causal efficacy may

---

37. Boyer, *Tradition as Truth*, 20 (emphasis original).

38. Ong, *Orality and Literacy*, 123.

39. Friesen, *Norming the Abnormal*, 154–93; Cartledge, *Charismatic Glossolalia*, fig. 3.1.

40. See Macchia, "Discerning the Truth," 67–71.

41. Giddens, "Post-Traditional Society," 65.

determine authenticity, Spirit baptism does not derive its truth from the literal quality of glossolalia but from their symbolic material, the dangerous potential, of speaking with tongues. Tongues *are* the language of Pentecost and its theology, a native expression of oral sacramentality,[42] because they can hold the symbolic material appropriate to communicate the truth of encountering the Spirit throughout the life of the tradition.[43] Pentecostals, however, have mistaken the correspondence of form for the carryover of value contained in the experience of Pentecost.[44] Hence, the insistence on glossolalia as a formulaic notion of authenticity assumes the whole meaning of Spirit baptism, which in turn is mistaken for the entire event of Pentecost communicated by the tradition.

As formulaic truth, neither tongues nor Spirit baptism can contain the collective memory of Pentecost. Instead, the communicative events we call "Pentecost" are manifested in a corresponding narrative that exists both in linguistic content and ritual embodiment, word *and* body, rather than beliefs and doctrines alone. Beyond tongues, identifying the truth of Pentecostal theology depends on recalling, preserving, and projecting the communicative events in the collective memory of the community. Amos Yong reminds Pentecostals that their "truth claims have to be assessed not as abstractly isolated propositions, but as members of the larger narrative sets . . . within which they find themselves."[45] For a global Pentecostal tradition, this means, first of all, to identify the set of conventional symbols associated with the communicative events of encountering Pentecost so that the meaning attributed to the events finds its greatest liberation rather than its most concise propositional articulation. Arguably, the historically most consistent and theologically comprehensive narrative set of events among Pentecostals is the full gospel.[46] The proclamation of Jesus as savior, sanctifier, Spirit baptizer, divine healer, and coming king offers a formulaic notion of truth that is hospitable to the symbolic material of Pentecost. In principle, the truth of this narrative depends on the meaning attributed to it by the collective memory of the community. The fact that Pentecostals have a four- or fivefold narrative suggests the significant influence of gatekeepers or guardians of what is considered the truth of the tradition.

42. Macchia, "Sighs Too Deep," 61.
43. See Yong, "'Tongues of Fire,'" 39–65.
44. Yong, "'Tongues of Fire,'" 64.
45. Yong, *Spirit-Word-Community*, 172. See also Yong, "Tongues of Fire."
46. See Vondey, *Pentecostal Theology*.

GUARDIANS OF THE PENTECOSTAL TRADITION

Tradition relies on guardians in Giddens's framework because "they are believed to be the agents, or the essential mediators, of its causal powers."[47] The guarding of the collective memory, its ritual communication, and narrative are necessary to prevent the tradition from becoming either arbitrary or routinized. Guardians are particularly responsible for preserving a tradition that is still developing, like Pentecostalism, that can be invented or re-invented, and that lends itself to conflicting interpretations. They are the guardians of the tradition, not because of their knowledge or competence, but because of the status attributed to them by the community.

For Pentecostals, the question of guardianship of their tradition has never been answered; it is inevitably bound up with a weak and undeveloped ecclesiology. The memory of Pentecost is deeply connected with the outpouring of the Spirit on sons and daughters, young and old, men and women (Acts 2:17–18). In the wider Christian tradition, where priests or prophets might be expected to serve as guardians, Pentecostals have vested status to the ideals of the priesthood and prophethood of *all* believers. Yet, Spirit baptism has remained a largely individualistic doctrine; glossolalia is seen as manifestation not of the collective memory but the individual narrative of empowerment. The institutionalization of global Pentecostalism reveals a dominance of sacerdotal and episcopal forms of ecclesiastical organization and a hierarchical view of the priesthood that contains features of vocational and ontological selectivity. In a movement where social status has been a significant aspect of its self-understanding, guardianship is often conferred to individual leaders (mostly men), pioneering figures (mostly Western), successful churches (mostly affluent), or influential (mostly political) fellowships. In a tradition of sacramental orality, Pentecostals have neglected that their guardians act not only *in persona Christi* but also *in persona ecclesiae*, representing a community that consists predominantly of women, the Majority World, the poor, the elderly, and the powerless.

The ideals of reconciliation, equality, and the renunciation of status in light of the outpouring of the Spirit struggle for realization amid the still dominant model of a global Western culture and patriarchal order, on the one hand, and the sobering global challenges of the prosperity

---

47. Giddens, "Post-Traditional Society," 65.

gospel, political corruption, racism, and migration, on the other. The colonial African guardianship of Pentecostal missionaries differs from the postcolonial tradition of African initiated churches.[48] The memory of African slave narratives among black Pentecostals remains largely foreign to the white cityscape plots of neo-Pentecostal and charismatic fellowships.[49] The memory of Pentecostal women accentuates a fundamental divide between the prophethood and priesthood asserted to all believers.[50] Oneness and Trinitarian Pentecostals serve as guardians of different theological traditions with no sustained attempt of reconciliation.[51] The emergence of a Pentecostal academy as potential guardian is largely ignored by the ecclesiastical leadership. The sacramental potential of Pentecostal theology (or what Pentecostals call the power of God) is bound by the chains of ethnicity, gender, age, nationality, educational background, and social and ecclesiastical status. The problem of the Pentecostal tradition is not that it has no guardians but that it has too many. What is at stake in a tradition with too many guardians is ultimately a proliferation and confusion of its normative content among too many authentic and non-authentic possibilities.

THE NORMATIVE CONTENT OF PENTECOSTAL THEOLOGY

In light of the preceding assessment, the content of Pentecostal theology cannot simply be listed. Statements of faith never take the step from Christian self-description to second-order reflection. The normative components of a tradition speaking with *other* tongues are not necessarily spelled out in well-worn doctrines and practices. Instead, Pentecost as communicative event, embedded in the sacramental orality and interpretive processes that guide its reenactment, is invested with robust emotional and affective underpinnings. For Giddens, tradition has binding force precisely because of its moral and emotional content.[52] Yet, although it has long been asserted that Pentecostal theology is an affective tradition, Pentecostals are generally unclear of the consequences

---

48. Kalu, *African Pentecostalism*, 3–146.
49. Vondey, "Making of a Black Liturgy," 147–68.
50. Qualls, *God Forgive Us*, 121–50.
51. Vondey, *Continuing and Building Relationships*, 268–90.
52. Giddens, "Post-Traditional Society," 65.

of this assertion.[53] We arrive at a normative theology of global Pentecostalism only when we can identify the affective epistemology operative in the "tongues" of the tradition. Important for the future of Pentecostalism as a global tradition is understanding its quest for the identification, solidarity, and transformation of the human condition rooted in the affections, desires, and transformative passions.

In a system of dysfunctional guardians, we cannot transfer the rituals and symbols of the collective memory exclusively to the material body; neither is it enough to emphasize the elusive anointing of the Spirit. Both incarnational theology and pneumatological imagination depend radically on the affective transformation resulting from the reception of the Spirit. The dangerous memory of Pentecost warns us that a pneumatological ontology does not automatically become a pneumatological epistemology apart from an authentic transformative encounter with the Spirit. Pentecostalism is a tradition of the Spirit because the encounter with the Spirit is a real and critical expression of authentic human transformation. To understand the normative content of Pentecostal theology, *narrating* the memory of Pentecost in the full gospel is therefore not enough—we need to identify where and how this authentic transformation actually takes place among Pentecostals.[54] Considering the oral sacramentality of Pentecostal theology and its roots in worship and witness, I suggest that the central and formative locus of this transformative encounter is the altar call and response.[55] The altar, as a place of encounter with Christ, is at the same time the fountainhead of the theological convictions that shape the Pentecostal tradition.

The affective memory of Pentecostal theology is born in the encounter with Christ at the altar and is structured by its transformative moments: Jesus is the *norma normans non normata* because he is encountered as savior, sanctifier, Spirit baptizer, divine healer, and coming king. These experiential moments with Jesus at the altar form the normative events of the global tradition because they are transformative moments of the *memoria salutis*. That the Pentecostal tradition "cannot keep from speaking" (Acts 4:20) of the full gospel results from the "overacceptance" of the Spirit who draws the community into and guides it alongside the encounter with Christ in a coming to, tarrying and transformation,

---

53. Land, *Pentecostal Spirituality*, 136.
54. Solivan, *Spirit, Pathos, and Liberation*, 1998.
55. Vondey, "Theology of the Altar," 94–107.

commissioning, and release from the altar. This altar narrative is normative because it is invested with the affective memory of human suffering and triumph bound up in the salvation of Christ's suffering and victory culminating with the outpouring of the Spirit.

The memory of Pentecost at the altar contains the anamnesis of Christ and extends it further through the epiclesis of the Spirit toward the coming kingdom of God. This eschatological reach of affectivity, although not unfamiliar to Giddens, extends beyond his idea of a mere anticipation of the future to its transformative power that cannot be colonized because it is identical with the presence of God. That the tongues of a global Pentecostal tradition are kindled at the altar signifies an eschatological transparency in which the present recapitulates the past only through an affective encounter with this future. Yet, Pentecostalism's global shift from an eschatological movement to a religion of the present has attenuated its affective repertoire. As a result, the altar is often reduced to an encounter of the moment in an endless repetitive circle of leaving and returning. The affections are directed to the altar and its memory of the past rather than to the apocalyptic event of the coming presence of God. As a post-eschatological tradition, Pentecostalism remains subject to the transformative events of its past only insofar as it rediscovers a future which profoundly challenges its self-sufficiency as a purely historical tradition.

CONCLUSION

The importance of the task to identify in the enormous diversity of Pentecostal groups worldwide a single theological tradition cannot be overestimated. Giddens's patterns of tradition suggest that Pentecostals have either ignored or abandoned this task prematurely in favor of identifying so closely as a localized revival or renewal movement that a unified global theological identity has become unnecessary. That Pentecostalism exhibits constantly changing forms has made the movement vulnerable to its own ideological, historical, and institutional critique of tradition. The greatest challenge of global Pentecostalism is how its theological distinctiveness is recognized and affirmed in the ideology, history, and institutions of the movement without reinforcing the stereotypes and extremes that have begun to dissolve this identity.

PART II

The Extension of the Question of Truth to Hermeneutical Experience

4

The Symbolic Turn in the Liturgy of Pentecostalism

EVERY LIVING COMMUNITY EXPRESSES itself publicly. This self-expression, on one hand, can take on various forms; on the other hand, there has to be a certain "coordinated system" of expressions that allows for the recognition and differentiation of a particular community. This understanding has been adequately developed in the ecclesiological insight that one essential "self-expression of the Church"[1] is the *liturgy*. In every true liturgy, Christ "continues the work of our redemption in, with, and through his Church"[2] (*opus Christi*). As such, liturgy is both the "self-definition"[3] and "self-realization"[4] of the church of Christ in the world. The liturgy of the world is "the primary and original liturgy"[5] of the continuous interaction between God and humanity (*opus Dei*).

---

1. See Schmidt, *Liturgy*. See also Flannery, *Vatican Council II*, 117, 122, quoting Paul VI, *Sacrosanctum Concilium*, 2 and 10.

2. *Catechism*, 1069.

3. See, e.g., Draper, "Christian Self-Definition," 362–77.

4. It is not just "the acts by which the Church exercises her power." Clynes, *Liturgy and Christian Life*, 5. Rather, it is also a continuous interaction between God and humanity in which the Church realizes itself as the community of God's people. For the relation of church and world in the liturgy, see also Seasoltz, "Anthropology and Liturgical Theology," 5–6.

5. Rahner, "Überlegungen zum personalen Vollzug," 282–301; see Rahner, "Kirche und Welt," 1336–57; Skelley, *Liturgy of the World*, 92.

The liturgy of the church is an "explicitly celebrated, stated, and appropriated"[6] expression of that interaction. This celebration only subsequently finds its particular manifestation in the church's celebration of the sacraments.[7] Liturgy "arises from a dynamic encounter of a given culture at a given moment with the church of always and everywhere as it celebrates its Lord in the Holy Spirit"[8] (*opus Spiriti*). It is this dynamic encounter that allows for the differentiation of a particular tradition and for a theology of liturgy of that community. Thus, liturgy is *primarily the explicit self-expression of the life of faith of the community and the individual within a creative and dynamic tradition*[9] *as celebration of the identity of the church in the world and in history.*

However, this dynamic encounter also contains the greatest potential for misunderstanding. Not every liturgy is equally developed and, consequently, recognized and understood. The liturgy of Pentecostalism presents a particular problem for the established churches[10] but also for the heterogeneous group of Pentecostal churches itself.[11] There exists today no common understanding of Pentecostalism as a theological tradition (see chapter 3). In addition, at a time when Pentecostals "are rediscovering the value of signs and the part which symbolic action plays in their personal and social lives,"[12] the acceptance of a perhaps symbolic interpretation of Pentecostalism appears all the more questionable. This "semantic cut"[13] is a threat to both the Pentecostal self-understanding[14] as well as to a better understanding of Pentecostalism by other Christian traditions.

   6. Rahner, "Theology of Worship," 147.

   7. "An act in which it [the church] actualizes its essence fully as the primordial sacrament of grace." Rahner, *Foundations of Christian Faith*, 417–18.

   8. Groupe des Dombes, "Holy Spirit, the Church," 21.

   9. For this term, see Groupe des Dombes, *Gift of Authority*, 17; Collins and Power, *Liturgy*, vii–viii.

   10. Just a few who voiced their critique of the lack of a Pentecostal "self-expression" are Moltmann, "Response," 59–70; Welker, *God the Spirit*; Volf, *Trinität und Gemeinschaft*.

   11. Considered among the most significant issues by Menzies, "Frontiers in Theology," 15–30. Robeck focused on the problem in "Making Sense of Pentecostalism," 1–34. See also Johns, "Adolescence of Pentecostalism," 3–18.

   12. They are more than twenty years behind this development in Christendom; see Groupe des Dombes, "Holy Spirit, the Church," 34.

   13. This term is explained in Chauvet, *Symbol and Sacrament*, 456.

   14. "The loss of correspondence between the Christian community's self-understanding and its liturgical expression endangers the existence of the community."

In this chapter, I will endeavor to explain and analyze the factors that contributed to the formation of a liturgy of Pentecostalism in order to provide a basis for (1) common ecumenical dialogue; (2) a Pentecostal sacramental theology; and (3) a Pentecostal theory of Christian and human existence. Rather than attempting a historical reconstruction, I will first focus on the question how Pentecostal identity can be expressed in a theology of liturgy. The basis for this theology is the thesis that an irreversible symbolic reinterpretation—a *symbolic turn*—initiated the birth and development of the Pentecostal tradition. I will therefore begin with a description of the meaning of the symbolic for the formulation of a theology of liturgy. This will lead to an explanation of what general factors contribute to a reinterpretation of the symbolic and how this *symbolic turn* affects the formulation of a liturgy. I will then relate this analysis to the formulation of a liturgy of Pentecostalism by first describing the *symbolic turn* that formed the basis for this liturgy, and second, by explaining how this interpretation is relevant for an understanding of the Pentecostal tradition.

THE SYMBOLIC TURN: ESTABLISHMENT, INTERPRETATION, AND COLLAPSE

If liturgy is the self-expression of the church, how is ecclesial identity expressed in the liturgy? Liturgy is foremost a symbolic act.[15] That is, it communicates the ecclesial reality in the form of verbal and non-verbal[16] symbols and signs "conditioned by historical forms of communication."[17] As a symbolic expression of Christian identity, liturgy is often frustrated by a lack of common definition of the symbolic and, consequently, the inability of many to dialogue with, to participate in, and to represent meaningfully the Christian tradition expressed in the liturgy. The formulation of a liturgy of Pentecostalism must therefore begin with a formulation of a common understanding of the symbolic.

Kilmartin, *Christian Liturgy*, 41–42.

15. "Reality is never present to us except in a mediated way . . . constructed out of the symbolic network of the culture which fashions us." Chauvet, *Symbol and Sacrament*, 84.

16. See Ganoczy, *Katholische Sakramentenlehre*, 107–35.

17. Kilmartin, *Christian Liturgy*, 45.

In 1915, the linguist Ferdinand de Saussure, in his widely influential work *Course in General Linguistics*,[18] was one of the first who faced the problems involved in constructing a comprehensive theory of language. Saussure considered signs as arbitrary, their value as purely negative and differential with the only essential requirement that one sign is not confused with another.[19] Saussure suggested a simple bipolar correlation[20] between the signifier, such as the *word* "pipe," and the signified, that to which it refers: a pipe. The *word* "pipe," he would say, does not refer to the *thing* itself, rather, it receives its meaning only within the entire system of language. The means by which, for example, the pipe is produced are completely unimportant because the system in which the sign exists is not affected; its value is received and its form matters only within this fixed system.[21] In other words, only a fixed system or code "makes it possible to have signs."[22] Taking this further, the architect Le Corbusier[23] concluded his influential book *Towards a New Architecture* in 1923 with the painting of a briar pipe as a symbol of pure functionalism.[24] To him, the pipe *was* a pipe and not the concept of a pipe; it is not a symbol of functionalism, it *is* functionalism.

The image of a pipe returned again three years later in a surrealist painting[25] by René Magritte, this time, it seems, as an answer to the concepts of both Saussure and Le Corbusier. Magritte's painting shows, to use the words of Michel Foucault, "a carefully drawn pipe, and underneath it (handwritten in a steady, painstaking, artificial script, a script from the convent, like that found heading the notebooks of schoolboys, or on a blackboard after an object lesson), this note: 'This is not a pipe.'"[26] The painting appears contradictory. The pipe, although perfect in its resemblance to a *real* pipe, is but the painting of a pipe, and who would

---

18. Saussure, *Cours de linguistique générale*.
19. Saussure, *Cours de linguistique générale*, 165.
20. Saussure, *Cours de linguistique générale*, 99. See Harris, *Reading Saussure*, 59.
21. Saussure, *Cours de linguistique générale*, 120.
22. Harris, *Reading Saussure*, 219.
23. Or Charles Edouard Jeanneret.
24. Le Corbusier, *Towards a New Architecture*, 289.
25. The painting is *The Treason of Images*. Hughes interpreted this as a "riposte to Corbusier's single-level rationalism" in *Shock of the New*, 244.
26. Foucault, *Not a Pipe*, 15.

THE SYMBOLIC TURN IN THE LITURGY OF PENTECOSTALISM 71

seriously contend otherwise? One may agree with Foucault and say, "My God, how simpleminded!"[27]

The symbolism of Magritte's painting speaks to us in an unusual way. It is saying, "Do not look . . . for a true pipe. It is the drawing . . . that must be accepted as a manifest truth."[28] Magritte, more than any other, seemed to have intended this exact likeness to a *real* pipe that allows for a new understanding of the visible: "What you see is *that*."[29] The pipe, so Magritte himself explained, is a visible description of thought; the visibility of the invisible, a symbol.

Magritte saw "no reason to accord more importance to the invisible than to the visible, nor vice versa."[30] With this he fully embraced the question of identity; to use Saussure's words: whether the signifier or the signified determine the identity of a symbol. How does the symbol receive its original meaning? What fixes the "code"[31] of its recognition? Magritte seems to concur with Saussure: it had to come from the "inside." However, for Saussure, inside the system "nothing apart from other signs"[32] exists—it is "a system of pure values which are determined by nothing but the momentary arrangement of its terms."[33] This is a crucial point in the understanding of liturgy as a "coordinated system" of symbolic order.

> The only necessary and sufficient condition for establishing the identity of any individual sign is that it be distinct from other signs. However, this can presumably only be so if the system as a whole is structured in such a way as to allocate to each sign its own semiological "space." Therefore Saussure . . . forces us to conclude that it can only be the total network of interrelations which establishes . . . individual signs . . . which in turn . . . explains *why altering just one set of relations disturbs the whole system*, and also why . . . it . . . encounters the passive *resistance of the entire structure*.[34]

27. Foucault, *Not a Pipe*, 19.
28. Foucault, *Not a Pipe*, 16–17.
29. Foucault, *Not a Pipe*, 34.
30. Letter of Magritte to Foucault, May 23, 1966. Foucault, *Not a Pipe*, 57.
31. "Code" is not an external and static device with which the symbol, once decoded, becomes somewhat less symbolic or mysterious. A symbolic code must evolve with the development of the community as part of the symbol's meaning within the liturgy as a whole.
32. Harris, *Reading Saussure*, 220.
33. Saussure, *Course in General Linguistics*, 80.
34. Harris, *Reading Saussure*, 220 (emphasis mine).

It is a "great illusion"[35] to consider a symbol as simply the union of signifier (a certain physical manifestation) and signified (a certain metaphysical concept). One symbol does not exist by itself but only as part of a "coordinated system" that allows for an understanding of that symbol. The symbol cannot exist apart from the whole of the liturgy; to approach a symbol as an autonomous subsystem that somehow explains the whole[36] perpetuates a confusion of signifier and signified that can eventually lead to a *symbolic turn*—the re-definition of the meaning and value of a symbol.

For Saussure it is the social fact alone, the community, which is necessary in order to "establish" a symbolic order.[37] The legitimacy (or credibility) of a liturgy as a whole and the validity of particular symbols is "thus linked directly to the '*symbolic capital*' . . . with which they are invested"[38] by the community. This symbolic order, nevertheless, is not stagnant. No "absolute immobility"[39] exists within any "coordinated system" (*liturgy*); it is rather part of an active system of symbolic meaning. This dynamic element further expands the problematic to the question of the identity of a symbol within a "coordinated system" which is continuously evolving.[40]

The confusion of signifier and signified is most evident in the *symbolic turn* of the concept "Messiah" in the Gospel of Mark. By the end of the Old Testament period, the signifier "Messiah" was understood clearly as "the Lord's Anointed" (1 Sam 24:6; 2 Sam 23:2; Ps 2:2), a divinely appointed ruler and high priest.[41] The messianic expectations were largely influenced by the royal interpretation of Moses (such as Isa 63:11; Exod 4:20), the divine choice of David (e.g., Pss 78:68; 89:20–21), the victorious servant of Isa 53 and the deliverer of Dan 7, placing the notion of a

---

35. Saussure, *Cours de linguistique générale*, 157.

36. For example, that an understanding of speaking in tongues (signifier) explains the "tongues movement" (signified), which in turn explains Pentecostalism (the whole liturgy).

37. Saussure, *Cours de linguistique générale*, 157.

38. Chauvet, *Symbol and Sacrament*, 348.

39. Saussure, *Cours de linguistique générale*, 110 and 193. Saussure was criticized for the lack of mobility his system allowed for. I do not attempt a critique of Saussure but rather an appreciation of his work within a theory of symbolic meaning.

40. See Saussure, *Cours de linguistique générale*, 159–60.

41. Schoeps, *Paul*, 92–94, points out that the prophets expected, not a person with supernatural power but an executive officer of God. See also Horbury, *Jewish Messianism*, 5–35.

suffering Messiah (Isa 53 and Zech 9 and 13) far into the background.[42] The established system allowed for the signified "Messiah" only to be one coming in power, the Davidic king who would restore Israel to its former glory.[43] Yet, the Gospel of Mark, for example, shows a "Messiah" who does not bring about fulfillment of the promise by the exercise of political power. Instead, Jesus redefines the meaning of the symbol as pointing to his rejection, suffering, death, and resurrection (8:31). This turn of the symbolic meaning of "Messiah" is really not completed until the recognition of Jesus as the Son of God at his crucifixion (15:39).

Peter verbalizes the traditional expectation of the "Messiah" (8:29) but rebukes Jesus' re-definition of the symbol. It is not until the rejected "Messiah" breathes his last that the established system, in form of a Roman centurion, recognizes the turn of the symbol from "Son of God" (3:11, 5:7, 9:7) to "Son of Man" (8:31, 9:31, 10:33, 14:62)—a crucified Messiah. The old meaning was not completely abandoned, yet it was fully transformed into a new symbolic order.[44] It is impossible to recognize this new symbolic meaning "without *ourselves* being called into question. . . . A reversal of desire is demanded here, a reversal that would not only confess our own injustice . . . but also simultaneously confess a God completely other than our infantile desire"[45] imagined. The historical reality of the cross, which redefined the meaning of the symbol "Messiah" once and for all, also demands a redefinition of those who are part of that symbolic order. The *symbolic turn* is not simply a shift from one meaning to another that concerns only one symbol—it is the overturn of the *whole* symbolic order.

"If God's revelation thus finds its decisive turn in Jesus' cross,"[46] a reading of the Gospel of Mark in light of the concept of this *symbolic*

---

42. Horbury, *Jewish Messianism*, 31–35. The Maccabean revolt as a consequence of the Seleucid persecution contributed to this understanding.

43. Cohn-Sherbok, *Jewish Messiah*, 44, 172.

44. This accounts largely for the semantic cut between Jewish and Christian interpretations of Jesus. The messianic interpretation of the Old Testament expected a new age of this world's history; in the New Testament this was transformed into a narrative of imminent messianic woes, cosmic transformation, the resurrection, the outpouring of the Holy Spirit, and the final judgment signifying the end of history. See Arrington, *Paul's Aeon Theology*, 89–170, 180.

45. This analysis of the last words of Jesus is given by Chauvet, *Symbol and Sacrament*, 501.

46. Chauvet, *Symbol and Sacrament*, 499.

turn poses several questions: first, the problem of *change*,[47] particularly the possibility of change for a *symbolic turn*; second, the problem of *causality*,[48] particularly the historical question of transition from one symbolic meaning to another; and, third, the problem of the *subject*,[49] particularly its role in the *symbolic turn*. Foucault locates the cause for change in the relation of power and knowledge that directly imply one another.[50] This power is not located in any central location, neither does it develop out of the relation of signifier and signified, but it is dispersed throughout the entire system in complex instances that interact with one another.[51] Change is brought about by a complex network of the knowing subject, the object to be known and the modalities of knowledge[52] that, as in Mark's Gospel, may ultimately overturn the system of power. Such a system is then no longer sufficiently "coordinated"; its liturgy has collapsed, and its self-expression is in need of redefinition.

Symbolic expression, of course, is not exhausted by language.[53] Jean-Francois Lyotard focused on the implications of change that take place inside the system (but outside the verbal discourse)[54] in the realm of social and political structures. Commenting on the relationship of symbolic meaning in the paintings of Magritte,[55] Lyotard concludes that meaning in a word is established by the (non-linguistic) image not the word itself. He "finds a figural opacity in the signifier which cannot itself be made into a matter of meaning."[56] Lyotard confers with Saussure that the basis for interpretation—and thus for change—is located *in* the community that endorses the symbol. But Lyotard goes beyond Saussure

---

47. See Foucault, *Order of Things*, xii.

48. Foucault, *Order of Things*, xii–xiii.

49. Foucault, *Order of Things*, xiii.

50. Foucault, *Surveiller et punir*, 32.

51. Foucault, *Surveiller et punir*, 197–229. Foucault, *Archeology of Knowledge*, 45.

52. Foucault, *Archeology of Knowledge*, 32.

53. "On peut dire que l'arbre est vert, mais on n'aura pas mis la couleur dans la phrase" (One can say that the tree is green but that does not put the color into the sentence). Lyotard, *Discours*, 52.

54. See particularly his understanding of "desire for change" (*désir de changement*), Lyotard, *Discours*, 223–25.

55. The attraction of Magritte's work, particularly *The Treason of Images*, is largely a Western European phenomenon. Magritte responded: "The famous pipe. How people reproached me for it! And yet, could you stuff my pipe? No, it's just a representation, is it not? So if I had written on my picture 'This is a pipe,' I'd have been lying!" Quoted by Torczyner, *Magritte*, 118.

56. Readings, *Introducing Lyotard*, 18.

when he formulates that it is *desire* that infiltrates the discourse through this non-linguistic act of interpretation.[57] This desire is the particular characteristic of the community that engages in the interpretation of a "coordinated system." Liturgy thus becomes "the symbolic expression of the human in its total corporality and as a being of desire"[58] as part of a community that expresses this desire—often as a "vision of a 'place which one must imagine without being able to conceive it.'"[59]

Desire is an expression of value. We desire that which we regard as possessing "desirable" value. The interpretation and acceptance of a particular symbolic order is based on the fact that a specific value is placed on the particular symbolic representation of the real. The social theorist Jean Baudrillard expresses this value in terms of a relationship of the symbol and its environment—a "political economy."[60] He responds to Saussure by assigning to the symbol "only an allusive value . . . its form is not that of the sign in general, but that of a certain organization which is that of the code."[61] This "code only governs certain signs"[62] and the existence of *a universal and eternal code* of value is consequently a (postmodern) illusion. This explains why Magritte's pipe (once again) becomes a "compromise formation"[63] between the functional and the symbolic that cannot be universally "decoded." The individual symbol institutes "a certain mode of signification in which all the surrounding signs . . . refer to each other."[64] Therefore, in order to formulate and understand a liturgy one must allow for the inapplicability of one's own code and first ask whether a different code is necessary in order to approach a particular liturgy.

Baudrillard criticizes the law of the code: "The reality principle *of the code* . . . extends over society in general. . . . You are asked only to consider value, according to the structural definition which here takes on its full social significance, as one term in . . . a multiple, incessant, twisting

57. "Il y a de figural dans le mot est avéré par l'image. C'est par cette polysémie non-linguistique que le désir s'infiltre dans le discours"; Lyotard, *Discours*, 412, note to plate 17; also 248–49, 271–73.

58. Chauvet, *Symbol and Sacrament*, 371.

59. Lyotard, *Economie libidinale*, back cover, quoted and translated by Dews, *Logics of Disintegration*, 133.

60. Baudrillard, *Pour une critique*, 229–55.

61. Baudrillard, *Symbolic Exchange and Death*, 7.

62. Baudrillard, *Symbolic Exchange and Death*, 7.

63. "Formation de compromise." See the critique of Magritte in Baudrillard, *Pour une critique*, 241–42.

64. Baudrillard, *For a Critique*, 191.

relation across the entire network of other signs."[65] Within this network all desire is regulated by the "common" code. If this code is broken "people no longer understand ('hear') one another."[66] The symbol remains as "an irreducible residue that comes to bar social relations and ... weighs down on us with all the abstraction of dead language."[67] The code becomes unacceptable because it can no longer provide the whole system with sufficient "coordination" to ensure a common understanding of both the individual symbol and the liturgy of which this symbol is a part in its representation of the real. It is this "death" of the code that brings about a *symbolic turn*. This understanding allows us now to consider the *symbolic turn* in the formation of a liturgy of Pentecostalism.

THE DEATH OF THE SYMBOLIC CODE AND THE FORMATION OF THE PENTECOSTAL VISION

The thesis of this essay is that a *symbolic turn* initiated the birth and growth of Pentecostalism and contributed to the formation and consolidation of a liturgy of Pentecostalism. By the end of the first decade of the twentieth century, which had seen the widely recognized Topeka Revival in 1901 and the Azusa Street revival in 1906, the *symbolic turn* had already occurred and a new "coordinated system"—Pentecostalism—had already formed. The first two stanzas of the following song by I. G. Martin from 1906 express this well:

> There are people, almost ev'rywhere, Whose hearts are all aflame
> With the fire that fell at Pentecost, Which made them all acclaim;
> It is burning now within my heart, All glory to His name!
> And I'm glad I can say I'm one of them. One of them, one of them,
> I am glad I can say I'm one of them; say I'm one of them.
>
> Tho' these people may not learned be, Nor boast of worldly fame,
> They have all received their Pentecost, Thro' faith in Jesus' name;
> And are telling now, both far and wide, His pow'r is yet the same,
> And I'm glad I can say I'm one of them. One of them, one of them,
> I am glad I can say I'm one of them; say I'm one of them.[68]

---

65. Baudrillard *Symbolic Exchange and Death*, 11.
66. Chauvet, *Symbol and Sacrament*, 350.
67. Baudrillard, *Symbolic Exchange and Death*, 202.
68. I. G. Marshall, "I'm Glad I'm One of Them" (1901), in *Church Hymnal*, 249. All

In order to locate a *symbolic turn* historically and to further assess its significance for the formulation of a liturgy of Pentecostalism, we must therefore first turn to the origins of classical Pentecostalism[69] at the end of the nineteenth century. It will be necessary to begin by describing the "death" of the symbolic code as a basis for a symbolic reinterpretation. I will then analyze the *symbolic turn* in Pentecostalism and its development in the context of the formation of a liturgy.

It is generally accepted that the immediate origins of Pentecostalism coincide with the rise of the Holiness movement in the nineteenth century.[70] The emphasis on holiness was not new to the church. *A Plain Account of Christian Perfection as Believed and Taught by the Reverend Mr. John Wesley*,[71] first published in 1739, served as a theological basis for much of the later Holiness movement.[72] "The Wesleyan spirituality embodied a specific catholic tradition of transformation which included Western and Eastern figures."[73] It centered on the desire for moral perfection—an absence to be filled—as taught in Scripture and as the attainable and ideal state of the Christian life. The Holiness churches were convinced that God was "calling each one of us to this same state [of holiness]."[74]

> Come one and all, both great and small,
> Whom sin has crippled by the fall,
> Through faith in Christ you may regain,
> Whose blood can wash from every stain.
>
> Cleansed from sin's degrading spot,
> Made new again, old things forgot,
> Now with our body, mind and soul
> We strive to reach the highest goal.[75]

---

hymns used in this essay are in the public domain.

69. This follows *The New International Dictionary of Pentecostal and Charismatic Movements* that uses the term "Classical Pentecostalism" (Synan, 219–22) to distinguish early Pentecostal churches from later "Neo-" and "charismatic" Pentecostalism.

70. E.g., see Anderson, *Vision of the Disinherited*, 28–46; Synan, *Holiness-Pentecostal Movement*; Synan, *Pentecostal-Charismatic Origins*; Dieter, *Holiness Revival*.

71. Jackson, *Works of John Wesley*, 9:366–488.

72. See Synan, *Holiness-Pentecostal Movement*, 13–32.

73. Land, *Pentecostal Spirituality*, 47.

74. Richardson, "Sainthood—Be and Live," 2.

75. Spurling, "For Unity" (1886), quoted by Beaty, "New Song," 4.

The established churches were frequently opposed to the Holiness theology.[76] The "political economy" of the mainline churches did not provide a "code" with which it could be interpreted and integrated; instead it assigned to the symbols of the Holiness movement a negative value due to its emphasis on individual transformation (a second crisis) as a continuation of salvation (a second work of grace) and the claim of Christian perfection (entire sanctification).[77] With the Holiness movement originated a desire that encountered both attraction to the doctrine of sanctification and repulsion of the "Holy Rollers"[78]—frequently found side by side. C. E. Jones explains that at this time "a new genre of Holiness-experience songs emerged" that "drew worshipers into sympathy one to another at the same time they were reinforcing teaching from the pulpit and creating a common doctrinal and behavioral standard."[79] The following excerpt from "We Will Sing and Preach Holiness" paints a vivid picture of this situation:

> When I first heard of holiness I thought it must be right;
> It seemed to fit the Bible, And be the Christian light.
> I heard the people singing and testifying too;
> They seemed to love their Savior, And Christians ought to do.
>
> I little thought of joining, I said I could not stand,
> To be among that people, That's called the "holy band."
> The world looked down upon them, And said they were so rash,
> They often spoke against them, And said they were but trash.
>
> But as I went to hear them, And saw the way they did,
> I saw they had a treasure, From worldly people hid.
> They seemed to be so happy, And filled with Christian love;
> When people talked about them, They only looked above.

---

76. See "Criticism and Controversy" in Synan, *Holiness-Pentecostal Movement*, 141–63.

77. Kelsey, *Tongue Speaking*, 72, remarks that the "social gospel became the teaching of most churches, and it was widely accepted that the task of the church was to reform the world. The Holiness movement offered the alternative of transformation from within." See also Womack, *Wellsprings*, 82–83.

78. A term frequently used for the early Pentecostals; see Conn, *Like a Mighty Army*, 158–59.

79. Jones, *Perfectionist Persuasion*, 38.

> My heart began to hunger, And thirst and burn within:
> I wanted full salvation, A freedom from all sin.
> I went to God for holiness, And called upon his name;
> He cleansed my heart completely, And filled it with the same.[80]

The movement would frequently point out that the desire for holiness originated with the symbol itself (sanctification) or with the group that endorsed it and that provided a code for its interpretation only insofar as this was understood as a response to the work of the Spirit (*opus Spiriti*). The message of this new symbolism was foolishness to the world,[81] a weakness of God, yet stronger than humankind.[82] The Holiness churches were "not primarily a social organisation but an institutional event, a real communication established between God and mankind."[83] This aspect of being more a spiritual community than a visible organization[84] has continued to be an obstacle. The application of the linguistic theory, presented earlier, does not allow for a full explanation at this point. As much as the community was necessary to establish the identity of the symbolic order through its public testimony, and as much as the desire for holiness was very much an individual "hunger," this experience of an "absence that had to be filled" was first and foremost a human response to divine grace. The desire was initiated by Christ (*opus Christi*):

> I can hear my Savior calling,
> I can hear my Savior calling,
> I can hear my Savior calling,
> "Take thy cross and follow, follow me."
> Where he leads me I will follow,
> I'll go with him all the way.[85]

---

80. Frank M. Graham in Winsett, *Songs of Pentecostal Power*, 213.

81. It is therefore insufficient to portray Pentecostalism as a mere social movement and a misconception to understand it primarily as a historical reactionary development.

82. See 1 Cor. 1:25; also 1:18, 21.

83. Groupe des Dombes, "Holy Spirit, the Church," 78, in Clifford, *Communion of the Churches*, 59–94.

84. For this language, see Paul VI, *Gaudium et Spes*, 40.

85. J. S. Norris, "Where He Leads Me" (1890), in *Church Hymnal*, 65. More precisely, Father, Son, and Spirit appear in their distinctive ways each as *principium personale* but also together as *causa efficiens* of the created grace; see Mühlen, *Heilige Geist als Person*, 305; Mühlen, *Una Mystica Persona*, 385.

The response of the Holiness people to the divine grace found its foremost expression in a strong desire for a closer relationship with Christ. Emphasis was placed on personal transformation as the beginning of an individual journey that, nevertheless, the church had embarked on together. "There is no evidence that the earliest holiness groups intended to form new sects or denominations."[86] Yet, the Holiness movement frequently criticized the established churches for having stifled this desire and replacing it with a formal system "not because they love holiness or the church but because they love honor, money, division, a great name and greetings in the markets, chief seats in the council, conferences and associations."[87]

> When their churches first begun,
> By the Holy Spirit they were run;
> But when their creeds each church had took,
> The Holy Spirit them forsook.[88]

The "formal system" was perceived as anti-spiritual. Richard G. Spurling, a former Baptist preacher, compared the church to the building and operating of a railroad: the train rolling on golden rails of God's law of love with liberty and equality forming the great drive wheels. The train is guided by the Holy Spirit, but

> one day in absence of the Guide, there being several engineers, firemen and porters (officers of the church) Satan tells them that other fire will run this engine as well as the fire from heaven, and that other rails would be lighter and easier managed than the golden rails (men-made creeds); they took out the golden link of God's law and set it on wooden rails. Then they tried to roll ahead, but alas . . . a great crash followed. For 1,500 years this golden link has been lost.[89]

Spurling located the origins of the "lost link" (the absence of a universal code) with the creed of Nicaea in AD 325. A "semantic cut," however, did not occur until this absence was realized in its full magnitude by the Holiness churches in the nineteenth century. The church had followed human laws (creeds) instead of God's law (love). For the

---

86. Conn, *Like a Mighty Army*, xxv.
87. Spurling, *Lost Link*, 30; written in 1897.
88. Spurling, *Lost Link*, 44.
89. Spurling, *Lost Link*, 15–16.

Holiness groups, the creeds, being contrary to God's law, had lost their social acceptability and with it their credibility and legitimacy. Nevertheless, it was not the creeds that were in need of "reform"[90] but the entire symbolic system. The transformation of the whole system (the liturgy of the church) was the envisioned fulfillment of what had to begin with the individual person. The Pentecostal vision was a global vision; yet it was not the vision of a church reformed but of a church reborn by the Spirit of God and as the work of Christ.

> Stand up, stand up for Jesus, ye soldiers of the cross,
> Lift high His royal banner, it must not suffer loss;
> From victory unto victory His army shall He lead,
> Till every foe is vanquished, and Christ is Lord indeed.[91]

The new emphasis permeated the literature of the nineteenth century frequently clothed in Pentecostal language and imagery.[92] George Hughes, a leading member of the National Holiness Association, envisioned a "world rocking revival of religion," which was to be "along pentecostal lines."[93] A widely circulating book, *The Tongue of Fire*, evoked Pentecostal language when calling for a "baptism with purifying flames of fire."[94] In 1871, Charles G. Finney addressed the Oberlin Council of Congregationalism on the "baptism of the Holy Spirit."[95] The late Holiness movement was characteristically looking back to Pentecost. But the use of this Pentecostal imagery remained rather thematic than dogmatic[96] until the Holiness groups accepted that it was not the "others" but they themselves that were called into question and that the global manifestation of God's Spirit would be completely other than what their desires had imagined. The change would occur only with the unexpected "fulfillment of the Pentecostal promise in visible, concrete, global manifestations."[97]

---

90. The Reformers "did not try to reform from creeds to God's law but tried to reform the creeds to a purer standard of faith"; Spurling, *Lost Link*, 20.
91. Duffield, "Stand Up for Jesus," quoted in Conn, *Like a Mighty Army*, 23.
92. See Dayton, *Theological Roots of Pentecostalism*, 65–73.
93. Quoted in Synan, *Holiness-Pentecostal Movement*, 141–42.
94. Arthur, *Tongue of Fire*.
95. Dayton, *Theological Roots of Pentecostalism*, 72.
96. See also Jones, *Perfectionist Persuasion*, 82–83.
97. Land, *Pentecostal Spirituality*, 69.

They were in an upper chamber, They were all with one accord,
When the Holy Ghost descended, As was promised by our Lord.
O Lord, send the power just now, O Lord, send the power just now;
O Lord send the pow'r just now and baptize ev'ry one.

Yes, this pow'r from heav'n descended With the sound of rushing wind;
Tongues of fire came down upon them, As the Lord said he would send.
O Lord, send the power just now, O Lord, send the power just now;
O Lord send the power just now and baptize ev'ry one.

Yes, this "Old time" pow'r was given To our fathers who were true;
This is promised to believers, And we all may have it too.
O Lord, send the power just now, O Lord, send the power just now;
O Lord send the power just now and baptize ev'ry one.[98]

The new Pentecostal emphasis on concrete manifestations moved the "Pentecostal" liturgy to a different level, accentuating it and thus distinguishing it further from the symbolic imagery of the established churches. Among the mainline churches "many were curious. Some were cynical. Others were openly hostile."[99] However, the "actor from one perspective . . . [was] simultaneously the 'acted upon' from another perspective."[100] The semantic cut that occurred at the outset of this new Pentecostal imagery drove the symbolic path of both the established and the Holiness churches further apart; the established churches claiming the possession of a "universal" but, in reality, inapplicable code; the Holiness churches witnessing the death of the universal code and simultaneously living the formation of a new liturgy. Since one symbol is established only within the whole network of symbolic meaning, as a consequence the whole church experienced a *symbolic turn*.[101] The desire of a few birthed the vision for many of that "place which one must imagine without being able to conceive it." This was a vision for the whole church, a vision that demanded immediate attention and was embraced with a strong sense of urgency:

---

98. Tillman, "Old Time Power" (1895), in *Church Hymnal*, 121.

99. Conn, *Like a Mighty Army*, 25, about the Shearer Schoolhouse revival in 1896.

100. Darrand, *Metaphors of Social Control*, 196.

101. It is thus inappropriate to say that only those writings concerned with Spirit baptism influenced the formation of Pentecostalism; see Hollenweger, *Pentecostalism*, 20–21.

Why do you wait, dear brother, O why do you tarry so long?
Your Savior is waiting to give you A place in His sanctified throng.
Why not? Why not? Why not come to Him now?
Do you not feel, dear brother, His Spirit now striving within?
Oh why not accept His salvation, And throw off thy burden of sin?
Why not? Why not? Why not come to Him now?
Why do you wait, dear brother? The harvest is passing away;
Your Savior is longing to bless you, There's danger and death in delay.
Why not? Why not? Why not come to Him now?[102]

THE SYMBOLIC TURN AND THE FORMATION OF A LITURGY OF PENTECOSTALISM

The *symbolic turn* occurred with a new symbol that would remove the new liturgy irrevocably from the symbolic order of the mainline churches. Spirit baptism, and its "visual" manifestation of speaking in tongues, completed the *symbolic turn*. With the manifestation of the Spirit baptism of over one hundred persons in North Carolina in 1896,[103] Agnes N. Ozman[104] and the Topeka revival in 1901, and the Azusa Street revival in 1906–1915, the new liturgy of Pentecostalism had come to its completion. Ideas that had been somewhat loosely connected with the Holiness movement,[105] such as a definite experience of Spirit baptism, supernatural healing, and expectations of the second coming of Christ,[106] now began to form a definite "coordinated system." And "in this context, the doctrine of entire sanctification became equated with the baptism of the Holy Spirit."[107] Two contributing factors for the consolidation of this liturgy of Spirit baptism were the reaction of the mainline churches and the unexpected expansion of the Pentecostal movement to international proportions. At the beginning of the *symbolic turn*, however, stood first of all the question of its symbolic interpretation: "What meaneth this?" (Acts 2:12 KJV).

102. George F. Root, "Why Do You Wait?" (1878), in *Church Hymnal*, 378–79.

103. See the account by Conn, *Like a Mighty Army*, 17–31.

104. Regarded by many as the beginning of Pentecostalism; see Dayton, *Theological Roots*, 179.

105. Bloch-Hoell, *Pentecostal Movement*, 16.

106. For an analysis of this shift see Faupel, *Everlasting Gospel*, 77–114.

107. Faupel, *Everlasting Gospel*, 80.

> "What meaneth this?"—the cry of the "devout men, out of every nation under heaven," when confronted with this initial appearance of the *glossolalia*. "What meaneth this?"—the cry of all thinking men who through the succeeding ages have contemplated this phenomenon of Pentecost. "What meaneth this?"—the cry of Bible students who through the centuries have read with wonder God's record of that extraordinary day. "What meaneth this?"—the cry which has lost none of its challenge though almost two thousand years have past since first it was uttered.[108]

The experience of Spirit baptism cut once and for all the ties of Pentecostalism with the symbolic interpretation of the mainline churches.[109] For those who had been filled with the desire for a Pentecostal experience as an expression of personal sanctification and intimate relationship with God, the code of interpretation was self-evident: the personal testimony and the witness of Scripture.[110] But for those who had distanced themselves from the Holiness movement, neither the first nor the latter was able to provide an adequate (and universal) code of interpretation.

(1) Spirit baptism was a symbol with no tradition; it was neither "to be confused with water baptism, be it by sprinkling, pouring or immersing. Nor can it be considered the same as the sacrament of confirmation, though this rite is believed by many in Christendom to convey the Holy Spirit to the participant."[111] (2) Spirit baptism was a symbol with no signifier; for Pentecostals, Spirit baptism was signified by the appearance of tongue speech, for non-Pentecostals *glossolalia* was a signifier of emotional excess or demonic influence.[112] (3) Spirit baptism was a symbol with no ritual; "Pentecostals maintain that no clergymen can ever perform this baptism," for it is Christ who baptizes—non-Pentecostals could not incorporate this symbol into a liturgy in which the minister acts in the person of the whole church.[113] The entire network of symbolic meaning

---

108. Brumback, *"What Meaneth This?,"* 21–22.

109. As well as with the old-school Holiness and fundamental churches; see Synan, *In the Latter Days*, 75–78.

110. Particularly important were Acts 1, 2, 8–11, 19; 1 Cor 12–14; John 3:34; Luke 24:49; Eph 5:18–19; Mark 16:17–18.

111. Durasoff, *Bright Wind*, 4.

112. See Hinson, "Significance of Glossolalia," 189–96.

113. In the established churches, even though it is Christ himself who baptizes, the minister acts *in persona totius Ecclesiae*; Aquinas, *Summa Theologiae*, III, q. 64, art. 9 ad 1; Augustine, *In Johannis Evangelium Tractatus* VI, 1.7, PL 35, 1428; Paul VI,

did not allow the established churches to interpret this symbol and with it the entire new structure of the liturgy of Pentecostalism. For the mainline churches a liturgy of Pentecostalism was non-existent—for the Pentecostal churches the liturgy of Christendom had collapsed.

Just as Jesus gave new meaning to the concept "Messiah" that could only be understood by forsaking the traditional code of its interpretation and experiencing its truth in light of Jesus' death and resurrection, the "Pentecostal experience" could only be understood if any former concept was forsaken in light of a vision that was not afraid of the death of the established code and that boldly embraced Spirit baptism as that "place" they had imagined without yet being able to fully conceive it. This vision thoroughly changed the understanding of Christianity for Pentecostals to a radical inbreaking of the kingdom of God in the now. For Pentecostals, "Pentecost has become a liturgical paradigm, an existential reality, and a dispensation of the Spirit in the last days."[114] The church has become a movement of the Spirit. The liturgy of Pentecostalism is therefore the liturgy of the *kenosis* of the Spirit of Christ into a church that is constantly being reborn at millions of Pentecosts.[115]

The reaction of the mainline churches, like Peter's rejection of the *symbolic turn*, further consolidated and isolated the liturgy of Pentecostalism, which "was denounced as 'anti-Christian,' as 'sensual and devilish,' and as 'the last vomit of Satan.' Its adherents were taunted and derided from the pulpit as well as in religious and secular press.... Those ministers and missionaries who embraced the Holy Spirit baptism were removed from their pulpits or dismissed by their mission boards."[116] The broken code of interpretation left the established churches with an irreducible symbolic residue that came to bar social and ecumenical relations. The anti-Pentecostal argument ranged from "the work of the devil" to excessive emotionalism and eccentric but harmless ideology.[117] The main argument, however, centered not around a *symbolic order*, that is, a liturgy of Pentecostalism, nor around the *symbolic significance*

Sacrosanctum Concilium, 7. However, Spirit baptism as a symbol, i.e., as a mediation in time and space, cannot be a reproducible symbol because the *causa efficiens* is the Spirit who as *principium personale* has the irreversible *auctoritas principii* toward the created grace. See also Mühlen, *Heilige Geist als Person*, 264–66; 292–304.

114. Land, *Pentecostal Spirituality*, 174.

115. "There was one Easter; there are millions of Pentecosts." Comblin, *Holy Spirit and Liberation*, 32. See also Groupe des Dombes, "Holy Spirit, the Church," 251.

116. Nichol, *Pentecostalism*, 70.

117. See Ward, "Anti-Pentecostal Argument," 99–122.

of Spirit baptism and therefore missed the life-giving center of the liturgy of Pentecostalism completely. It rather exclusively focused on the validity and credibility of the apparently only signifier: *glossolalia*.[118] As a result of the rejection of tongue speech (as signifier), Spirit baptism (as the signified) was also disregarded and with it the entire symbolic network of the Pentecostal community. The self-expression of Pentecostalism as the fullness of the church, necessary for the establishment of a common *liturgy of Pentecostalism*, remained to a large extent the self-im-pression of a system that appeared "coordinated" only to those who were themselves a dynamic part of it.

On the other hand, the liturgy of Pentecostalism was not easily ex-pressed. The manifestation of Spirit baptism was experienced at the same time in countries around the world,[119] bringing with it a global *symbolic turn*: the disturbance of the whole of Christendom. Yet, the expansion of Pentecostalism must not merely be understood as the world being "overwhelmed by a sweeping revival campaign."[120] Rather, it was much of Pentecostalism itself that was overwhelmed. The force of the *symbolic turn* was directed much toward the movement itself: it wiped out "whatever ideas or views you may have adopted, or systems you may have formed."[121] The newly emerging system reflected a hierarchy of truths (*hierarchia veritatum*)[122] very different from that of the established churches, with a liturgy that developed first of all as the exclamation that "Pentecostals believe in more than tongues!"[123]

---

118. Mainly the inapplicability of *glossolalia* in the book of Acts, the temporary nature of tongue speech, the inferiority of *glossolalia*, and a psychological explanation of *glossolalia* as a human phenomenon. Synan, *Pentecostal-Charismatic Origins*, 119. It is thus a misrepresentation that the Pentecostal movement for some reason favored glossolalia as one symbol over others, isolated this symbol from the common liturgy, and formed its own liturgy around it.

119. Pentecostal revivals were experienced in Europe, Latin America, Russia, and Asia. See Synan, *In the Latter Days*, 55–69.

120. Bloch-Hoell, *Pentecostal Movement*, 30.

121. Barratt, *In the Days*, 31.

122. See *Unitatis Redintegratio* in Flannery, *Documents of Vatican II*, 499–524; and "Notion of Hierarchy," 561–71.

123. See Anderson, "Pentecostals Believe," 53–64.

PENTECOSTAL LITURGY AFTER THE SYMBOLIC TURN

The *symbolic turn* has not created a liturgy of Pentecostalism *about* which one could now write as a mere object and as if it stood at the end of a fully completed development. It is the necessary and independent but *partial* cause of a liturgy of Pentecostalism that unfolds as an eternal covenant promise of God in our times (Acts 2:16–21) and which requires the continuing commitment of the human person to this covenant as a mutual and personal act.[124] Spirit baptism is a *distinctive* symbol of this covenant; it is distinctive to the development and formation of the Pentecostal tradition. Yet, Spirit baptism is not the foundation of a Pentecostal hierarchy of truths. At the Azusa Street revival, William J. Seymour expressed this in Pentecostal language:

> Tongues are one of the signs that go with every baptized person, but it is not the real evidence of the baptism in the every day life. Your life must measure up with the fruits of the Spirit. . . . Many may start in this salvation, and yet if they do not watch . . . they will lose the Spirit of Jesus, and have only gifts which will be as sounding brass and a tinkling cymbal, and sooner or later these will be taken away.[125]

As much as an understanding of "Messiah" cannot be reduced to the *symbolic turn* embedded in the temporal manifestation of the crucifixion,[126] one can also not reduce an understanding of Pentecostalism to the *symbolic turn* embedded in Spirit baptism—much less to its signifier *glossolalia*.

Aimee Semple McPherson[127] summarized a more inclusive basis for a liturgy of Pentecostalism in an often-quoted statement from 1922:

> Jesus saves us according to John 3:16. He baptizes us with the Holy Spirit according to Acts 2:4. He heals our bodies according

---

124. For a distinction of the *causae partiales*, see Mühlen, *Heilige Geist als Person*, 71–72, 78–81.

125. Seymour, *Apostolic Faith*, 2.

126. See the critique by Bonhoeffer of Heidegger's ontology in *Act and Being*. The symbol of "Christ crucified" (1 Cor 1:23) represents the fullness of the *kerygma* (1 Cor 15:1–10).

127. Founder of the International Church of the Foursquare Gospel.

to James 5:14–15. And Jesus is coming again to receive us unto Himself according to 1 Thessalonians 4:16–17.[128]

This summary represents an early attempt to integrate the liturgy of Pentecostalism into the liturgy of the church. Yet, these four themes must be read as only representative of a much wider and more complex understanding of the *opus Christi*. Pentecostalism subsequently emphasized other themes in their own right, and within a liturgy of Pentecostalism, the distinctive themes are "not a goal to be reached . . . but a door [to] . . . a greater fullness of life in the Spirit."[129] Without the ability to once and for all define the liturgy, a specific Pentecostal liturgy remains grounded upon the *symbolic turn* the church experienced in the form of Spirit baptism. The church continues to be transformed by that event in an eschatological transformation. A sacramental liturgy of Pentecostalism is still being written on the basis of that eschatological reinterpretation of the liturgy of Christendom. At the same time, the *anamnesis* of the Pentecostal tradition today is characterized by the struggle to reconcile Easter with Pentecost. To do so, Pentecostalism is reaching out to the liturgy of the world *and* the church. It is the whole world that is participating in this event.

CONCLUSION

A liturgy of Pentecostalism is still being written. This study presented how this liturgy could emerge and what factors contributed to its formation. There can be no universal understanding of Spirit baptism as the distinctive symbol of this liturgy without integration of the coordinating system it is embedded in and vice versa. In the liturgy of Pentecostalism, God is rewriting the liturgy of the world *and* of the church; it is conditioned by the response of those who are a part of it as much as by those who think they are not. Those who are have found in it a form of self-expression, which requires a conscious giving up of that which constitutes the interpretation of reality, and the acceptance that Pentecostalism is neither *this* (modern Pentecost) nor *that* (biblical Pentecost) but a continually engaging reality that is constantly being moved by the Spirit

---

128. Quoted in Cox, *Four-Square Gospel*, 9.

129. Lee, "Pneumatological Ecclesiology," 38, quoting "A Proposed Description of the Nature and Purpose of a Dialogue Between a Group of Pentecostals and Roman Catholics Under the Sponsorship of the Secretariat for Promoting Christian Unity."

of God as the work of Christ in, with, and through his church. Those who distance themselves from Pentecostalism will find in it a constant challenge to their own symbolic interpretation of reality and sacramentality. It is impossible to acknowledge Pentecostalism without ourselves being called into question by the historical and concrete reality of a liturgy that has as its center the always initiating Spirit of God.

5

Worship, Spirituality, and the Making of a Black Liturgy

IN THE STUDY OF African American worship and spirituality, Pentecostalism has received only marginal attention. The reverse statement is also applicable: in Pentecostal studies, the African American dimension has not received the attention it deserves.[1] These statements are all the more surprising in light of a prominent emphasis on the African roots of Pentecostalism, in general, and of African American Pentecostalism, in particular. The veracity of this relationship has never been fully explored despite suggestions that Pentecostalism is at heart characterized by a Black liturgy. The history and shape of this Black Pentecostal liturgy remains uncharted territory. As a result, the role of Black worship and spirituality for the unity of the racially and ethnically diverse Pentecostal movement remains unidentified.

This chapter begins to trace the connection between African, African American, and Pentecostal religion in the context of the liturgical environment of North America. I argue that the making of a Black liturgy, a form of spirituality and worship rooted deeply in the religion of African slaves and ritual practices emerging from the American camp meeting, functions as a basis of resemblance and unity among North American Pentecostal churches. The initial development of this Black liturgy is attributable to

---

1. See Yong and Alexander, "Black Tongues of Fire," in *Afro-Pentecostalism*, 1–18.

the pervasive processes of migration and urbanization in North America during the nineteenth and twentieth centuries. The resulting Black liturgy is both uniquely African American and Pentecostal.

The journey into the making of a Black liturgy begins with a look at the contemporary argument on worship and spirituality in the context of Pentecostalism. This introduction initiates the conversation between studies on African American worship and Pentecostalism. The conversation is then taken to an exploration of African slave narratives and the American camp meetings appropriated by Pentecostals. The study concludes with an investigation of the effects of migration and urbanization on the making of a Black Pentecostal liturgy and suggestions for future directions in the study of Afro-Pentecostalism.

BLACK LITURGY IN PENTECOSTAL WORSHIP AND SPIRITUALITY

The term "liturgy" is foreign to most of the literature of Pentecostal scholarship (see chapter 4). To speak of a Black liturgy in the context of African American Pentecostal churches stands in sharp contrast to the widespread neglect of the liturgical development of Pentecostalism and its frequent stereotyping as a movement without liturgical sensitivities.[2] In a similar vein, Pentecostalism is almost completely absent from the tradition of liturgical and ritual studies.[3] The term "liturgy" must therefore be used carefully. In the broadest possible sense of the word, liturgy refers to any activity designated as a "work of the people" (*leitourgia*).[4] In the context of Pentecostalism, the term comprises both a form of spirituality and a form of worship concentrated in the encounter with God. The emphasis of the term is on the free response to this encounter with God rather than an order or a structure provided for the possibility of that encounter.[5] The only path to integrate Pentecostalism in the existing and often highly structured liturgical landscape is through a rather loose attachment of the term "liturgy" to the practices of spirituality and worship, a connection I shall refer to as an "open arrangement."

2. See Alexander, "Non-Liturgical Holiness-Pentecostalism," 158–93; Albrecht, "Pentecostal Spirituality," 107–25; Alexander, "Pentecostal Ritual Reconsidered," 109–28.

3. See Albrecht, *Rites in the Spirit*.

4. See Vondey, "Symbolic Turn," 223–47.

5. See Vondey, *Beyond Pentecostalism*, 109–40.

The emphasis on liturgy as an open and holistic mixture of spirituality and worship often resisting formalization is also a strong emphasis of the African American community.[6] African American liturgical traditions are held together mostly by the rather broad scheme of singing, preaching, prayer, and fellowship, and the emphasis on experience and empowerment.[7] Dialogical style and prophetic elements including the frequent attention to celebration, liberation, and improvisation diversify African American churches and distinguish them from other liturgical traditions.[8] Black worship and spirituality are part of a nurturing process that involve the interrelated components of the personal, interpersonal, and social dimensions of life interwoven with the story of God, the Christian heritage of faith, and the personal and communal encounter with the divine.[9] This process is permeated by a dominant emphasis on the Holy Spirit that is characteristic for both Black and Pentecostal communities.[10] At least in principle, Pentecostalism and African American churches display similar patterns of spirituality and worship.

The term "liturgy" in these contexts is perhaps best described as what African American scholars have called "embodied spirituality"[11] or what Pentecostals call "action-reflection in the Spirit."[12] While worship as embodied spirituality can be ritualized, the process of formalization and structuring is slow. In this sense, the term "liturgy" always remains closer to spirituality and worship and resists formal structure, whether imposed by church or culture. The making of a Black "liturgy" therefore refers more broadly to the actualization of a reflection on the Christian life than to the ordered performance of spirituality in worship. African American scholars have referred to this aspect as the importance of worship in the invisible institution rather than the official structures of churches and congregations.[13] This somewhat pre-critical and pre-ecclesiological appreciation of liturgy is particularly typical among African American Pentecostal congregations; it paints the image of liturgy in the colors of

---

6. See Costen, *African American Christian Worship*.

7. Costen, *African American Christian Worship*, 127–34. See Costen and Swann, *Black Christian Worship Experience*.

8. See Maynard-Reid, *Diverse Worship*, 53–107.

9. See Floy-Thomas et al., *Black Church Studies*, 179–200.

10. See Hinson, *Fire in My Bones*.

11. Wilson Bridges, *Resurrection Song*, 83; Battle, *Black Church in America*, 163–82.

12. Land, *Pentecostal Spirituality*, 119.

13. Costen, *African American Christian Worship*, 36–49.

tarrying and waiting for an encounter with God and the response to that encounter.[14] At the moment of encounter, all liturgy ceases.

The close connection between Pentecostalism and African American religions has led some scholars to speak of the African and African American roots of the Pentecostal movement.[15] The classic study on Pentecostalism by Walter J. Hollenweger, in particular, suggests that a Black, oral liturgy is central to the characterization of global Pentecostalism.[16] However, the precise character of this liturgy has not been examined. Hollenweger situated the liturgical origins of classical Pentecostals at the Azusa Street Mission and revival of 1906, concentrated in the black preacher William J. Seymour who, according to Hollenweger's assessment, "inspired his congregation to develop its own liturgy."[17] Hollenweger later attributed the roots of Seymour's liturgical sensitivity to "his black heritage," yet continued to infer that it was Seymour's personal initiative that shaped the Pentecostal revivals.[18] Surprisingly, even among African American Pentecostals, little research has been done on the origins and development of a "Black" liturgy. On the basis of contemporary research, Seymour, and even the Azusa Street revival and mission, are too insufficient a basis to explain the character of such a liturgy in the broader American and Pentecostal socioreligious contexts.

The construction of a broader support for an African American basis of a Black liturgy requires two premises that have been established only recently by contemporary scholarship. First, Pentecostal origins are deeply connected with African American spirituality.[19] While the argument for African roots of classical Pentecostalism is not new, it is more precise to speak of the African roots of Pentecostal liturgy.[20] Second, this African spiritual heritage was exposed in the North American context to interracial and complex religious impulses of European, Hispanic,

---

14. See Daniels, "Until the Power," 173–91.

15. See Lovett, "Black Origins," 123–41.

16. See, in particular, Hollenweger, *Pentecostals*; Hollenweger, "Social and Ecumenical Significance," 207–15.

17. Hollenweger, "Social and Ecumenical Significance," 208.

18. Hollenweger, "Black Roots of Pentecostalism," 40.

19. See, for example, MacRobert, *Black Roots*; MacRobert, "Black Roots of Pentecostalism," 295–309; Paris, *Black Pentecostalism*; Sanders, "African American Worship," 105–20.

20. A step in this direction was made by Beckman, "Trance," 11–26.

and other cultures.[21] From this perspective, it is clear that a Pentecostal liturgy did not originate within the medieval European context of the traditional liturgical environment. On the other hand, we cannot speak at any point of a "pure" African liturgy in the North American context. In order to trace the birth and formation of a Black Pentecostal liturgy, this chapter follows the hypothesis that from the plantation prayer grounds of African slaves and the camp meetings of the American South an African American spirituality was carried to the urban centers of the American heartland where, shaped by the social, cultural, and religious conditions of the new environment, it emerged as a new liturgical form labeled "Pentecostal" and in its sensitivities uniquely American.

THE AFRICAN ROOTS OF THE PENTECOSTAL LITURGY

The African religious heritage has long been a focus of the study of African American worship and spirituality.[22] Cultural, social, psychological, and aesthetic connections to the experience and history of slavery penetrate the discussion with particular force.[23] The rediscovery of slave narratives in recent scholarship has unearthed that the African slaves formed a "unique and coherent understanding of Christianity" from often "illegal and hidden religious practices" and "in radical distinction to white Christianity . . . in their own language and idiom."[24] The forced Christianization of the slaves did little to extinguish the notions of African indigenous religion brought to the North American context, particularly the ritual sensitivities of the African life.[25] These sensitivities included a preference for nature, the field and barns, bushes, and forests, over buildings, churches, and pews.[26]

---

21. See Baer and Singer, *African American Religion*, 1–26. In the context of Pentecostalism, Daniels, "'Everybody Bids You Welcome,'" 222–52.

22. See Costen, *African American Christian Worship*, 25–35.

23. See Woodson, *History of the Negro Church*.

24. Hopkins, "Slave Theology," 1–2.

25. See Wood, "Jesus Christ," 1–7; Jernegan, "Slavery and Conversion," 505–27.

26. Hopkins, "Slave Theology," 5–7.

> Us could go to de white folk's church, but us wanted ter go whar us could sing all de way through, an' hum 'long, an' shout—yo' all know, jist turn loose lack.[27]

Nature and creation formed the space of the early African American rituals. While much of this exposure to the outdoors in North America was forced upon the slaves by their white masters, the rural prayer grounds shaped significantly what was expected and what was possible in the worship experience.

> We jes made er bush arbor by cutin' bushes dat was full of green leaves an' puttin' em on top of four poles reachin' from pole to pole. Den sometimes we'd have dem bushes put roun' to kiver de sides an' back from der bottom to der top. All us get together in dis arbor fer de meetin'.[28]

The formal liturgies of the established churches seemed disconnected from the needs and demands of the African American faith community. As George C. L. Cummings has shown, the thematic framework was shaped decidedly by two key theological loci that I have highlighted as significant elements of the Pentecostal imagination: the presence of the Holy Spirit (pneumatology) and the expectation of the kingdom of God (eschatology).[29]

> Getting religion was manifested in a variety of ways. Some slaves had visions, others shouted and walked, and still others bore witness to the creative power of the Spirit. The Spirit possessed the physical being of the slaves, and as a consequence they shouted; spoke of great visions of God, heaven, or freedom; and engaged in physical activity that manifested the Spirit's presence.[30]

The presence of God's Spirit was perceived as a liberating occurrence of freedom, experienced temporally in the prayer grounds, and nurturing a vision of ultimate freedom in the future. "Concomitantly," Cummings states, "the eschatological hopes and aspirations of the slave community became evident in the Spirit who guarantees the future as one of freedom and justice."[31] This orientation toward the ultimate freedom of life in the

---

27. Emily Dixon, quoted in Hopkins, "Slave Theology," 6.
28. Arthur Greene, quoted in Hopkins, "Slave Theology," 6.
29. Cummings, "Slave Narratives," 33–46.
30. Cummings, "Slave Narratives," 34.
31. Cummings, "Slave Narratives," 43.

Spirit profoundly shaped the early African American liturgy, which was greatly impacted by the slave work ethic.

Work, for the slaves, meant forced labor. As Joan Martin observes,

> This made the nature of the work they were required to do evil. It was evil because it grew out of the sinful human will to subjugate and exploit others. . . . Their lives demonstrated that the result of such evil was unwarranted, unearned, and undeserved suffering.[32]

This work ethic stood in contrast to the freedom and justice associated with God. For the African slaves, ritual action was not a "work" of the people but the freedom from compulsion, exploitation, duty, and performance. The often coded opposition to forced labor could be seen (and heard) over and over again in the Negro spirituals and slave songs during monotonous and hard labor.[33] Yet nowhere else was the African spiritual tradition retained more explicitly than in the fields and bushes, where the slaves were free to pray, sing, dance, shout, and "jist turn loose lack." In elemental African spiritual practices such as the "ring shout," the slaves broke free from outward conformity.[34] Even when performed in a formal religious environment, these practices resisted formalization. Worship meant enthusiasm, life, and freedom—liturgy as play.[35]

The prayer grounds lacked the structural liturgical framework of medieval liturgical performance. As Charles Joyner noted, "Slaves did not so much adapt to Christianity . . . as adapt Christianity to themselves."[36] The African folk religion was based on an oral traditioning process, centered on narratives, songs, plays, and other forms of communication that preserved the story of the slaves and their values, affections, and rituals.[37] The architecture, language, movements, scripts, music, processions, vestments, and vessels of the traditional Christian liturgy did not function in the secret worship meetings. The worship of the slaves was dominated by prayer, preaching, and singing, and although oriented along European ritual, these liturgical aspects were transformed by the imagination and

---

32. Martin, "Perseverance and Unwearied Industry," 127.
33. See Allen et al., *Slave Songs*.
34. See Johnson and Johnson, *Books*, 31–34.
35. See Bridgeman Davis, "Go Play with God," 26–32.
36. Joyner, *Down by the Riverside*, 141.
37. MacRobert, *Black Roots*, 11–12; MacRobert, "Black Roots of Pentecostalism," 299–301.

rhythm of their African roots.[38] Liturgy was not a "confining structure" but an "open arrangement" oriented along the necessities of the situation and the possibilities provided by the presence of God's Spirit. The "openness" of the liturgical arrangement was most clearly seen in the dominance of unrehearsed participation rather than structured performance.[39] Spontaneous responses to the sermon, shouting, stomping, singing, sighing, dancing, swaying, clapping, humming, and an entire array of kinesthetic activities emerged out of a sense of spiritual liberty. While these practices were often inherited from African religious tradition, they found new meaning in the African American context.[40]

> The phenomenon of spirit possession, one of the most significant features in African religion . . . was reinterpreted in Christian terms to become a central feature of expressive behavior in African-American Christianity and a necessary part of the conversion experience. Conversion was the climax of a spiritual journey called "seeking." A prolonged period of praying "in the wilderness" included an ecstatic trance without which conversion was not considered authentic.[41]

The orientation toward nature, the pneumatological imagination, and the broad array of kinesthetic responses to the spiritual awareness of God's presence undoubtedly emerged from African antecedents.[42] The experience of the presence of the Holy Spirit provided a contrast to the performance-oriented work environment of the day. The pneumatological and eschatological setting of African American worship provided a refuge from the harsh realities of everyday life and offered a sense of empowerment and freedom.[43] Here, the slaves were free to engage God in the fullness of their being and affections.

---

38. See Duitsman Cornelius, *Slave Missions*, 8–12, 16–20.
39. See Joyner, "Believer I Know," 25–36.
40. See Mbiti, *Introduction to African Religion*.
41. Mbiti, *Introduction to African Religion*, 30.
42. See Magesa, *Anatomy of Inculturation*, 171–88.
43. Andrews, *Practical Theology*, 34–37.

THE CAMP MEETING ROOTS OF
THE AMERICAN SOUTH

The integration of the freed slaves into the established ecclesiastical and liturgical structures presented one of the greatest challenges after the Civil War.[44] It was the camp meeting of the rural South that provided the premier environment for the mixing of liturgical temperaments.[45] The camp meetings had already exerted a powerful influence on the conversion of the slaves to Christianity and continued to be extremely popular.[46] As Albert Raboteau states in his classic study on slave religion, the camp meetings "presented a congenial setting for slaves to merge African patterns of response with Christian interpretations of the experience of spirit possession."[47]

In the traditional Christian environment, these meetings were closest in nature to the prayer ground meetings of the African slave community as they created room for the intermingling of different denominations, races, language groups, worship practices, and musical forms.[48] The emancipation of the slaves did not immediately prevent continued segregation, yet the camp meeting environment offered the opportunity for those who followed more expressive rituals to move to a secluded area without thereby forsaking the entire religious event.[49] The African liturgy thus came in contact with the "institutional" liturgy of those churches in North America that embraced the camp meetings as means of religious revival and evangelization.

Participants arrived at the camp meetings prepared to engage in not only a religious but also a social event. Similar to the "bush arbors" of the slave community, these events were initially held at rural, outdoor, and transient encampments that did not resemble the structural framework and liturgical environment of the established churches.[50] Arrangements

---

44. Andrews, *Practical Theology*, 12–30; Joyner, "Believer I Know," 18–46.

45. See Johnson, *Frontier Camp Meeting*; Conklin, *Cane Ridge*; Brown, *Holy Ground*; Brown, *Holy Ground Too*; Stephens, *Fire Spreads*.

46. See Baer and Singer, *African American Religion*, 3–12; Andrews, *Practical Theology*, 12–16; Raboteau, *Slave Religion*, 132.

47. Raboteau, *Slave Religion*, 72.

48. See Eslinger, *Citizens of Zion*.

49. See Baer and Singer, *African American Religion*, 12; Wesche, "Revival of the Camp-Meeting."

50. The most detailed documentation still comes from Brown, *Holy Ground Too*, 26–68.

were often spontaneous and haphazard, the meeting tents crowded, sleeping quarters sparse, and opportunities for eating, resting, and reflection frequently ignored.[51] Camp meetings resisted standardization into a particular pattern and were characterized loosely by their outdoor experience, the independent support of the participants, and the openness to all social strata among the churched and the unchurched.[52] The environment itself came to closely define the level of action and interaction for the liturgical consciousness of classical Pentecostalism. The rapidly growing Methodists and Baptists, and the Holiness Movement in particular, carried the camp meetings to the twentieth century and into the arms of the emerging Pentecostal movement.[53]

Despite the impact of camp meeting revivals on the history of modern evangelism, the liturgical structure of the meetings has not received much theological attention. The comparative dimensions of the liturgy, however, allow for an integration of camp meetings into a heuristic framework that takes account of both liturgical and dramatic theory. Hesser and Weigert suggest that such an analysis can be divided into an actional and an interactional level.[54] If we adopt this distinction, then the camp meetings clearly reshaped the involvement of place, time, actors, gestures, objects, vestments, and language that defined the traditional liturgical setting on the actional level. The meetings were not ecclesiastical in nature but resembled more "a temporary occupancy of the summer woods where the trees and hills are especially sanctified."[55] Usually, the celebrations were temporally restricted only by the exhaustion and weariness of the participants; bad weather and nightfall rarely shortened the meetings. The language was that of the people, not of liturgical manuals. Physical structures reflected simplicity of construction rather than symbolic character. Formal liturgical vestments were absent, and liturgical "props" were limited to few sacramental vessels.[56] As a result, the meetings were interactional on all levels, ranging from the dissolving of formal procedures and a lack of definition of the situation to spontaneous participation and unrehearsed responses to whatever the situation seemed to demand. A

51. Eslinger, *Citizens of Zion*, 233–35.
52. For a critique of formal definition, see Brown, *Holy Ground Too*, 27.
53. Westerfield Tucker, "North America," 607–10.
54. Hesser and Weigert, "Comparative Dimensions of Liturgy," 215–29.
55. Cooley, "Manna and the Manual," 132.
56. For first-hand accounts see Hughes, *Days of Power*; Mead, *Manna in the Wilderness*; Wallace, *Modern Pentecost*.

liturgy was not "performed"; the whole event rather "played" out as the circumstances permitted and where the Spirit of God led. Camp meetings were ordered not by formal liturgical structures but by opportunities to respond to an imagination that envisioned the camp ground as a sacred outdoor temple.[57] Understandably, the denominations that associated with the meetings, among them most prominently Baptists, Methodists, and the nineteenth-century Holiness movement, were especially attractive to African American spirituality.[58] The classical Pentecostal liturgy emerged more fully out of this environment.

The Holiness movement adopted the camp meetings not only for their effectiveness in evangelism and church growth but for the particular purpose of propagating the message of the holiness imagination.[59] Even a superficial glance at the liturgical environment of the camp meetings reveals that the claim is unfounded that they were essentially non-liturgical. The Presbyterian and Methodist heritage of the meetings preserved the liturgical sensitivities of those traditions, including the usual arrangement inside the tents, the placement of liturgical props, and celebration of the Lord's Supper (and more rarely and spontaneously water baptism).[60] However, the outdoor environment of the camp meetings altered the performative qualities of liturgical action and interaction, and it is therefore more adequate to speak of a quasi-liturgical framework. Adherents to the Holiness movement frequently contrasted the ritualism of established liturgical structures with the spiritual freedom experienced at the revival meetings.[61] A structurally planned worship service was typically taken as an indication of nominal Christianity.[62] For the participants of the camp meetings, the hills, the trees, and the meadows were the sanctuary of God's Spirit. They were surrounded by a "forest temple"[63] or, liturgically speaking, a "forest of symbols."[64] Similar to the prayer ground meetings of the African slave community, people often came directly from their work in the fields. Church buildings were replaced by tents and rough-hewn timber structures. The altar was not a place of sacramental action

57. Cooley, "Manna and the Manual," 137–45.
58. See Baer and Singer, *African American Religion*, 11.
59. See Dieter, *Holiness Revival*, 81–99.
60. See Vincent, *Wesleyan Grove*.
61. See Westerfield Tucker, "North America," 615–16.
62. See Wacker, *Heaven Below*, 100.
63. Synan, *Holiness-Pentecostal Movement*, 33–54.
64. Turner, *Forest of Symbols*.

but of repentance and sanctification, often represented only roughly by a pulpit or the area where the word of God was preached. Gestures were generally not visible from afar, but the spoken word traveled well in the otherwise quiet valleys and hills. Traditional liturgical vestments were avoided since they were not only impractical in the rural environment but their meaning was interpreted differently by those attending. The language was usually plain and outspoken.

The celebration of the sacraments presented a particular difficulty in the camp meeting environment. As the meeting places became established and more solid structures were built, little emphasis was placed on sacramental performance. The construction of the camp shed was influenced more heavily by the demands and potential of the moment. Central within such structures, the pulpit replaced the altar of the traditional liturgical setting. Even though worship at the pulpit was sometimes called the "altar service,"[65] this notion referred not to a sacrificial or sacramental place of worship but to a communal response to an invitation or challenge given in the sermon for the purpose of seeking salvation, repentance, or the baptism of the Holy Spirit. Considerations of performance did not influence the participation and response of the participants at these occasions. A Pentecostal camp meeting publication illustrates the event:

> As we pulled into the camp ground, which is shaded by a large grove of beautiful trees, carpeted with blue grass, surrounded by large fields of corn and alfalfa . . . we were soon overjoyed to see the tents that were up. . . . The campers increased until the tents numbered 195 and several house cars and trucks on top of that. The estimation of the people camping is from 700 to 900 throughout the camp meeting. . . . People were surely getting through in every morning service. Many were being slain under the power, at one time I counted 22 lying under the mighty power, being filled with the Holy Ghost and power. At various times it seemed that the power just came like sheets of rain and great shouts of praise would sweep over the whole congregation. . . . A number fell under the hand of the Lord.[66]

The rural, outdoor environment of the camp meetings represented a melting-pot for the amalgamation of liturgies among many Christian groups, including the "open arrangement" of the African American

65. See Newburn, "Significance of the Altar," 168–74.
66. Shields, "Camp-Meeting Special," 18.

liturgy characterized by both the preservation of existing elements of liturgical traditions and the resistance to formalization and structure evident among those traditions, embracing sensitivities to both the traditions represented and immediate demands or unusual circumstances.[67] The urbanization of the camp meetings further altered the liturgical landscape and removed the African origins of classical Pentecostalism and the camp meeting sensibilities further from the established liturgical structures of the institutional churches.

THE URBANIZATION OF THE PENTECOSTAL LITURGY

While the rural adherents of the camp meetings were exposed to the African American liturgy, two main factors influenced the expansion of this mixed heritage among Pentecostals. On the one hand, the National Camp Meeting Association for the Promotion of Christian Holiness contributed to the rapid expansion of camp meetings and to the transfer of the meetings from their original rural environment to larger urban areas.[68]

On the other hand, the mobility of the African American community after the emancipation of the slaves and especially with the Great Migration took the agrarian roots of the Pentecostal liturgy to the northern, northeastern, and western borders of the United States.[69] The unexpected migration of African Americans in general incurred strong, negative reactions.[70] The Holiness movement, on the other hand, "provided an unprecedented cultural context for legitimizing the African-derived liturgy of plantation praise houses."[71] The rural transplants attempted to "recreate" in the urban context the liturgical environment of the prayer grounds and camp meetings.[72] In this way, the teachings and values of the Holiness movement and the rituals of

---

67. See Vondey, *Beyond Pentecostalism*, 122–25.

68. Dieter, *Holiness Revival*, 81–82. On the rural-urban transition, see Smith, *Revivalism and Social Reform*.

69. See Arnesen, *Black Protest*; Sernett, *Bound*.

70. See Marks, *Farewell*, 110–36.

71. Kossie, "Move Is On," 62. On the Holiness movement and the migration, see also Jones, *Perfectionist Persuasion*, 79–88.

72. See Frazier, *Negro Church in America*, 58–60.

African liturgy meshed in urban areas, and exposed Pentecostals in the storefront churches to the revival rituals of the forest temples.

As a result of the urbanization, the traditional organization of the African American community was changed significantly: the cities demanded a reorganization of life and religion.[73] The urban surroundings provided a radically dissimilar environment for the actional and interactional dimensions of the rural liturgy. In the cities, the liturgy was exposed to utilitarianism, economic progress, population growth, social mobility, radical individualism, anonymity, the separation of work and residence, the emancipation of religion, as well as racial, ethnic, and religious diversity.[74] Los Angeles, often considered the birthplace of classical Pentecostalism, marked a particularly stark contrast to the environment of the rural Pentecostal communities, and the urban character of the Azusa Street Mission revival was markedly different from the roots of the Pentecostal liturgy in the camp meetings of the rural South. Nonetheless, under the leadership of William J. Seymour, the pastor of the Azusa Street Mission, together with his predominantly African American congregation, the liturgical framework of the camp meetings was kept alive in the urban environment.

The reenactment of the camp meetings at the Azusa Street Mission encountered numerous challenges. Most significantly, the open, outdoor sanctuary was replaced by the limitations of a city structure, a tight, hot, and sparsely illuminated enclosure. Cecil M. Robeck Jr. paints a vivid picture of the circumstances:

> The building in which they met was "tucked away" in a transitional neighborhood. It was nothing to look at—little more than a poorly whitewashed, burned-out shell with makeshift essentials. On its sawdust-covered dirt floor sat a collection of nail kegs and boards, and an assortment of discarded chairs. Because it lacked insulation and air-conditioning, and its ground floor was built of rough-sawn studs with only the outside lumber as walls, during the summer months the building grew intensely hot. . . . In spite of these problems—the substandard facilities, intense heat, lack of ventilation, and swarms of flies—people came by the thousands.[75]

73. See Frazier, *Negro Church in America*, 52–80; Stephens, *Fire Spreads*, 67–69.

74. The difference of urban and rural revivalism in North America is one of the central arguments in Smith, *Revivalism and Social Reform*. On the impact of urbanization on religion see Cox, *Secular City*.

75. Robeck, *Azusa Street Mission*, 129–31.

The urban environment could not maintain the "open arrangement" of the quasi-liturgical framework of the camp meetings and African American prayer grounds. In addition, the Azusa Street congregation provided interracial impulses and a multicultural environment for liturgical celebration that soon spread to other parts of the country.[76] Embedded in this environment were the influences of a variety of religious experiences that significantly expanded the horizon of liturgical perspectives among Pentecostals. The uniqueness of classical Pentecostalism is that its liturgical experience differed from the Anglo-European religious and cultural arrangement, crafting a new, and often radically different, ritual arrangement on the American religious scene. The new practices were often received with rejection by outsiders to the movement and encountered criticism even within Pentecostal ranks. At Azusa Street, the accusations of Pentecostal pioneer Charles F. Parham, for example, vividly illustrate the situation:

> There was a beautiful outpouring of the Holy Spirit in Los Angeles. . . . Then they pulled off all the stunts common in old camp meetings among colored folks. . . . That is the way they worship God, but what makes my soul sick . . . is to see white people imitating unintelligent crude negroisms of the Southland, and laying it on the Holy Ghost.[77]

Observers frequently reported "scenes that duplicate those of the negro revival meetings of the South."[78] The racial tensions contained in the makeup of this transformed spirituality and worship are undeniable.[79] In the urban environment of the early twentieth century, the mixture of African American worship and camp meeting tradition had changed into a new "Pentecostal" liturgy radically dissimilar from the traditional Anglo-European structures yet retaining the quasi-liturgical dimension of the camp meetings.

Robeck's seminal work on the Azusa Street Mission places at the heart of the new liturgy such elements as worship through prayer, song, singing in the Spirit, preaching and discussion, gathering at the altar, testimony, deliverance and conversion, sanctification, and the

---

76. See Daniels, "Everybody Bids You Welcome," 225–33. For the criticism, see Synan, *Holiness-Pentecostal Movement*, 110–12, 178–84; Robeck, "Past."
77. Parham, "Sermons," 9–10.
78. Robeck, *Azusa Street Mission*, 137.
79. See Vondey, *Pentecostalism*, 111–31.

baptism in the Holy Spirit.[80] Medieval liturgical structures were absent, established North American forms of the liturgy were not dominant, and liturgical manuals were rarely consulted. Instead, the altar service established itself as the heart of the urban liturgy, including opportunities for singing, testimony, conversion, deliverance, sanctification, and Spirit baptism. Robeck vividly describes the diverse expressions of urban Pentecostal worship.

> The intensity of their encounter with God led many at the mission to respond in ways that before their encounter they could "only imagine." It was a life changing-moment, a transformative time that produced a range of responses. There were those who . . . broke into dance. Others jumped, or stood with hands outstretched, or sang or shouted with all the gusto they could muster. Others were so full of awe when they encountered God that their knees buckled—they fell on the floor, "slain in the Spirit." Some spoke, rapid-fire, in a tongue they did not know, while others were struck entirely speechless.[81]

The established churches in the urban environment were ill-prepared to engage the emerging Pentecostal liturgy, which was seen as differing in both form and substance from orthodox Christian worship.[82] American Christianity at the turn of the twentieth century was characterized by widespread ecclesiastical turmoil. The American heartland had experienced an unprecedented religious transition from the established and organized churches, particularly Baptist and Methodist, but also Mennonites, Quakers, and Presbyterians, to radical new fellowships with very different, often unprecedented, liturgical settings.[83] European immigrants entering the country remained largely attached to the liturgical traditions of their homeland churches and introduced them to the complex reality of religious migration on the new continent.[84] This diversity of old and new, marked by a hybridity of cultural, ethnic, racial, social, ecclesiastical, and theological convictions and practices, resulted in a direct confrontation of established liturgical traditions with the new Pentecostal liturgy.

80. Robeck, *Azusa Street Mission*, 138–86; Daniels, "Gotta Moan Sometime," 5–32.

81. Robeck, *Azusa Street Mission*, 131.

82. Scholarship has only recently refuted that position; see Gaede, "Pentecost and Praise," 5–8; Baer, "Quaker Silence, Catholic Liturgy," 151–64.

83. Wacker, *Heaven Below*, 1; Dieter, *Holiness Revival*, 81–99; Dayton, *Theological Roots of Pentecostalism*, 35–84.

84. See Westerfield Tucker, "North America," 586–632.

The ritual practices of the movement were generally seen as "a symbolic rebellion on the part of socially disenfranchised Pentecostals."[85] These Pentecostals, however, were themselves unsure about the complexity of the liturgical practices that were emerging among them. Their liturgy had been shaped by African roots that were confronted with the sociocultural context of slavery in North America, exposed to the religious impulses of camp meetings and the Holiness movement, and transformed in the multicultural contexts of migration and urbanization. In these regards, the emergence of Pentecostalism represented at the same time the emergence of distinct liturgical sensitivities shaped by the diverse American contexts that contributed to their formation.

CONCLUSION

This chapter has charted the initial development of a Black liturgy that is both American and Pentecostal. Today's Black liturgy is a pervasive liturgical practice throughout Pentecostalism and beyond African American churches. The making of this liturgy indicates that Pentecostalism is a liturgical movement based on spirituality and worship experience rather than doctrinal consensus. The Black liturgy therefore functions as a basis of resemblance and unity at least among North American Pentecostals. The shared and pervasive experience of spirituality and worship forms the basis for ecumenicity and reconciliation in the Pentecostal movement.

The implications of this argument reach beyond the African American community and the makeup of North American Pentecostalism. If Pentecostalism is fundamentally a liturgical movement with Black spirituality and worship, then neither the African American community nor Pentecostal scholarship can continue to avoid addressing the liturgical identity of the movement. The isolation of the making of a Black liturgy from the dominant Anglo-European liturgical structures and its exposure to the North American cultural and ecclesiastical contexts has contributed to a destructuralization of the traditional conceptual framework that usually constitutes liturgical action.[86] In its place has emerged an alternative liturgical sensitivity, born in the sanctuary of nature, shaped by a revival mentality, and expanded by the opportunities and challenges of urban life.

85. Alexander, *Victor Turner Revisited*, 71.

86. For the Pentecostal dimensions, see Alexander, "Pentecostal Ritual Reconsidered," 109–28; for African American concerns, see Williams, "Worship and Anti-Structure," 161–74.

In contrast to the structural Anglo-European liturgy to which many of the established American churches adhered, with its conceptually fixed, written, priest-centered, and performance-oriented framework of sacramental celebration, Pentecostalism as a liturgical movement exhibits a destructuralizing, flexible, oral, participation-centered, and pneumatologically oriented "open arrangement" of worship, prayer, and praise. By the time the liturgical movement took hold on the American continent, classical Pentecostal denominations had already been formally organized and remained largely unaffected by the problems that concerned the liturgical renewal in the established churches.[87] In turn, from the perspective of the established Anglo-European liturgical traditions, Pentecostalism has essentially lost contact with the formal orthodox framework for a structural composition of ritual celebration.

If this assessment is correct, it has been incorrectly interpreted as an indication that Pentecostalism possesses no liturgy at all; a judgment uncritically accepted by many Pentecostals. As a result, the so-called non-liturgical character of Pentecostal faith and praxis has become the epitome of what many perceive at the root of a worldwide liturgical crisis. At the same time, Pentecostals hold the structural framework of the institutional churches responsible for the lack of freedom, openness, and flexibility in contemporary Christian worship and spirituality. This potential impasse demands a shared investigation of liturgical sensitivities by both Pentecostal and non-Pentecostal communities.

More work needs to be done to understand the dispersion of the Black liturgy through mass media and technology among Pentecostals beyond the African American community. Similarly, the reverse penetration of an urban Black liturgy into rural Pentecostal congregations demands further investigation. The effects of the popularization of the Black liturgy on the original Pentecostal character and African roots of that liturgy also have not been widely studied. Little attention has been paid to the effects of institutionalization, clericalization, and secularization on Pentecostal spirituality and worship. The ritual features and elements of the Black liturgy need further study in African, African American, white, and transethnic Pentecostal communities. In these diverse contexts, worship and spirituality should be considered a hallmark of racial and ecumenical reconciliation. The impact of a Black liturgy on the (self-)understanding of modern-day Pentecostalism has to be reevaluated.

---

87. See Fenwick and Spinks, *Worship in Transition*, 187–94.

6

Religion at Play and the Transformation of a Secular Age

PENTECOSTALS HAVE AVOIDED THE conversation on secularization. Ten years after Charles Taylor wrote *A Secular Age*, few Pentecostals have engaged his seminal proposal and monumental genealogy.[1] One of the reasons may be the general reluctance of scholarship on secularization to engage Pentecostals in the telling of the story. In Taylor's narrative, Pentecostals are examples of embodied, ecstatic, and "festive" countermovements that help not to exaggerate the reach of secularization, but that otherwise play no dominant role.[2] However, a more convincing reason for the reluctance of Pentecostals seems to be precisely their lack of awareness of their own place within the secular. The question we need to ask is where Pentecostalism fits Taylor's narrative of a secular age, and, perhaps more importantly, whether Pentecostals fit this telling of the story in the first place. Taylor leaves room here for Pentecostals in his account of modern conversions, or re-conversions, back to a nostalgic image of Christendom. Yet, I suggest that this room does not fit, that Pentecostalism is not a reconstruction of disillusioned modernists who wish to return to the premodern world but an alternative experience of the

---

1. Taylor, *Secular Age*. For details on Taylor's understanding of Pentecostalism, see the second part of this essay.
2. See Taylor, *Secular Age*, 244, 314, 455, 512, 552, 554, 766.

sacred in which the plausibility of the secular is suspended. The metaphor I want to invoke here for Pentecostals is that of religion as play, a ludic way of the religious life that engages with the secular without accepting the conditions that lend it authority. Religion at play is comfortable with observable and repeatable but often exaggerated, precocious, daring, and autotelic behavior with no immediately recognizable function and structural boundaries.[3] Pentecostalism is a manifestation of the divine at play *with* the religious and the secular, a divine festival, to use Taylor's image. In order to follow this argument, I engage with Taylor's foundational proposal of the central conditions of premodern life that have made room for our modern, secular world and demonstrate how and why these conditions are *not* met in Pentecostalism. I then examine the notion of play in Taylor's genealogy in order to illuminate more closely the ill fit of Pentecostalism in the history of the secular. I conclude that Pentecostalism represents a condition of religion that resolves the tension between sacred and secular unaccounted for in Taylor's work. At the same time, the notion of play also casts a critical shadow on the concept of "religion" as a term *sui generis*.[4] In the uncontested terrain of the secular supernova we call modernity, with its explosive multiplicity of alternative options, Pentecostalism is the nucleus of a different religious age.

PENTECOSTALISM AND THE CONDITIONS OF THE SECULAR

A Secular Age offers a complex history of secularization, not in the sense of the emptying of religion from public spaces (secularity 1) or the waning of religious belief and practice (secularity 2) but in a third sense of the secular manifested in changing conditions of belief (secularity 3) "from a society in which it was virtually impossible not to believe in God, to one in which faith . . . is one human possibility among others" (p. 3).[5] Taylor's work should be read primarily with this focus on identifying the conditions of the secular, and any critique from the perspective of Pentecostalism depends on its fit within this third type of secularity.

3. See Burghardt, "Defining and Recognizing Play," 9–18.
4. I use the term "religion" as a noun following Taylor's work, although the adjectival use of "religious," suggested by Smith, *How (Not) to Be Secular*, 1–25, would be more consistent with its opposition to "secular" and the critique to religion as a category inherent in the notion of play.
5. Page numbers from *A Secular Age* are given in parenthesis.

The impression that Pentecostalism does not fit a master narrative of secularization has emerged only sporadically in recent years. David Martin, whose political sociology of religion joins interests in secularization and Pentecostalism, suggests that the Pentecostal movement "was discounted because it was presented as politically the wrong kind of modernity or treated as an alarming case of reactive fundamentalism or dismissed as simply a phase before genuine modernity set in."[6] If Martin is correct, then the place of Pentecostalism can be identified with regard to the instrumental changes that, for Taylor, mark the transition from the premodern to the modern age and which form the conditions for the possibility of unbelief in a secular age: (1) the disenchantment of the modern world; (2) the disengagement from others; (3) the loss of equilibrium; (4) the instrumentalization of time; and (5) the discovery of the universe. The following account begins with Taylor's definition of each condition, identifies where the narrative meets Pentecostalism, and suggests how Pentecostals challenge the notion of a secular age.

The Enchantment of the Disenchanted

Taylor's account begins with the disenchantment of the enchanted premodern world. Investment in a world of spirits, demons, and devils is replaced by a process of internalization and introspection in which meaning is determined entirely by the human mind (pp. 29–41). Disenchantment is a shift in naïve understanding, where meaning can reside in the world independently from and external to human beings (p. 32), to the secular conviction that the outside world impinges on the human being no longer through its own exogenous power but only through the inward space of the mind. Whereas the premodern human being was a "porous" self, vulnerable, or more favorably, "healable" to benevolent and malevolent forces (p. 36), the modern self is "buffered" (p. 37) in a very different existential condition of choice to disengage "from everything outside the mind" (p. 38). Hence, the modern person has the option of disbelief in God, whereas this is not an option to the healable premodern self.

Taylor illustrates the change of boundaries with relation to spirits, also referencing the work of Birgit Meyer on Pentecostalism in Ghana (p. 39).[7] The modern, secular age, Taylor suggests, has replaced spirits

---

6. Martin, *Future of Christianity*, 25.
7. See Meyer, *Translating the Devil*.

with spirituality, that is, "not 'real' bodies or spirits but rather ways of talking about secular, modern mystifications."[8] Meyer challenges Taylor's proposal precisely on the premises of Pentecostal pneumatology. She points out that Pentecostals in a modern secular state do not simply exhibit the unexpected choice of a buffered self to return to a premodern age and rejects Taylor's "temporalization of cultures" as unacceptable in "a heavily pentecostalized public sphere in which ... spirits ... are not just there, as signs of a traditional past, but *reproduced* under modern conditions."[9] In response, Taylor holds on to the idea that Pentecostalism represents merely a "transition phenomenon" although questioning at another place whether secularization applies inevitably to all religions.[10] Meyer suggests that what Pentecostals exhibit are at once both secular and religious lives intersecting in the category of "spirit" and hence in a secular world of enchantment.[11] Pentecostals belong to what we might call "enchanted secular religious" movements, a porous entanglement of spirits that reaches from the secular to the religious and back again because the notion of "spirits" takes seriously all dimensions of created existence in a way that undercuts any awareness of either enchantment or disenchantment. Hence, Pentecostals can be enchanted naturalists, interventionist, or non-interventionist supernaturalists.[12] Disbelief is not an option in the encounter with spirits.[13] Yet, this extensive "pneumatological imagination" lies not in the choice of the individual mind but in a complex intersection of the acts, objects, and contexts of spirited existence.[14] Pentecostal spirit-awareness is profoundly embodied in a community undergirded by and interwoven with "spirits" who are experienced in a radically social imaginary of both socioreligious and secular engagements.

---

8. Taves and Bender, "Introduction," 18.
9. Meyer, "Religious and Secular," 88.
10. Taylor, "Future," 243.
11. Meyer, "Religious and Secular," 89.
12. Smith, *Thinking in Tongues*, 89–99.
13. For a nuanced evaluation see Anderson, *Spirit-Filled World*.
14. See Yong, *Spirit-Word-Community*, 219–310.

The Engagement of the Disengaged

The possibility of disengagement marks the second condition in Taylor's account of a secular age. The social life of the porous premodern self, including the "spiritual forces which impinged... on us as a society" and which were previously defended by "deploying a power that we can only draw on as a community" (p. 42), has turned into an atomic individualism where "disbelief no longer has social consequences."[15] The secular, already marked in Taylor's account by the absence of spiritual power, is unable to locate such power in society itself because the buffered self now has the option not to participate in collective rites aimed at harnessing the spirits. Since secularity as disengagement is the consequence of disenchantment, all realms of religious imagination are now disassociated from one another and from the sacred. The result is both a society no longer grounded in shared religious beliefs and religious beliefs that no longer require a social framework.

Pentecostalism does not easily fit this pattern. On the one hand, Pentecostals are clearly bound up in a socio-spiritual network where the self exists always as part of a community of "sons and daughters, young and old, men and women" (see Acts 2:17–18) filled with God's Spirit and engaging other spirits within the social realm of the secular.[16] On the other hand, spiritual empowerment among Pentecostals is also bound up with concerns for individual well-being and autonomy, even resisting traditional social obligations.[17] Yet, this spiritual autonomy of the Pentecostal self should not be misunderstood as simply the replacement of social bonds with a secular individualism. Rather, ethnographic studies point instead to a redefining of the principles of kinship through a restructuring of socio-spiritual bonds.[18] It is precisely the enchanted worldview that necessitates these structures, not as a departure from social bonds but as a transformation of community for the sake of spiritually *and* socially embodied lives.

Embodiment refers to the materiality of practices that form and are informed by an enchanted worldview in which meaning is spiritually,

---

15. Smith, *(Not) to Be Secular*, 31.

16. See Wells Davies, *Embattled but Empowered Community*; Brodwin, "Pentecostalism in Translation," 85–101; Williams, *Black Pentecostal Church*.

17. See McClendon and Riedl, "Individualism and Empowerment," 119–44; Marshall, *Political Spiritualities*; Meyer, "Make a Complete Break," 182–208.

18. See Quiroz, "Relating as Children"; Dijk, "Religion, Reciprocity, and Restructuring," 173–96; Meyer, *Translating the Devil*, 179–204.

and thus physically, socially, and culturally communicated.[19] Contemporary studies of Pentecostalism affirm certain foundational rites as the consistent practices and traditions of the Pentecostal life.[20] The role of embodiment, materiality, affectivity, and experience is evident throughout all facets of Pentecostalism.[21] Pentecostal theology heralds a form of enchanted, thoroughly material and transformational, attachment in its proclamation of the so-called full gospel and the expectations that in a personal encounter with Jesus Christ the human being and the community experience salvation, sanctification, baptism in the Holy Spirit, divine healing, and the coming of God's kingdom. Genuine fullness, the human experience of meaning and significance, and an important category for Taylor (pp. 5–12), rather than a projection of the human mind, is "believed" only because it is *experienced* in embodied practices and rituals which are shaped by and which shape social living. Pentecost is unthinkable as privatized, atomic disengagement from the languages, cultures, and social life of the secular world. It is the festival of enchanted social attachment that forms the symbol of Pentecostalism.

The Festival of Enchanted Attachment

With Pentecost we arrive at the enchanted and embodied Christian festival par excellence. The continuing experience of Pentecost also identifies the heart of the problem of situating Pentecostalism in Taylor's account. He identifies the third feature of the premodern world as "an equilibrium in tension ... between the demands of total transformation which the faith calls us to, and the requirements of ordinary ongoing life" (p. 44). Whereas medieval Christendom possessed the spectacle of carnival as a mechanism of restoring the equilibrium, "periods in which the ordinary order of things was inverted" (p. 45–46), the modern secular age has abandoned the festival for functionalist structures, boundaries, and order. Employing the ritual theory of Victor Turner, Taylor argues that secularity eclipses the festival and its "anti-structure" to social norms and expectations.[22] What is dissolved in a secular age is

---

19. See Vondey, "Embodied Gospel," 46–72.
20. See Albrecht, *Rites in the Spirit*.
21. Vondey, *Pentecostal Theology*. See also Wilkinson, "Pentecostals and the World," 373–93; Bialecki, "Affect," 95–108.
22. Turner, *Dramas, Fields, and Metaphors*, 237. Cited by Taylor, *Secular Age*, 47.

the sense of complementarity and coexistence in all forms of public and religious life, so that the "traditional play of structure and anti-structure is no longer available to us" (p. 53).

The biblical account of Pentecost, with the first Christians behaving as if they were drunk, speaking in tongues, preaching in the streets of the city, speaking of a Spirit poured out on all flesh, should readily lend itself to a comparison with Taylor's notion of the lost festival. Indeed, Taylor alludes to the festive element in Pentecostalism, yet without further explanation, as "a crucial dimension of contemporary religious life" (p. 470).[23] Pentecostals have been acutely aware of the demands of enacting and reenacting the festive nature of Pentecost in the modern world. Bobby Alexander's examination of Turner's ritual studies in African American Pentecostalism proposes that charismatic practices establish a ritual anti-structure by placing Pentecostals in a liminality that generates alternative social arrangements that allow for the ecstatic display of the Spirit.[24] Pentecostal rituals here function as instruments of social change redressing established behavioral norms within a suspended environment of freedom, spontaneity, and enthusiasm.[25] Jean-Jacques Suurmond and André Droogers have described this liminal realm in Pentecostalism as a form of play. Suurmond highlights the anti-structural manner of Pentecostal play in contrast to the "goal-oriented, play-corrupting attitude" of society.[26] For Suurmond, play resides between order (supplied by the word of God) and chaos (supplied by the Spirit) in a ludic realm characterized by relative purposelessness.[27] Droogers proposes that Pentecostals exhibit a form of methodological ludism which he defines as the "capacity to deal simultaneously and subjunctively with two or more ways of classifying reality."[28] In my own analysis of Pentecostalism, I have suggested that this play constitutes a consistent expectation and imagination, which among Pentecostals suspends established social structures and performative expectations.[29] The festival of fools, as Harvey Cox has called it, is seen in the Pentecostal resistance to imposed structures, rules, and boundaries in

---

23. See also Taylor, *Secular Age*, 554.

24. Alexander, "Correcting Misinterpretations," 32–41. See also Alexander, "Pentecostal Ritual Reconsidered," 109–28.

25. See Alexander, *Victor Turner Revisited*.

26. See Suurmond, "Church at Play," 252.

27. Suurmond, *Word and Spirit*, 29; Suurmond, "Church at Play," 248–50.

28. Droogers, "Methodological Ludism," 53; Droogers, "Third Bank," 285–313.

29. Vondey, *Beyond Pentecostalism*, 136–40.

the secular city.³⁰ Nimi Wariboko's response to Cox and to my own work challenges Pentecostals to consider that the real principle of Pentecostalism may lie in the inherent secularization at the core of the movement.³¹ He speaks of play as "pure means" and "purposelessness": play is religion as a form of principal human action that exhibits our existence in the secular.³² Whereas Cox seemed uncertain that Pentecostals can engage a secular age, for Wariboko, the playful carnival not only brings Pentecostals into the secular city but transforms that city into a charismatic world.³³ These accounts of Pentecostalism challenge Taylor's argument of the lost equilibrium. The chief problem lies in defining Pentecostalism exclusively as a religious phenomenon. That Pentecostals show the festival with particular force should also not indicate that they are aware of their place amid the secular. Breaking out in unknown tongues, prophecies, words of wisdom or praise, exorcising demonic spirits, laying on of hands, jumping over pews, soaking in prayer, or falling out in the Spirit—and any other manifestations of Pentecost, whether in the first century or today—belong strictly neither to the religious nor to the secular realm.³⁴ Pentecost is not the opposite of the secular, in order to bring out an equilibrium, but a divine in-between: Pentecostalism as a religious festival is a necessary part of the secular in order to bring the whole world into the rhythm of God's time and promise.

The Transformation of Secular Time

From the perspective of Pentecostalism as a continuation, extension, and revival of the festival of Pentecost, it is easy to agree with Taylor that the carnival possesses its own time. In his account of the changing conditions of the secular, the time of the premodern festival is a higher time, filled with kairotic and eschatological "moments whose nature and placing calls for reversal" of ordinary time (p. 55). If there was a secular time in the premodern world, it existed "in a multiplex vertical context, so that everything relates to more than one kind of time" (p. 57). But in the modern

---

30. Cox, *Festival of Fools*. See also Cox, *Religion in the Secular*, 240–61.
31. Wariboko, "Fire from Heaven," 391–408.
32. Wariboko, *Pentecostal Principle*, 161–95.
33. Wariboko, *Charismatic City*.
34. This idea emerges clearly in the African context of Pentecostalism where the Africanization of Christianity and the Pentecostalization of Africa overlap. See Meyer, *Translating the Devil*, 134–40.

age, the "secular" comes to represent its own time, an ordinary time against religion and eternity. For Taylor, the secular age eschews God's time for the fixed and unvarying resource of measurable time (p. 59) so that the secular world disconnects from the premodern sense of eternity because it no longer participates in the life of God. Today's church continues to participate in eternity through its liturgical enactment but can no longer fill the disenchanted, homogeneous, and empty cosmic time of the secular with the common experience of eternity.

The festival of Pentecost, with its enchanted engagement of the religious and the secular amid a time filled with the activity of God's Spirit, resists also this fourth facet of Taylor's account. As I have previously argued, a pneumatological understanding of time suggests that eternity is determined by the perpetuation of the present moment in the activity of the Holy Spirit through, across, and beyond ordinary time. Put differently, the festival as an encounter with the divine Spirit always relates to more than one time. Pentecostals in their present experience of Pentecost relate also to the biblical Pentecost and to the coming Pentecost of God's kingdom. Yet, this present "lived" time is in an important sense neither the "higher" time of the divine nor the "lower" time of the world; Pentecost is a time "between": God's eternity is brought low, so to speak, into the world and into the secular, while ordinary time is lifted toward the eternal kingdom. To use a common Pentecostal parlance, Pentecost marks a time of the inbreaking of God's kingdom where human beings are "saved, sanctified, filled with the Spirit, healed, and on their way to heaven." At Pentecost, the times of promise and fulfillment overlap in the present realization of God's activity in the world. Pentecostal experiences, as much as they are religious markers of a liturgical time that belongs to the church, are the playful, irrational, unexpected, and foolish markers of the kingdom of God breaking into the secular. At the spectacle of Pentecost, secular time encounters God and is suspended in visions and dreams and encounters with eternity. In response, the religious behavior of Pentecostals is the observable form of the unspeakable and inexpressible charismatic encounters with God's Spirit. This realm of the "charismatic" cuts through the "secular" age and muddles the distinction between transcendence and immanence and what belongs to each realm.[35] Charismatic time ticks within a porous cosmos.

---

35. See Taylor, "Western Secularity," 31–53.

The Porous Cosmos

The final element in Taylor's account, deeply connected with the idea of secular disenchanted time, is the transformation of the idea that we live in a divinely instituted, meaningful and limited cosmos into the scientific notion of an unbounded self-governing universe. The premodern hierarchy of beings is replaced with "exceptionless natural laws" (p. 60) which no longer evolve around human meaning. The language of a universe "has altered the terms of the debate, and reshaped the possibilities both of belief and unbelief, opened up new loci of mystery, as well as offering new ways of denying transcendence" (p. 61).

Pentecostals have been rather disinterested in scientific cosmology and often hostile to evolutionary accounts of existence.[36] The reasons for this hostility are rooted in the enchantment of the Pentecostal worldview that is dominated by theological concerns for salvation. The doctrine of creation is subsumed under soteriology as an indication that the meaning of the universe is found not in the product or act of creation itself but in the redemption of the cosmos.[37] Creation is the economy of salvation in a Pentecostal narrative that begins and ends with God punctuated by the experiences and interaction of human beings with different powers in a "spirit-filled" cosmos that engages perichoretically four porous and overlapping spheres: (1) the divine; (2) the human; (3) the natural world; and (4) the realm of evil.[38] This metaphysics of a porous cosmos rejects a strict distinction between God and the economy of salvation in favor of a kenotic realism of the divine persons in the world.[39] What we find in this cosmology is not a dialectic of secularization and religion, as argued by David Martin and endorsed by Taylor, but the interpenetration of transcendence and immanence, sacred and secular, Christianization and secularization, at all levels.[40] The porous cosmos speaks of material deliverance, sanctification, and salvation of the world deeply dependent on spiritual beings, powers, and God. The entire cosmos, not just the individual, is porous and healable. The Pentecostal cosmos is, to use Taylor's idea of the premodern world, finite and bounded, and thus open to disaster and destruction as

---

36. See Smith and Yong, *Science and the Spirit*; Yong, *Spirit Renews*.

37. Vondey, *Pentecostal Theology*, 155–74.

38. See Yong, *Spirit of Creation*, 175–84; Baker, "Angels," 179–94; Macchia, "Repudiating the Enemy," 194–213; Mutungu, "Response to M. L. Daneel," 127–31.

39. Vondey, *Beyond Pentecostalism*, 98–108.

40. See Martin, *On Secularization*. See also Martin, *General Theory of Secularization*.

much as to miracles and deliverance. Universe and cosmos are not identical but overlapping realities confronting each other in an eschatological tension which expects the dissolution of the secular and religious divide with the arrival of a new creation.

PENTECOSTALISM AND THE HISTORY OF THE SECULAR

In the previous section, I examined the conditions of premodernity identified in Charles Taylor's account as obstacles to the rise of a secular age and found them still to be present in the contemporary Pentecostal movements. Put differently, the mechanisms of secularization do not readily apply to Pentecostalism. I have identified the alternative mechanisms in place as a form of religion at play evident in an enchanted worldview, socio-spiritual attachment, the festival of Pentecost, the transformation of secular time, and a porous cosmos. What emerges from this proposal is a significant challenge to the identity of the secular as a historical construct, a temporal "age" in contrast to the premodern. Pentecostalism challenges the authority of the secular that Taylor's historical narrative assumes behind the conditions emerging with modernity. In contrast, the festival we label "Pentecostalism" engages in a play of the divine and the world in a way that locates meaning in the intentions of God and thus places the mechanisms of this play outside of the history of religious and secular reality. In order to demonstrate this impact, the following section takes a closer look at the notion of play in Taylor's genealogy of the secular in order to situate Pentecostalism more firmly in the tumultuous history of religion. The intention is to critically examine the nature of the historical narrative of a secular age along the contours of play. I begin with a brief analysis of Taylor's observations on the idea of play in the Romantic age and then suggest how Pentecostalism (as play) transcends the historical narrative of the religious and the secular.

Play in the History of the Secular

David Martin's suggestion, noted at the beginning of this essay, that Pentecostalism was discounted in the history of the secular is followed by his alternative theory that Pentecostalism identifies a "subculture

[that] runs alongside modernization in a mutually supportive manner"[41] producing its own major narrative of modernity.[42] Taylor's foreword to Martin's revised theory of secularization highlights its main achievement as identifying alternative models of the history of secularity.[43] Yet, despite Taylor's noticeable dependence on Martin's work for integrating Pentecostalism in his own narrative, he makes little use of Martin's suggestion that Pentecostalism presents a major alternative route to the modern and that its success is rooted, as Martin explains, in the Pentecostal espousal of "story and song, gesture and empowerment, image and embodiment, enthusiastic release and personal discipline."[44] Neither Martin nor Taylor make use of these principal observations of Pentecostalism as identifying an alternative model of modern religion.[45] Still, the qualitatively distinctive nature of Pentecostalism lies for Martin in its mobilization of self-consciousness and voluntary association.[46] These elements appear also in Taylor's work in the context of diverse attempts at navigating the modern "supernova" of possible options confronting the buffered self. It is here that the contrast of Pentecostalism to the history of the secular emerges with clarity in the notion of play.

Navigating the nova, Taylor insists, is the true "malaise of modernity" (p. 299), and he presents play as one of its historical solutions precisely for its capacity to express human self-consciousness and the full realization of human nature. Taylor's account of the notion of play begins with the Romantic philosopher, historian, and poet Friedrich Schiller, in a line of thought which continues in two diametrically opposed directions, on the one hand, the ideals of a liberated humanism and, on the other, the religious fascination of the Pietistic and modern Pentecostal movements.[47] Taylor does not expand on how one may understand Pentecostals as children of the Romantic age, but the integration of the notion of play in the narrative of secularization offers significant possibilities for advancing its role as a model for a religious age in balance with the secular.

41. Martin, *On Secularization*, 5.
42. Martin, *On Secularization*, 141–55.
43. Martin, *On Secularization*, ix–x.
44. Martin, *On Secularization*, 142.
45. See also the subsequent discussion in Martin, *Secularisation, Pentecostalism, and Violence*, 136–54, 170–84.
46. Martin, *Future of Christianity*, 63–83.
47. Taylor, *Secular Age*, 314–17, 358–59; 609–10.

Schiller introduces the term "play" in his *Letters on the Aesthetic Education of Man* as the highest fulfillment of human self-realization in the sense of a gratuitous and spontaneous freedom "by which we create and respond to beauty."[48] Play is the expression of the aesthetic instinct of human existence which completes the sensuous and formal instincts of humankind.[49] In play, passion, feeling, and reason are in harmony, liberated from the demands of law and necessity for the pursuit of beauty as their ultimate object.[50] More precisely, for Schiller, sensuous impulses precede rational impulses and human consciousness and therefore present the key to the realization of human liberty.[51] The human being finds its full realization when sensibility and reason become the mutually balancing powers of an aesthetic imagination that sees no conflict between form and uselessness.[52] The human being, bound to history, finds an existential freedom beyond the limitations given to the individual by life's phenomenal domains: "To give freedom to freedom is the fundamental law of this realm."[53] Consequently, although the instinct of play exists in every human being, Schiller concludes that its actualization is the real task of the self-realization of humankind in history.

Despite Taylor's aim of crafting a universal genealogy of the secular, he does not take up Schiller's notion of play as an essential solution to secularity but only as a line of further historical controversy (p. 320). Of course, Schiller's critique of Enlightenment anthropocentrism reacts both to the inadequacies of an unqualified moralism and to the uncritical affirmation of desire. Yet, the crucial problem for Taylor is that the inclusion of God in the pursuit of beauty, while still an option, is not a necessity but can evolve in the imagination of the buffered identity into a mere symbol (p. 360). While Schiller may convince us that what is missing from human self-realization is an aesthetic imagination, the ontic commitments of play remain undefined and thus allow for the direction of unbelief (p. 400). Play as the pursuit of beauty may speak to a division within human nature or to a separation of human communal nature or to a loss of the enchanted ideals of the past without engaging religious concerns (p. 315). Hence, the concept is taken up by Nietzsche eventually

---

48. Taylor, *Secular Age*, 358.
49. Schiller, *Letters on the Aesthetic*, ch. 14. See Wertz, "Reader's Guide," 80–104.
50. Schiller, *Letters on the Aesthetic*, ch. 15.
51. Schiller, *Letters on the Aesthetic*, ch. 20.
52. Schiller, *Letters on the Aesthetic*, ch. 27.
53. Schiller, *Letters on the Aesthetic*, ch. 27.

in deliberate contrast of the aesthetic realm to the moral (p. 359). The cross-pressures of secularization following Schiller ultimately leave the transformation of desire unresolved in modern Western culture and thus deny success to the human pursuit of beauty.

Schiller continues to appear as a paradigm in Taylor's work, yet his notion of play holds no significance for the continuing narrative. Taylor seems to find in the Romantic idea of play only a particular historical reaction to human fragmentation, disengagement of reason from the senses, isolation of bodily existence, neglect of feeling, and loss of creativity resulting from the Enlightenment.[54] In this sense, Pentecostalism is one possible re-articulation of the Romantic protest amid the winded history of secularity. The importance of the physical and the moral life in the Pentecostal worldview speaks to the Romantic idea of balance and transformation.[55]

It is Schiller's aesthetic dimension, however, the realm of beauty, not the activity of play, that identifies for Taylor the heart of the Romantic ideal. In this sense, Pentecostalism does not appear to be a child of the Romantic age since its "selective assumption of disciplines" (p. 493) (rather than their playful engagement) yields no clear aesthetic model. Moreover, the notion of beauty (and thus of play) remains tied to the historical conditions and rules internal to the Romantic age, which are ostensibly absent from Pentecostalism.[56] This struggle to integrate Pentecostalism in Taylor's account of play is the direct result of the Pentecostal resistance to the loss of premodern conditions that characterize Taylor's master narrative. Yet, underlying this problem is the more fundamental difficulty to fit Pentecostalism in the history of ideas, not as unfolding chronologically but, as it were, idealistically. Martin's account of Pentecostalism offers historically compelling reasons for the neglect of Pentecostalism in the master narrative. Taylor's account, in contrast, seeks to tell the history of ideas by relying on the history of events. Here we arrive at the central questions for considering Pentecostalism's relation to the secular. If Pentecostalism represents a different narrative of modernity, one that resists the historicizing of the religious and the secular (and their fundamental opposition), how is that narrative to be told? The answer may lie in the telling of the story of Pentecostalism as

---

54. See Taylor, *Secular Age*, 379, 381, 400, 476, 609–10, 615–16, 642.
55. Taylor, *Secular Age*, 552–53.
56. Vondey, "Spirit and Nature," 30–35.

religion at play throughout and ultimately beyond the historical distinction of the religious and the secular.

Pentecostalism Beyond the Religious and the Secular

Taylor's primary interest in the secular as a social imaginary is based on the way we experience the world rather than our ideas (pp. 171–72).[57] Consequently, he situates the Romantic protest in the modern age as a historical response to the Enlightenment (pp. 358, 372). Even when considering the Romantic appeal as an axis of ideas, the resulting "subtler language"[58] of the Romantics exists only because of and in contrast to the premodern conditions.[59] Schiller's notion of play is not seen as a transcendental attempt to realize the fullness of human nature but as an aesthetic located in history and aimed at rediscovering what is lost with the turn to the modern. Taylor's continued attempt at historicizing the conditions of the secular to uncover the experiences of the world underlying them presses him further to define the aesthetic in the material sense as art, and the heart of the artistic ideal in the production of Romantic literature.[60] In this way the demand for the history of the secular deconstructs the idea of play for the sake of constructing the social imaginary of beauty. As an expression of the latter, the appeal to beauty can transcend history only when it enables "people to explore ... meanings with their ontological commitments as it were in suspense" (p. 351) and thus opening the way for both belief and unbelief. This conclusion, however, is acceptable only if the conditions of the premodern world have been removed and room is made for non-religious and non-theistic ontology (or even the possibility of suspending ontological commitments in the first place). If the "premodern" conditions are still operative, either in ignorance of the need to question them or in deliberate rejection to do so, the ontological presuppositions accompanying this social imaginary cannot be suspended.

James K. A. Smith recently related Taylor's notion of the social imaginary to Pentecostalism and proposed that a Pentecostal social imaginary arises first of all from "a constellation of spiritual practices

---

57. See also Taylor, *Modern Social Imaginaries*.
58. A phrase borrowed from Wasserman, *Subtler Language*.
59. See Taylor, *Secular Age*, 356–61.
60. See Jager, "This Detail, This History," 166–92.

that carry within them an implicit understanding."[61] For Smith, the Pentecostal social imaginary is an aesthetic in its relentless pursuit of the experience of the divine in the world. More exactly, embedded in Pentecostal practices is an implicit ontological commitment to a world where "the miraculous is normal"[62] because "nature is always already suspended in and inhabited by the Spirit such that it is always already *primed* for the Spirit's manifestations."[63] This pneumatological ontology is tied to an epistemology of the Spirit that is radically open to the possibility of any social imaginary beyond the confines of particular historical manifestations. As I suggested previously, the Pentecostal aesthetic lends itself to a surreal rather than a realist version of history.[64] Probing Smith's idea of this ontological surrealism further, Nimi Wariboko speaks of existence in the Pentecostal cosmos as a "continual opening and reopening" of history to the divine.[65] The novum, to use Taylor's term, arises from the emergent and disruptive creativity of the Spirit who is neither (or both) immanent and transcendent to history.[66] The freedom of the Spirit allows for both crisis and opportunity in historical time and is both (or neither) fundamentally religious and radically secular.[67] For Wariboko, the experience of the Spirit is "pure mediality" disinterested in productivity or functional enactment (as measured by the secular or the religious realms) and as unended action represents "pure potentiality" in and beyond history of the self-realization of humanity.[68] The mechanism of this self-realization prevalent in Pentecostalism he designates as play.

Although neither Smith nor Wariboko engages Schiller's notion of play, their ideas can be seen as a radical extension of the Romantic appeal to the aesthetic.[69] Wariboko presses the understanding of play (and Pentecostalism) further through an ontological analysis that identifies play as the foundational principle of Pentecostalism as a religion that radicalizes grace. In Schiller's terms, the radicalization of grace

61. Smith, *Thinking in Tongues*, 30–31.
62. Smith, *Thinking in Tongues*, 98–99.
63. Smith, *Thinking in Tongues*, 101.
64. See Vondey and Green, "Between This and That," 243–64; Vondey, "Symbolic Turn," 223–47. See Smith, *Thinking in Tongues*, 80–85.
65. Wariboko, *Pentecostal Principle*, 51; see also 51–59.
66. Wariboko, *Pentecostal Principle*, 53.
67. Wariboko, *Pentecostal Principle*, 87–88; following Paul Tillich's idea of *kairos*.
68. Wariboko, *Pentecostal Principle*, 99–100.
69. The preface mentions Schiller briefly; Wariboko, *Pentecostal Principle*, xi.

is its "aestheticization of desire"[70] for all freely evolving potentialities of human existential self-realization with no regard for the difference between secular and sacred.[71] Play reorganizes religion by depriving religion of necessity, want, and purpose so that it functions within the secular but outside of its laws.[72] That is, the object of religion is the rendering inoperative of the law of purpose (whether perceived as beauty or morals). Taylor's criticism of Schiller's aesthetic as allowing in principle for the pursuit of beauty apart from God does not hold for Pentecostalism because the ontology with which the Pentecostal aesthetic operates is bound to the continuing expectation of the encounter with the divine Spirit in the world. Put theologically, the state of grace is the fulfillment of Schiller's vision of the mutually balancing powers of an aesthetic imagination that avoids any distinction between form and uselessness. Pentecostalism exhibits religion as play beyond its historical form (at the end of a development begun with Pietism or evangelical revivalism) in its existential manifestation as an aesthetic of desire which seeks by all means the continuing participation in the evolving potentialities of encountering the divine in the world. To speak of this as the "purpose" of Pentecostalism would mean to once again subscribe to the laws made necessary by the identification of a secular age.

The problem of forcing Pentecostalism in a secular age finds its fullest expression in the historical narrative applied to both secularization and religion. Taylor's genealogical account is indebted to Herder's genetic-historical method, which demands that ideas and actions originate always in a specific historical context and must therefore be understood according to the laws internal to that moment.[73] Tied to the historical narrative, Pentecostalism can be seen only as a subsequent development of prior forces of the secular/religious divide, as revival or re-conversion or re-action to particular (preceding) constellations. While this account has been successfully applied to Pentecostal historiography in North America,[74] it relates only with difficulty to Pentecostalism as a global phenomenon.[75]

70. Wariboko, *Pentecostal Principle*, 176.
71. Wariboko, *Pentecostal Principle*, 151–54, 173–74.
72. Wariboko, *Pentecostal Principle*, 185.
73. See Adler and Menze, *Johann Gottfried Herder*. Jager, "This Detail, This History," 181–83, argues that Taylor's genealogy is a shift away from Herder's genetic history.
74. See Cerillo and Wacker, "Bibliography and Historiography," 382–405.
75. See Bundy, "Historiography of Pentecostalism," 405–17.

The difficulty to understand Pentecostalism as an expression of religion, which differs in its internal makeup as widely as the tensions visible in global Pentecostalism and which resists a simple fit in the narrative of the secular, is amplified by the exclusive methodological choices for the telling of this narrative. Taylor's genealogy must disperse the essence of Pentecostalism into the energies of often overlapping and contradicting historical developments subordinate, as it seems, to the dominance of the secular and the religious as the only true competing essences at work in the narrative.[76] Talal Asad's critique of the genealogies of religion, in general, identifies the alternative in Kant's attempt to explain religion *sui generis* as "a fully essentialized idea . . . which could be counterposed to its phenomenal forms."[77] The distinction between the essentialization of religion, on the one hand, and its historicization and temporalization, on the other, comes to a point in Schleiermacher's distinction between the inner essence and the outer appearance of religion.[78] We can find the perpetuation of this distinction in the tendency of contemporary scholarship on Pentecostal Christianity to over-contextualize the movement in its phenomenological, historical, and sociological manifestations or to essentialize Pentecostalism as a historical metaphenomenon often located in a pneumatological or revivalist account. What should have become evident throughout this brief study is that Pentecostalism resists the exclusive pull of either direction. Play suspends both "secular" and "religious" as uncontested critical categories.[79] What is visible in Pentecostalism is not the distinction between secular and religious, and all the derivative binaries that grasp at this distinction, including essence and phenomenon, idea and history, premodern and modern, transcendent and immanent, sacred and profane, but the expression of one in terms of the other, not by accident or by pure determination but by the unexpected and incalculable dynamic of play.

Religion as play writes the history of the essence of Pentecostalism in both the narrative and the counternarrative to our secular age. Pentecostalism suggests that the secular and religious binary is suspended because play is disinterested in either side's exclusive claim at human

76. See Butler, "Disquieted History," 193–216.
77. Asad, *Genealogies of Religion*, 42.
78. See Jager, "After the Secular," 301–22.
79. This is consistent with the recent critique of religion by scholars such as Jonathan Z. Smith, Russell T. McCutcheon, Timothy Fitzgerald, Craig Martin, Tomoko Masuzawa, and others.

self-realization and liberty. That is, any purpose of religion at play is at once functional, counter-functional, and non-functional, resisting normative secular and religious expectations, even if operating within them, while transcending, absorbing, and transforming them toward what always lies ahead and beyond their reach. The festival of Pentecostalism is an aesthetic imagination in which history itself is subject to transformation. That the narrative of this transformation cannot be written apart from history is evidence for the importance of understanding the ontological, epistemological, and aesthetic commitments of religion. At the same time, that this narrative must transcend history demands a different reading of religion at play. For this task, Pentecostalism represents a leading opportunity.

CONCLUSION

A critical examination of the fit of Pentecostal Christianity into Charles Taylor's account of secularization suggests that Pentecostalism represents a condition of religion unaccounted for in this dominant narrative. Pentecostalism does not show the absence of the central conditions of premodern life that have made room for our modern, secular world because it suspends the secular/religion binary foundational to the narrative. The integration of Pentecostalism demands a different narrative in which religion is disinterested in itself as religious understood exclusively and in contradistinction to the secular. Instead, religion as play suspends the authority of any finite reality (religious or secular) and engages all things for the goal of the existential self-realization of humankind in relation to the divine. Discovering religion as play calls for a telling of the narrative of religion in which Pentecostalism is included neither as an exception nor as ultimate fulfillment. The particular Pentecostal narrative of religion as play finds its manifestation throughout and beyond history as the festival ("Pentecost") of the eternal Spirit. Those who are caught up in this cosmic play find their Pentecost beyond the secular and the religious divide in a redemptive festival penetrating and transforming the nature of all things.

PART III

The Ontological Shift of Pentecostal Hermeneutics Guided by Liturgy

PART III

7

Gospel as Principle of Pentecostal Theology

IN 2004, LUTHERAN AND Pentecostal representatives entered into exploratory conversations that preceded the approval of official dialogue between the Lutheran World Federation and Pentecostal churches. The central theme for the conversations was the experiential concern, "How do we encounter Christ?" The report of the conversations, published in 2010, appears in a generally hopeful tone but nonetheless ends on a cautious note: Pentecostals wondered if Lutherans believed in something "less than the full gospel," while Lutherans were concerned if Pentecostals held to "more than the pure gospel."[1] Despite its explanatory power, the aphoristic juxtaposition of *full gospel* and *pure gospel*, identified as the central tension between Lutherans and Pentecostals, is only marginally explored (and explained) in the document. The conversation focuses only on identifying the respective positions but does not engage in a comparative analysis of the two modifiers "full" and "pure" or question if the concept of the "gospel" held by each side indeed allows for such comparison.

Considering the ongoing neglect to study the charismatic renewal among Lutherans and the Lutheran response to Pentecostalism,[2]

---

1. *Lutherans and Pentecostals in Dialogue*, 12.
2. See Appold, "Lutheran Reactions to Pentecostalism," 58–84; Blomquist, *Lutherans*

clarifying the veracity of this central tension might affirm foundational differences between the two groups, provide direction for further (official) investigation, and offer ecumenical opportunities for theological reconciliation. This essay intends to close this gap by offering a theological assessment of the distinction between the so-called pure gospel and full gospel paradigms. The modest goal of this essay is an etymological study of the notion of "gospel" on historical and theological grounds between Lutherans and Pentecostals. The first section identifies the respective understandings of the notion of "gospel" held by Lutherans and Pentecostals and evaluates its comparative usage. The second section traces the development of the notion of "gospel" from the Reformation to the birth of twentieth-century Pentecostalism. The investigation begins with Martin Luther's theology and traces the development of Lutheran theology and its influence on Protestant and Pentecostal notions of the gospel. The final part contrasts the modifying terms "pure" and "full" applied to characterize the theological principles of each perspective and offers an evaluative analysis of both paradigms.

GOSPEL AMONG LUTHERANS AND PENTECOSTALS

Luther's criticism of the charismatic movement of his days is well known.[3] His understanding of the gospel emphasized faith rather than charisma, albeit not at the cost of rejecting spiritual gifts but with the intention to offer an integrative principle of participating in God's work of salvation.[4] Luther's concern was to protect the gospel against the fanaticism of the enthusiast and a complete subjectivizing of revelation. Lutheran confessional strictures point to the "Smalcald Articles," which are typically seen as an unambiguous expression of Luther's denial that these movements were of the Holy Spirit.[5] Contemporary appropriations of Luther's critique, such as the report of the Commission on Theology and Church Relations of the Lutheran Church—Missouri Synod in 1972, have continued to reject Pentecostal and charismatic movements on the basis of Luther's apparent disavowal of the "claim that God communicates directly with

---

Respond to Pentecostalism; Lindberg, *Third Reformation*; McDonnell, *Presence, Power, Praise*; Christenson, *Charismatic Renewal Among Lutherans*.

3. Ji, "Work," 204–13.
4. See Föller, "Martin Luther on Miracles," 333–51.
5. Maier, "Fanaticism," 173–81.

believers through prophecy, visions, tongues, or other means."[6] Whether this is a correct reading of the "Smalcald Articles" can be debated.[7] Surprisingly, however, Lutheran interpretations have focused more on the pneumatology and psychology of Luther's criticism than on his emphasis on revelation and definition of "gospel."

In turn, Pentecostals have generally looked favorably at Luther, who is seen as a restorer of sound doctrine at the cost of entering into conflict with religious, political, and spiritual powers.[8] When referencing Luther, Pentecostal pioneers frequently highlighted his advocacy for the gospel and embraced Luther's emphasis on the good news in its pure form, even identifying particular biblical texts with Luther's help as "the chief book of the New Testament" and "the purest Gospel."[9] For most Pentecostals, Luther had preached the gospel as "the doctrine of atoning blood to slumbering Europe."[10] Classical Pentecostals widely identified with the evangelistic and missionary thrust of the Reformation. Contemporary Pentecostals, however, often distinguish between Luther and Lutherans, challenging the tradition's lack of emphasis on charismatic practices yet without questioning what precisely Luther meant by his notion of "gospel."

For both Lutherans and Pentecostals, the Gospels of the New Testament form the heart of the Christian message of salvation offered by God in Jesus Christ. The Gospels form the core narrative of the Christian faith and thus the ground for Christian confession and witness. From the New Testament context, both Lutherans and Pentecostals typically identify the "gospel" as the "good news," a word-for-word translation of the old English *gōd-spell*, derived from the Greek *euangélion*, and in the Latin, *evangelium*, rendered in Luther's German as *Evangelium*. Similarly, Pentecostals are not shy to use the term "evangel" in some form for the title of their publications, assemblies, churches, and educational institutions to emphasize the missionary intent and soteriology of the movement.[11] Both

---

6. Lutheran Church—Missouri Synod, *Charismatic Movement*, 34.

7. See Jungkuntz, "Sectarian Consequences," 166–67.

8. See "Pentecostal Baptism Restored," 1; "Church's Privileges," 14; "Daily Portion," 9; "Satan and Martin Luther," 2.

9. Flower, "Spirit of Life," 10.

10. "World's Supreme Need," 18.

11. See, e.g., "The Pentecostal Evangel" (1913–), "The Church of God Evangel" (1910–), "Evangelio Pentecostal" (1995–), Evangel University, Evangel Pentecostal Church, Evangel Pentecostal Assembly.

traditions therefore use the term "gospel" in the twofold sense of referring to the biblical texts and to the content of these texts, a distinction that deserves more attention in the ecumenical conversation.

Luther and Gospel

In his preface to the New Testament, Luther explains the notion of "gospel" precisely through reference to the biblical proclamation: the gospel is the message of the Gospels. Consequently, "there is only one gospel . . . because the gospel . . . is . . . the proclamation of Christ the son of God and of David, truly God and man."[12]

> By his death and resurrection, He has conquered sin, death, and hell for us and all who believe in Him. The gospel may be proclaimed in few words or in many; one writer may describe it briefly and the other at length. If at length, then many of the works and words of Christ will be set down, as in the case of the four evangelists. Those who write it briefly . . . tell succinctly how He conquered sin, death, and hell by His own death and resurrection on behalf of those who believe in Him.[13]

Arguably, Luther's idea of "gospel" is located precisely in his concern for the proper confession of the revelation of Christ.[14] Consequently, thesis sixty-two of the "Ninety-Five Theses" describes the gospel not only as "the glory and grace of God" but as "the true treasure of the church."[15] One might argue that, for Luther, revelation and gospel are two interdependent aspects of the responsibility of the church, which is to be upheld in its doctrines. In the "Smalcald Articles," Luther consequently orders all Christian teaching around the proclamation of the gospel and exclaims, "The first and chief article is this, that Jesus Christ, our God and Lord, 'was put to death for our trespasses and raised again for our justification' (Rom 4:25)."[16] At the same time, Luther subsequently identifies the gospel not only as the gift of God but by its "peculiar office"[17] to the world manifested in the ministry of the church.

---

12. Luther, "Preface," 16.
13. Luther, "Preface," 16–17.
14. See Rosin, "Luther Discovers the Gospel," 147–60.
15. Luther, "Disputation of Doctor Martin Luther," 1:29–38.
16. Luther, "Smalcald Articles," 2.i.
17. Luther, "Smalcald Articles," 3.4.

Lutherans have appropriated this task in a twofold sense, denoting with the responsibility to the gospel both the proclamation of God's saving work in Christ and its application to those who believe.[18] The "Formula of Concord" distinguishes similarly between the gospel in the proper sense, identifying "solely the preaching of God's grace" and the gospel in the general sense, referencing "the entire doctrine of Christ, our Lord, which He proclaimed in His ministry upon earth, and commanded to be proclaimed in the New Testament."[19] It was the affirmation of this dual responsibility as the foundation for protecting the authority of the gospel that was to be restored by the Reformation movement.

Pentecostals and Gospel

Luther's emphasis on the Gospels as the proclamation of Christ is echoed by Pentecostals, however, with a strong emphasis on the historical narratives of the church. Although not exclusively, the Gospel of Luke and the book of Acts are widely heralded as the focus of Pentecostal hermeneutics.[20] The Pentecostal emphasis is on the "power of the gospel" (1 Thess 1:5) contained in the saving work of Christ as made evident in the outpouring of the Holy Spirit at Pentecost (see Acts 2). While Luther frequently preached on Pentecost, he held no lectures on the Acts of the Apostles.[21] In contrast, Pentecostals often see Luke–Acts as a single, continuous Gospel narrative in which the good news of Jesus Christ (in Luke) is reinterpreted with the day of Pentecost through the work of the Spirit of Christ (in Acts). Pentecostals consequently agree on the essential core of the gospel, namely that "in Christ God was reconciling the world to himself" (2 Cor 5:19).[22]

At the same time, Pentecostal rhetoric has emerged from various revival movements during the nineteenth and twentieth centuries and emphasizes the experience of the gospel rather than its historical or intellectual content. The gospel as the proclamation of Jesus Christ is therefore the proclamation of the experience of Jesus, which advocates a narrative of Jesus' ministry as savior that highlights also the diverse experiences of

---

18. See Campbell, *Gospel*, 43–54.
19. "Formula of Concord," Solid Declaration, 5.3–6.
20. See Mittelstadt, *Reading Luke–Acts*.
21. See Loewenich, "Luthers Auslegung der Pfingstgeschichte," 181–90.
22. See the report in Vondey, *Pentecostalism*, 164.

Jesus as sanctifier, Spirit baptizer, divine healer, and coming king. It was this appropriation of Jesus' ministry as the foundation for the power of the gospel that was to be restored by the Pentecostal movement.

GOSPEL FROM THE REFORMATION TO PENTECOSTALISM

Luther's quest to protect the authority of the gospel from the revelatory claims of the enthusiasts was a motivating factor in articulating the Protestant principle *sola Scriptura*.[23] For Luther, Scripture functions as the rule and norm of the gospel because it contains revealed doctrine.[24] In turn, the gospel forms the uncontested internal principle of Scripture in its revelation of Jesus Christ.[25] However, the exact relationship of Scripture to gospel has become a subject of debate among Lutherans exacerbated with the theological distinction between the form and matter of revelation.[26] Put succinctly, *sola scriptura* ("scripture alone") is not identical with *solum evangelium* ("gospel alone")! From the perspective of this distinction, it is not the "content" of revelation, the biblical texts, but their inner "form," where the authority of the gospel is located.[27]

The Form and Content of Revelation

The "Formula of Concord" is one of the earliest indications of pursuing a twofold theological sense of "gospel." Noteworthy in the theological content of the document is not only the identification of "gospel" in terms of "doctrine," and the latter in terms of its opposition to the law, but the distinction drawn between the nature and content of the gospel itself. Accordingly, the "Formula of Concord" identifies the nature of the "gospel" as "that doctrine [sic!] which teaches what a man should believe in order to obtain the forgiveness of sins from God, since man has failed to keep the law of God and has transgressed it, his corrupted nature, thoughts, words, and deeds war against the law, and he is

---

23. See Oberman, *Dawn of the Reformation*, 270–88; Kropatscheck, *Schriftprinzip der lutherischen Kirche*.
24. See Braaten, "Can We Still Hold," 189–90.
25. Wood, "Luther's Concept of Revelation," 149–59.
26. See Hägglund, *Heilige Schrift*, 77–81, 105–18.
27. Hägglund, *Heilige Schrift*, 105–7.

therefore subject to the wrath of God, to death, to temporal miseries, and to the punishment of hell-fire."[28]

At the same time, the document highlights that "the content of the Gospel is this, that the Son of God, Christ our Lord, himself assumed and bore the curse of the law and expiated and paid for all our sins, that through him alone we reenter the good graces of God, obtain forgiveness of sins through faith, are freed from death and all the punishments of sin, and are saved eternally."[29] The identification of "gospel" in the twofold sense noted above and the further equation of gospel (in this twofold sense) with Christian doctrine have forged a unique theological identity in Lutheran theology.

Among early Lutherans, this distinction between form and content is perpetuated in the influential systematic account of orthodox Lutheran theology by Johann Gerhard[30] who suggested that one was justified to speak also of a formal and material principle of Christian doctrine.[31] J. W. Baier's *Compendium of Positive Theology* and Johann Philipp Gabler's theology were influential in weaving this fundamental distinction into the theological training of generations of Lutheran pastors since the end of the seventeenth century.[32] Gabler argued that the only *material* foundation of the Christian religion could be a *doctrine* that would serve as the source of all other teachings.[33] From a Lutheran perspective, Luther's doctrine of justification was the clear champion to serve as the highest material principle.

However, Gabler questioned whether it was possible to offer a single material principle as the chief teaching of the gospel that could also serve as the supreme principle of Lutheran theology.[34] He insisted that the theological task was guided instead by a *formal* principle, and not by a matter of content.[35] This distinction opened the way for the longstanding historical discussion on the integral principle of Protestant thought.[36] Its

---

28. "Formula of Concord," Solid Declaration, 5.20.
29. "Formula of Concord," Solid Declaration, 5.20.
30. See Hägglund, *Heilige Schrift*, 9–16; Congar, *Revelation of God*, 154–55.
31. See Vondey, "Wesleyan Theology," 70–85.
32. Baier, *Compendium of Positive Theology*, 1, 25.
33. Gabler, Review of *Summa theologiae*, 587–600.
34. Gabler, Review of *Summa theologiae*, 594–96.
35. Gabler, Review of *Summa theologiae*, 599.
36. Ritschl, "Ueber die beiden Principien," 397–413.

most immediate and far-reaching consequence is the (theo)logical separation of Scripture, doctrine, and gospel.

Scripture, Doctrine, and Gospel

In contrast to Luther's intentions, *sola Scriptura* came to serve the historical evaluation of the Reformation and the resulting confessions; it delineated a formula for identifying the principle of contemporary Protestantism rather than aiding in protecting the authority of the gospel.[37] In other words, if the gospel serves as the *formal* principle of the Lutheran worldview, it has to be supplemented by a *material* counterpart from within the system of Lutheran doctrines. In this way, the doctrine of justification retained its positions as the material principle of the theological enterprise, which, understood as a compendium of propositional, dogmatic truths, still demands adherence to the authority of Scripture on formal grounds but can find its core identified with a particular doctrine rather than the narrative content of the Gospel.

The problematic nature of these distinctions was formally recognized by a report of the Lutheran Church—Missouri Synod in 1972.[38] The confusion is evident in the report itself, which initially acknowledges that some "have in effect made the Bible, rather than the Gospel, the heart and center—the 'material principle'—of their faith"[39] while later explaining in reverse that "today there is a frequent confusion of these principles, with the result that the Gospel, rather than the Bible, is employed as the norm of our theology."[40] The same report identifies that most Lutherans see the formal principle as *sola Scriptura* and the gospel as the material principle.[41] Yet, at a later point still it is suggested that "the material principle of Lutheran theology is in reality only a synopsis and summary of the Christian truth" and "when Lutheran theologians speak of justification by faith as the material principle of theology, they merely wish to indicate that all theological thinking must begin at this article, center in it, and culminate in it."[42]

---

37. Ritschl, "Ueber die beiden Principien," 405–11.
38. Lutheran Church—Missouri Synod, *Gospel and Scripture*.
39. Lutheran Church—Missouri Synod, *Gospel and Scripture*, 2.
40. Lutheran Church—Missouri Synod, *Gospel and Scripture*, 23.
41. Lutheran Church—Missouri Synod, *Gospel and Scripture*, 2.
42. Lutheran Church—Missouri Synod, *Gospel and Scripture*, 23, where the text quotes Meier, "Formal and Material Principles," 545 and 548.

Finally, the report suggests that the term "gospel" could be applied in a minimalist sense and not mean to cover all church doctrine and practices. In response, the report recommends that while the gospel is the norm of Scripture, the gospel is not normative for Lutheran theology in the sense of a basic principle. In turn, Scripture is the norm of the gospel because the latter is derived from the former as the word of God. Formal and material principles are therefore interdependent insofar as "Lutheran Symbols are correct expositions of Scripture, [and] they teach the Gospel purely."[43]

This confusion is symptomatic not only for Lutherans; we can find a widespread disagreement among evangelical and Protestant traditions on the nature of the relationship between Scripture, gospel, and doctrine.[44] Moreover, there exists a fundamental impasse of reconciling a formal with a material principle of theology: either both principles are given equal authority, which would elevate doctrine to the same status as revelation and effectively equate justification with the gospel, or one principle supersedes the other, which would separate gospel and doctrine.[45] The only logical alternative is a separation of the formal element from the material, which in fact separates the doctrine of justification, as the material principle of the gospel, from Scripture as the formal principle of Protestantism.[46] This separation has allowed the doctrine of justification at times to emerge as a synonym for the Lutheran understanding of the gospel. Beyond the Lutheran fellowship, this equation suggests that it is appropriate to make similar distinctions in ecumenical conversations with other traditions: if the gospel is the formal principle of Pentecostalism, then what is the material principle identifying the chief teaching of Pentecostal doctrine?

PURE GOSPEL

Demands for the purity of the gospel are not unique to Lutherans and can be found among a variety of Christian traditions and thinkers, including Pentecostals.[47] The history of the notion of gospel among

43. Lutheran Church—Missouri Synod, *Gospel and Scripture*, 19.
44. See Pinnock and Callen, *Scripture Principle*.
45. Ritschl, "Ueber die beiden Principien," 411.
46. See Ratschow, "Einleitende Analyse der Themafrage," 4; Gennrich, *Kampf um die Schrift*, 1–9.
47. See Kim, *History and Theology*; Fletcher, *Doctrines of Grace*; Goodwin, *Discourse*.

Lutherans suggests that the phrase "pure gospel" can refer as a formal principle both to the purity of the gospel, thus emphasizing the content of Scripture ("gospel") and its proclamation of Christ (*solus Christus*), and to the purity of doctrine, thus emphasizing the content of the church's teaching as "purely gospel" or the "gospel alone." However, Lutheran theology demands historically that the pure proclamation of the gospel of Christ alone is identified by a further material principle, which qualifies the purity of the church's teaching. At Luther's time, the notion of a "pure" gospel carried the substantial undertones of his dissatisfaction with the way the church (Catholics, enthusiasts, and others) proclaimed and protected the good news of Christ.

Strictly speaking, Luther was not concerned with the purity of the gospel as such, since it is the word of God, but with the purity of the church's proclamation. Hence, when Luther warned "that many have the gospel but not the truth of the gospel,"[48] his concern was in fact that the truth of the gospel revealed by Scripture was reflected in the church's "pure doctrine."[49] In the same vein, the "Augsburg Confession" defines the church as "the assembly of all believers among whom the gospel is purely preached and the sacraments administered according to the gospel."[50] For Luther, and for Lutherans, the purity of the gospel and the demand for the purity of doctrine are at the core identical.[51]

Law and Gospel

Luther's demand that the church's doctrine must proclaim the pure gospel is clearly distinguished from Luther's equally stern rebuke that the proclamation of the gospel must be radically distinguished from the law. The distinction of law and gospel was maintained by the "Augsburg Confession" and with the "Formula of Concord" became a general hermeneutical principle.[52] This contrast is significant for understanding the Lutheran demand of a "pure" gospel insofar as the disabuse of the law (understood as God's absolute demand that cannot be satisfied by humankind) is the

---

48. Luther, *Lectures on Galatians*, 115.
49. Luther, *Lectures on Galatians*, 41–42.
50. "Augsburg Confession," 7.
51. See Stoltzfus, "Martin Luther."
52. See Bente and Dau, *Triglot Concordia*, 135 and 503.

presupposition for the authority of the gospel.[53] The "law-gospel" dichotomy represents for many the *de facto* material principle of the Reformation contained within the single term "gospel" and as a hermeneutical principle identical with the heart of the biblical message.[54] The understanding of a "pure" gospel here emerges from the contrast to the law, as is well preserved in C. F. W. Walther's classic treatise *The Proper Distinction Between Law and Gospel*, which ends, in the North American context of rising revelatory claims made by various marginal Christian groups, with Walther's admonition that the "pure gospel" is presented correctly as "pure doctrine" only if law and gospel are not confused.[55]

Influential contemporary works, including Edmund Schlink's *Theology of the Lutheran Confessions*, therefore warn that the church must always bear witness to the gospel and not to herself.[56] Even faith must not be seen as a condition for salvation, and any emphasis on repentance, sanctification, and other works necessary for salvation pollutes the objective nature of justification granted by faith alone. The distinction of law and gospel, for Schlink, is not a matter of logical deduction or formal adherence but "takes place . . . by experience alone," that is, by faith.[57] Contemporary Lutheran concerns maintain that the gospel must be received in the experience of faith apart from the law so that even the authority of dogma is based on the promises of God.[58] Pure gospel is encapsulated by pure doctrine only with the singular emphasis that "faith alone" (*sola fide*), apart from the works of the law, leads to justification. For Lutherans, the singular emphasis on justification therefore preserves the purity of doctrine because it defines the role of Christian works for salvation precisely by negating their significance.

FULL GOSPEL

The emphasis on a "full" gospel emerged historically in relative isolation from the Reformation debates and the Lutheran emphasis on justification, law, and gospel. Instead, the idea developed originally from the

53. Hummel, "Law and Gospel," 181–207.
54. Hummel, "Law and Gospel," 191.
55. See Walther, *Proper Distinction*.
56. Schlink, *Theology*.
57. Schlink, *Theology*, 136.
58. See Gritsch and Jenson, *Lutheranism*, 2–15.

attempt among Pentecostal pioneers to narrate their experiences with God in their encounter with Christ. The most widely known framework for narrating the set of Pentecostal experiences emerging on the ground is the so-called four- or fivefold gospel.[59] The pattern has endured the short history of modern-day Pentecostalism as a consistent narrative for articulating the spirituality and theology of the movement.[60] The larger, five-fold pattern proclaims, usually in kerygmatic form, the good news that Jesus Christ brings (1) salvation; (2) sanctification; (3) baptism in the Spirit; (4) divine healing; and (5) the impending arrival of the kingdom of God.[61]

Rather than elements of propositional doctrine (formal or material), these patterns form a narrative framework for identifying the centrality of encountering Christ manifested in several underlying experiences of the Holy Spirit.[62] All elements of the gospel and their reflection in contemporary Pentecostal theology are more immediately subjected to integration in the narrated experience of the "full" gospel (whether in the four- or fivefold pattern) than in a strict doctrinal framework. One might say that for the practices of the gospel, experience is more hospitable among Pentecostals than their articulation as doctrine. The articulation of Pentecostal theology today continues to be challenged by the integral demand that the doctrines of Pentecostals reflect the hospitality of their experiences.

The Catholicity of the Full Gospel

The order and content of the full gospel is not strictly defined and varies historically and geographically, since the four- or fivefold pattern is not the result of systematic theological reflection or received interpretation of Scripture but functions as a descriptive mechanism of Pentecostal spirituality shaped by a range of personal and communal experiences. The full gospel motif should therefore not be understood in a reductionist fashion as a definitive formula for the content of Pentecostal

---

59. Simpson, *Four-Fold Gospel*.

60. See Cartledge, "Early Pentecostal Theology," 117–30; Thomas, "Pentecostal Theology," 3–19; Land, *Pentecostal Spirituality*, 183; Dayton, *Theological Roots of Pentecostalism*, 15–23.

61. See Dayton, *Theological Roots of Pentecostalism*, 21–23.

62. See Kärkkäinen, "Encountering Christ," 5–19.

doctrine.⁶³ The elements are not logically isolated or adhere to a strict theological sequence, since the experiences underlying the motif have occurred in diverse fashion among Pentecostals.⁶⁴ Hence, the greatest challenge of engaging Pentecostal theology ecumenically is a reduction of the full gospel to the propositional ideas of salvation, sanctification, Spirit baptism, divine healing, and the coming kingdom, or worst, to merely one of those elements.

What is lost in any reductionism is the hospitable character, or catholicity, of the experiences and the ensuing transformation, reflection, and practices, which stand at the core of each element and of the full gospel narrative as a whole.⁶⁵ In the sense of this hospitality, Pentecostal theology resists the distinction between the form and content of revelation and its application to doctrine.⁶⁶ While salvation is arguably a dominant (formal) theological concern, soteriology is not a central Pentecostal "doctrine" among others but dispersed among the experiences narrated by the full gospel. In turn, the full gospel itself is not an analytical exposition of a Pentecostal order of salvation but rather an open narrative of the way of participating in all events of the gospel.

The Pentecostal *Via Salutis*

The articulation of a *full* gospel underscores the dominance of "salvation" for articulating a Pentecostal theology not merely by its primary position in the narrative but by its distribution throughout. One could say that the full gospel is soteriological from beginning to end: all elements are potential entry points on the way to salvation.⁶⁷ In other words, soteriology can be identified as the formal name for a narrative account of Pentecostal theology, which originates from, tends toward, and is supported throughout by the doctrine of salvation. Consequently, when Pentecostals say that salvation marks the beginning and overall direction of their theology, this should not be construed as a definitive Pentecostal *ordo salutis*. The full gospel motif as the framework for Pentecostal key experiences may give the impression that the good news of Jesus Christ

---

63. See Archer, "Fivefold Gospel," 7–43.
64. See Sutton, *Aimee Semple McPherson*.
65. Kärkkäinen, "Beyond Augsburg," 45–48.
66. See Vondey, *Beyond Pentecostalism*, 47–77.
67. See Yong, *In the Days*, 121–358; Yong, *Spirit Poured Out*, 83–90.

as savior, sanctifier, Spirit baptizer, divine healer, and coming king is marked by an uncompromising four- or fivefold order.

Indeed, classical Pentecostals have adopted in their history a Protestant *ordo salutis* that obscures the full gospel motif and its hospitality.[68] The global Pentecostal movements accentuate the single importance of salvation for Pentecostal theology, the centrality of Jesus Christ, and the pneumatological orientation reflected in the full gospel. Salvation does function in a sense as the Pentecostal equivalent for the Lutheran emphasis on justification, although the two terms are not identical.[69] However, a much broader palette of soteriological experiences becomes visible among Pentecostals worldwide that suggests that *all* elements of the full gospel are works of grace and thus possible entrance points to the way of salvation (*via salutis*).[70] The concern for the "full" gospel is thus, in the first instance, a concern for the fullness of salvation made available through the gospel and its proclamation and practice in the church.

PURITY AND FULLNESS

The distinction between full gospel and pure gospel reflects a complicated historical and rich theological development, which undoubtedly impacts official conversations between Lutherans and Pentecostals. However, the two phrases talk at cross purposes and do not simply identify a shift in perspective on the same object: pure gospel is an attempt to condense the notion of the gospel to a central core in the effort to protect its form and content in the church's proclamation; full gospel is an attempt to extend the notion of the gospel in the effort to protect the hospitality of all possible experiences narrated by the Gospels.

On the other hand, the different emphases do not mutually exclude one another: full gospel is an attempt to protect the purity of the gospel by showing the consistency between the gospel of Christ and its appropriation by the church; pure gospel is an attempt to identify with a singular principle the entirety of the biblical message and its proclamation by the church.

---

68. Studebaker, "Pentecostal Soteriology and Pneumatology," 248–70.

69. See Macchia, *Justified by the Spirit*. However, cf. Land, *Pentecostal Spirituality*, 18.

70. See Archer, "Nourishment for Our Journey," 79–96; Gause, *Living in the Spirit*.

Nonetheless, the two perspectives operate on two radically different presuppositions. Pure gospel signifies a principle of doctrine whereas full gospel denotes a narrative of experience. The former contests religious experiences not readily identifiable with the form and content of the gospel, while the latter struggles with theological doctrines not readily observable in (or contradicting) religious experiences. When Lutherans take for granted the reflection of their own theological principles in the formation of Pentecostal thought, the notion of the full gospel is likely to be distorted into the idea that Pentecostalism adds either to the formal principle of the gospel a different standard or to the material principle a different content. When Pentecostals expect Lutheran theology to reflect the hospitality of their own experiences, the notion of a pure gospel is likely to become distorted into the idea that Lutherans exclude religious (and charismatic) experiences on principle as a valid source of revelation.

Purity and fullness of the gospel are indicative of how the two groups express their respective experiences of Christ. The future of dialogue between the two traditions will therefore depend initially less on the reconciliation of doctrine than on the mutual sharing of their experiences as valid manifestations of the same gospel.

8

Sacramentality and the Hermeneutic of the Altar

PENTECOST—FOR MOST PENTECOSTALS—WAS AN unscripted event. Pioneers of the Pentecostal movement rarely describe the day of Pentecost in formal liturgical patterns. What occurred that day happened in a mix of "wonderful excitement" and "a blaze of Holy Ghost power and glory."[1] Pentecost was the work of the Spirit of Christ, and the work of the people (*leitourgia*) on that day "sprang fresh from his hands."[2] Pentecostals might view the day of Pentecost as the unencumbered manifestation of the end of days, unfettered by human plans, and in all its signs and wonders an eschatological threshold to the kingdom of God.[3] And yet Pentecostals also describe the day of Pentecost with liturgical overtones, often identifying the work of the church as "the grandest and most effective display"[4] of the gifts of the Holy Spirit among God's people. This effectiveness is typically measured by the three thousand souls converted to God and added to the church (Acts 2:41, 47)—a result attributed as much to the power of the Holy Spirit as to the work of the people. Pentecost stands implicitly as the liturgical fountainhead for the manifestation of the life

---

1. Woodworth-Etter, "Signs and Wonders," 26.
2. Tomlinson, *Last Great Conflict*, 100.
3. See Jacobsen, *Thinking in the Spirit*, 34–50, 80–84, 101–10, 123–27.
4. Bosworth, "All Speak in Tongues," 142.

of the Spirit. For Pentecostals, the events of Pentecost are not an isolated occurrence but a repeatable celebration essential to the mission of the church.[5] The day of Pentecost is the first day in a sequence of revivals that have ushered in the contemporary global Pentecostal movements.[6] Nonetheless, the exact liturgical qualities of Pentecost (and thus of Pentecostalism) remain largely unstated.

The liturgical quality of Pentecost became quickly the focus of both advocates and critics of contemporary Pentecostalism. The former see in the day of Pentecost a prototype for the church and its ministry, the latter find in this interpretation and in the emerging Pentecostal practices severe disregard for established liturgical conventions.[7] Although Pentecostals have undoubtedly ritualized the events of Pentecost, the contemporary movement has generally resisted the temptation to articulate a formal liturgy and thus to tradition their biblical and theological perspectives.[8] In the previous chapters, I have argued that the liturgical development of Pentecostalism is a product of specific religious and sociocultural, economic, and political forces at play during the early twentieth century.[9] I suggested elsewhere that Pentecostals have transformed the notion of liturgy from a conceptually fixed, written, and tradition-based framework to a spontaneous, improvisational, liminal, and anti-structural notion of ritual.[10] And I proposed that the reality of this Pentecostal liturgy—in its broadest sense—can be characterized by the notion of sacramentality.[11] While the argument that Pentecostal spirituality is fundamentally sacramental is not new,[12] it remains to be shown how exactly this sacramentality is practiced among Pentecostals today.

In this chapter, I suggest that the Pentecostal worldview is existentially sacramental, albeit primarily on ecclesiological and pneumatological grounds. At the heart of the Pentecostal liturgy stands a theology of the altar—an archetype of Pentecost—that is the summit and source of sacramentality among Pentecostals. In order to substantiate this claim, I

5. See Hodges, *Theology of the Church*, 32–36.
6. See Anderson, *Ends of the Earth*, 11–36.
7. See Brumback, "What Meaneth This?," 24; Dayton, *Theological Roots of Pentecostalism*, 19–23.
8. See Chan, *Pentecostal Theology*, 40–72.
9. Vondey, "Making of a Black Liturgy," 147–68.
10. Vondey, *Beyond Pentecostalism*, 109–40.
11. Vondey and Green, "Between This and That," 243–64.
12. See, e.g., Gunstone, *Pentecost Comes to Church*.

begin with a sacramental reading of the day of Pentecost in Luke–Acts. This narrative is followed by a construction of the theological language for Pentecostal sacramentality in conversation with the Roman Catholic Constitution on the Sacred Liturgy (*Sacrosanctum Concilium*). With this help, the third part constructs a Pentecostal theology of liturgy from a theology of the altar. The final part elevates this proposal to a discussion of the pneumatological foundations for a Pentecostal theology of sacramentality.

A SACRAMENTAL READING OF PENTECOST

Pentecost is a hermeneutic, a concise hermeneutical framework for Pentecostalism.[13] The records of the event are above all contained in the biblical texts of Luke–Acts. Although these texts offer insight into the proceedings of the day, a sacramental reading has not been attempted.[14] I suggest that any such attempt among Pentecostals reveals an inherent sacramentality marked by four distinct moments: (1) the creation of a sacramental environment; (2) a call to personal participation in the divine-human encounter, (3) personal and communal response, and (4) transformation and manifestations of the effects of the encounter.

The day of Pentecost was a ritual event on the calendar of ancient Israel (see Exod 34:22; Deut 16:10) celebrating the giving of the Law on Mt. Sinai; its advent was expected and planned. However, Jesus announces an unusual significance of the coming days for the disciples who tarry in Jerusalem (Luke 24:49) and who are promised power from the Holy Spirit and effective witness to the gospel (Acts 1:8). The disciples accordingly assemble in preparation and prayer in Jerusalem (1:14) and meet "all together in one place" (Acts 2:1). The arriving feast day coincides with the fulfillment of the promises of Jesus. The stage is set in an ordinary context of the liturgical life of the Jewish community for the unfolding of the extraordinary circumstances of the work of God revealed in the person of Jesus Christ.

The ordinariness and ritual character of the day are interrupted with the sudden sound of "a violent wind" filling "the entire house" (2:2). Precisely, this occurrence is identified as the outpouring of the Holy Spirit on "all of the disciples," in a place "where they were sitting" with

---

13. Smith, *Thinking in Tongues*, 23.
14. See Bock, *Theology*; Mittelstadt, *Reading Luke–Acts*.

the appearance of divided tongues "on each of them" and the speaking in other languages "as the Spirit gave them ability" (2:4). The outpouring of the Spirit signifies a divine–human encounter indicated by physical (visible and audible) manifestations. This encounter of the disciples with the Holy Spirit becomes a signifier for others in the neighborhood who gather at the sound and the languages spoken (2:6). The Spirit-filled disciples do not disperse into the city but remain gathered in a sacred environment that attracts a plurality of others in bewilderment, amazement and astonishment (2:8), and widespread perplexity (2:12). Theologically, the divine–human encounter of this event is signified not by the incomprehensibility of the acts of the apostles but by what Michael Welker has called the "overcomprehensibility" or "a totally unexpected comprehensibility and . . . unbelievable, universal capacity to understand and act of understanding."[15] This comprehensibility of "God's deeds of power" (2:11) establishes the threshold toward an overthrow of the existing symbolic network of the "devout Jews from many nations" (2:5) and its comprehensive reinterpretation in the terms of a renewed Christian existence.[16] The existential work of the church now originates from this space created by the outpouring of the Holy Spirit "on all flesh" (2:17) and manifested in the succinct work of the disciples encountering the crowd in Jerusalem.

The reality of the divine–human encounter is further delineated by the apostle Peter who, "standing with the eleven" (2:14), issues an explanation and interpretation of the events (2:14–36) to those drawn by the physical manifestations to the threshold of the encounter with God. The work of the disciples, now fulfilling Jesus' anticipation of their witness to the gospel, is carried out in the power of the Spirit, explaining, exhorting, and instructing the ethnically diverse population in attendance (2:38–40). The audience, already astonished and perplexed, is eventually "cut to the heart" and issues, from the perspective of Pentecost, a fundamental question regarding the transformation of their lives: "What should we do?" (2:37).

The answer to this existential question is Peter's call to "repent, and be baptized" (2:38), followed by the promise of the gift of the Holy Spirit to all those who respond. With this call, Peter not only beckons the audience to move into the sacred encounter with God, he also expands this

---

15. Welker, *God the Spirit*, 230–33.
16. See Chauvet, *Symbol and Sacrament*, 159–89.

human–divine meeting in an ongoing Pentecost beyond the spatial and temporal confines of the house and the disciples to the Jews present, their subsequent generations, and "all who are far away" (2:39).[17] In response, several thousand "welcome" the message and enter into fellowship with the disciples (2:42) accompanied by the continued signs, wonders, faith, and worship of the church (2:43–47). Teaching and formation, communion, water baptism, and the breaking of the bread are all integrated in the comprehensive embrace of the sacramentality of Pentecost.

TOWARD A PENTECOSTAL ARTICULATION OF SACRAMENTALITY

My reading of the biblical account of Pentecost suggests that contemporary Pentecostalism (in its explicit dependence on Pentecost) possesses an implicit sacramentality that has not yet been fully articulated. What is lacking in this formulation is above all a connection to the Christian spiritual traditions. Comparisons with the liturgical traditions have typically led to a critical distinction from established ritual practices.[18] Pentecostal commentary emphasizes the renewal rather than the imitation of traditional liturgy in the churches.[19]

A milestone in the history of liturgical reform, the first document promulgated by Vatican Council II (1962–1965) was *Sacrosanctum Concilium*, which was widely hailed for its liturgical vision and depth of reform. It represents a suitable dialogue partner for Pentecostal ambitions to reform liturgical practices while challenging Pentecostals not only with its historical and theological depth but also with the breadth of liturgical practices and sacramental implications.[20] The Constitution expands the reach of liturgical reform from traditional sacramental practices to the instruction of the clergy, liturgy professors, liturgical training in seminaries and in religious houses, and the education of the laity.[21] The liturgical dimension of renewal envisioned in this document has expanded the original vision of the Council even to the charismatic renewal

---

17. See Yong, *Spirit Poured Out*, 83.

18. See Alexander, "Non-Liturgical Holiness Pentecostalism," 158–93.

19. See Suurmond, "Church at Play," 247–59; Gunstone, "Spirit's Freedom," 4–16.

20. See Jackson, "Theology of the Liturgy," 101–28; Cessario, "Sacraments of the Church," 129–44.

21. Senn, *Christian Liturgy*, 629–30.

movements.[22] A Pentecostal theology of liturgy can take its impetus from the central affirmations of the Catholic document.

Sacrosanctum Concilium is fundamentally oriented toward ecclesiology. The liturgy is the principal manifestation of the church; it expresses both the nature and purpose of the church and the concrete practices of ecclesial action.[23] This significance is most clearly expressed in the statement that "the liturgy is the summit toward which the activity of the church is directed; it is also the source from which all its power flows."[24] The reason for this affirmation is the soteriological significance attributed to the liturgy "through which 'the work of our redemption takes place.'"[25] The presence and action of Christ in the liturgy is the central concern for any liturgical practice.[26] At the heart of all liturgical celebrations mediating the redemptive work of Christ stands the sacrifice of the Eucharist "to which all other activities of the church are directed, as toward their end."[27] Hence, liturgical celebration is in character sacramental, not "an accidental unity composed of a theology of the sacraments"[28] but a sacramental system fully ordered by the reality of sacred signs: Christ the primordial sacrament; the church, sacrament of Christ; and the Eucharist, the royal sacrament of the church to which other sacraments are directed.[29] On these theological dimensions the Council then promulgated its vision of liturgical reform and instruction.

The most far-reaching principle of the liturgical reform envisioned here is the "active participation" and "liturgical formation" of all the faithful.[30] Since the liturgy is human participation in the divine reality, the reform of the liturgy aimed at "elements subject to change" that "not only may be changed but ought to be changed with the passage of time, if they have suffered from the intrusion of anything out of harmony with the inner nature of the liturgy or have become less suitable."[31] The purpose of the reformed practices is that all people of faith "should be able

---

22. See Vondey, *Heribert Mühlen*, 161–262.
23. Rocha, "Principal Manifestation," 3–26.
24. Paul VI, *Sacrosanctum Concilium*, 10; Flannery, *Vatican Council II*, 122.
25. Paul VI, *Sacrosanctum Concilium*, 2; Flannery, *Vatican Council II*, 117.
26. Schmidt, *Constitution de la Sainte*, 154.
27. Paul VI, *Sacrosanctum Concilium*, 10; Flannery, *Vatican Council II*, 123.
28. Kiesling, "Sacramental Character," 385.
29. See Schmidt, *Constitution de la Sainte*, 169–79.
30. Paul VI, *Sacrosanctum Concilium*, 14. See Jungmann, "Constitution," 1:1–87.
31. Paul VI, *Sacrosanctum Concilium*, 21; Flannery, *Vatican Council II*, 126.

to understand them easily and take part in them in a celebration which is full, active and the community's own."[32] The church, identified by its liturgy, is thus conceived as a liturgical space or place in which all texts, rites, materials, and actions are continually directed toward active participation in the worship of God.[33]

A Pentecostal appropriation of the *Sacrosanctum Concilium* must engage both the liturgical and sacramental dimensions of the ecclesial life. Few Pentecostals will find it difficult to adopt the emphasis placed on the context of salvation history, the redemptive work of Christ, the concrete place of the church's assembly, and the active participation of all people. On the other hand, two central concerns present themselves immediately in this attempt to appropriate the Catholic document for Pentecostal purposes. First, *Sacrosanctum Concilium* is remarkably short on references to the Holy Spirit, Pentecost, and the charismatic life of the church. Although the renewal of the liturgical life is seen as "a movement of the Holy Spirit,"[34] nothing substantial is said about the pneumatological dimension of the liturgy or the sacraments for the life of the church and its worship "in Spirit and in truth" (John 4:24). Second, the Eucharist does not occupy a central position in Pentecostal ecclesiology, although efforts have been made to develop eucharistic and sacramental theologies among Pentecostals.[35] While regularly celebrated in Pentecostal churches, the Lord's Supper is not a central ritual of Pentecostal spiritual praxis.[36] A Pentecostal theology of worship can be scripted ordinarily without a central eucharistic celebration although not without central liturgical and ritual practices.[37] Nonetheless, these two obstacles can be resolved within a Pentecostal affirmation of sacramentality similar to the vision of the liturgy in *Sacrosanctum Concilium*.

A Pentecostal affirmation of sacramentality is rooted in the sacramental character of Pentecost as the originating event of the church and its liturgy. While sacramental theology has an obligation to start from a Christological principle rooted in the mystery and history of the salvific work of Christ, Pentecostal sacramentality is also governed by a pneumatological

---

32. Paul VI, *Sacrosanctum Concilium*, 21.
33. See Diekmann, "Place of Liturgical Worship," 67–107.
34. Paul VI, *Sacrosanctum Concilium*, 43; Flannery, *Vatican Council II*, 133.
35. See Green, *Toward a Pentecostal Theology*; Tomberlin, *Pentecostal Sacraments*, 153–91; Biddy, "Re-Envisioning the Pentecostal Understanding," 228–51.
36. See Albrecht, *Rites in the Spirit*.
37. See Cartledge, *Testimony in the Spirit*, 36–46.

principle rooted in the visible birth of the church through the Spirit of Pentecost.[38] Pentecost represents a change to the Jewish liturgy. At the heart of the Christian liturgy celebrated in its place, Pentecostals find the outpouring of the Holy Spirit and its physical manifestations that together create a sacramental environment in the church. Characteristic of this environment are the active participation and transformation of all people in a Spirit-filled encounter with God. The most widely used symbol for this environment among Pentecostals is the altar.

THE ALTAR: SUMMIT OF THE PENTECOSTAL LITURGY

Most Pentecostal churches do not have a physical altar—neither in the sacrificial sense of the biblical writings nor in the eucharistic sense of *Sacrosanctum Concilium*.[39] Rather, mimicking the events of Pentecost, for Pentecostals, the altar exists in the sacramental action of the community facing a divine–human encounter. The distinct moments of the sacramentality of Pentecost delineated above are ritually present in the life and worship of Pentecostals constituted by the creation of the sacramental environment, a call to participation, the response, and the ensuing transformation of the community.

The creation of the sacramental environment of the altar can take different forms among Pentecostals. The aesthetic of the altar as a sacred space often possesses few material or architectural markers.[40] In classical Pentecostalism, derived from the plantation prayer grounds of African slaves, the camp meetings of the rural American south, and the influence of the Church of England and early Methodism, the altar can be identified by a walking of the aisle or jumping on pews or, less dramatically, the simple assembly of people at the end of a church building where the word of God is preached (see chapter 5).[41] In charismatic churches with historical roots in the established liturgical and sacramental traditions, the formally established sacred space of the sanctuary, including the altar

---

38. See Chauvet, *Symbol and Sacrament*, 487. For an exposition of these principles, see Vondey, *People of Bread*.

39. On the altar in *Sacrosanctum Concilium* see Diekmann, "Place of Liturgical Worship," 91–97.

40. See Martin, "Latin American Pentecostalism," 138–60.

41. See Vondey, *Beyond Pentecostalism*, 122–25; Murray, *Revival and Revivalism*, 185–87.

and tabernacle, delineates the spatial boundaries of the divine–human encounter.[42] In neo-Pentecostal communities, the idea of the "sacred space" with a central focus point ("altar") is shifting from clear architectural identifiers in the past at the back end of a church building to the more symbolically and experientially identified center of worship in the congregation.[43] In the vast diversity of physical space among Pentecostal churches worldwide—from megachurches to rooms in shopping malls, sheds on the outskirts of a village or open-air benches—the space of human–divine encounter is typically identified by the congregation's manifest (and sometimes pre-cognitive) activity of worship.[44] The Pentecostal altar exists in the ritual space of preaching, prayer, anointing, conversion, singing, dancing, praise, and ministry in various forms, including the laying on of hands, healing, exorcism, testimony, teaching or tarrying before the Lord, and the practice of spiritual gifts. In his extensive study of Pentecostal rituals, Daniel Albrecht summarizes,

> The altar space reveals something important in Pentecostal liturgy and spirituality: "meeting with God" is a primary purpose of the entire ritual. The altar space functions symbolically as an *axis mundi* in Pentecostal spirituality . . . [that] most clearly symbolizes and helps to focus the human–divine convergence.[45]

In the language of *Sacrosanctum Concilium*, the altar is the liturgical summit toward which the activity of the whole church is directed.

The *altar call* is a foundational rite of Pentecostal churches, although no ecclesiology has yet been based on the concept. The call is constitutive of the sacramental reality of the altar, which is generally made explicit in a verbal representation of the divine and human meeting that has occurred in the worship of the church. The altar call is typically an invitation issued by the pastor or evangelist to the congregation to "bring themselves" (i.e., their lives, faith, sins, circumstances, illnesses, problems, fears, hopes, etc.) to a meeting with God.[46] The call from the platform or the front of the church may be a general invitation or follow a specific emphasis of the service; at other times, the call may not be

---

42. See Ryle, "Laying Our Sins," 68–97.
43. See Gold, "From the 'Upper Room,'" 74–88.
44. Miller and Yamamori, *Global Pentecostalism*, 129–59.
45. Albrecht, *Rites in the Spirit*, 133.
46. Tomberlin, *Pentecostal Sacraments*, 103–4. See Thompson, "Public Invitation as Method."

SACRAMENTALITY AND THE HERMENEUTIC OF THE ALTAR 153

voiced explicitly from the leaders of the worship but erupt spontaneously through a tongue or revelation in the congregation.[47] The altar call can be made to begin a new dimension in the worship of the community (e.g., communal prayer), to initiate the main focus of the service (e.g., a healing service), or to integrate other ritual practices and usher in the celebration of the sacraments (typically the Lord's Supper but also water baptism). The formal celebration of the sacraments represents in this larger context "an opportunity to invite the saints of God once again to the altar to encounter the Holy Spirit."[48] The invitation alone does not establish or constitute the altar space; it presents in a strict sense only an "offer" to the congregation that has yet to be accepted.

The acceptance of the invitation is ritually displayed in some form of audible or visible *response*, often accompanied by other physical and charismatic manifestations of individuals or the entire congregation. If the altar call is the offer to enter into a sacramental environment, the response to the call is the acceptance of that offer by the worshiping community.[49] More precisely, the response is a physical manifestation of the active participation of the faithful in the divine–human encounter that establishes the altar as the space of that meeting. This response is in a sense an "overaccepting" of the invitation issued by the church and thus of the promises and gifts of God.[50] The congregation does not only acknowledge and submit to the grace of God but overabundantly responds to the Spirit in "an active way of receiving . . . without losing the initiative."[51] The abundant participation of the worshipers includes sometimes a congregational move forward into the holy place, sometimes a gradual reorientation of some, at other times a jumping and running of the aisle by individuals. The bringing of oneself to the altar may be the actual walk of a person or manifested only by a groaning in the spirit, a singing of the congregation into the presence of God, or the eruption of tongues and prophecies and prayers that in a manner of speaking bring the altar to the people. For Pentecostals, over-accepting the presence of God is the hallmark of signifying their willingness for transformation and redemption.

---

47. Albrecht, *Rites in the Spirit*, 165–66.
48. Tomberlin, *Pentecostal Sacraments*, 103.
49. See Knight, *Pentecostal Worship*, 97–98.
50. On the notion of over-accepting, see Wells, *Improvisation*, 131–40.
51. Wells, *Improvisation*, 131.

The goal of the Pentecostal liturgy is *transformation* through the encounter with the actual presence of God. The altar space is a threshold to the real presence of Christ in the Spirit, a presence that can be encountered through the sacraments as much as through the baptism of the Holy Spirit or the practices of healing, deliverance, anointing, and other ministries.[52] The sacraments are not the prime symbols of Pentecostal sacramentality, but these "sacramental ordinances" are integrated in the larger sacramental journey of the community.[53] The active participation of the faithful in the sacramentality of the altar call is an affirmation of the divine presence "in full expectation that God would act uniquely and powerfully in and through these rites."[54] Only the experience of transformation can resolve in Pentecostal worship the "fundamental tension" between the expectation of an immediate encounter with God and the necessarily mediated nature sacramentality.[55] Pentecostals embrace the mediatedness of the human condition as the necessary means of not only encountering or receiving God's grace but of the effects manifested in the human being and the community. All human mediatedness is sacramental in this experience of the transformation at the altar. For Pentecostals, this mediation is utterly dependent on the transforming work of the Holy Spirit.

THE PNEUMATOLOGICAL FOUNDATIONS OF PENTECOSTAL SACRAMENTALITY

The symbol of the altar offers a pneumatological entrance to the construction of the liturgy. The central emphasis of this pneumatological direction is not only the possibility of a liturgical experience of the Spirit beyond the ritual structures of a cultic framework but the requirement that all sacramental participation must involve the epiclesis of the Spirit. The baptism in the Holy Spirit remains the central metaphor for Pentecostal sacramentality as a participation in God's redemptive presence.[56]

---

52. See Albrecht, *Rites in the Spirit*, 256; Tomberlin, *Pentecostal Sacraments*, 107–258.

53. See Archer, "Nourishment for Our Journey," 79–96.

54. Green, *Toward a Pentecostal Theology*, 178. What Green says about the sacraments in early Pentecostalism can be extended to the notion of sacramentality among Pentecostals in general.

55. See Poloma, "Symbolic Dilemma," 105; Arteaga, *Forgotten Power*, 21–55.

56. See Macchia, *Baptized in the Spirit*, 247–56.

The Spirit is called upon not for the sake of the Spirit alone but always in Trinitarian communion with the Father and the Son.[57] Hence, the Pentecostal liturgy exists only in the economy of salvation in which the Father's sending of the Son and the Spirit are primary, and "the church and its sacraments are *secondary salvific gifts* which naturally proceed from the Son and the Spirit."[58] Although the traditional Christological focus of the sacraments is maintained, it is supplemented by an explicit pneumatological attention in which the Spirit accentuates, completes, and continues the work of Christ in the community. Put differently, sacramental action among Pentecostals refers to the presence and action of Christ as the gift of the Father insofar as this gift is manifested by the Holy Spirit in the church. Sacramentality is a principle of ecclesial reality, an action of the community extending to any manifest encounter with Christ as the primordial gift of God, through the Spirit as the gift of Christ, in the church as the gift of Christ and the Spirit, and among the faithful as those filled with the Spirit.

Liturgically speaking, the sacramental environment of the altar is a pneumatological expansion, not replacement, of the traditional emphasis of the sacraments. This extension of the salvific work of Christ beyond the sacramental ordinances, and even beyond the Lord's Supper, invites a broad theological reconstruction of how soteriological and ecclesiological concerns meet in the concrete encounter of Pentecostal worship. The suppression of the celebration of sacraments among some Pentecostals is the unfortunate result of inherent anti-ritual tendencies accentuated by a misappropriation of the fideism of the Protestant Reformation and the critical experience (or hearsay) of ritual activities that fail to manifest the presence of God.[59] Worship among Pentecostals shows that the Pentecostal liturgy is able to integrate all accentuations of sacramental celebration ranging from the centrality of the Lord's Supper in some churches to a moderate ritual celebration in others and to a variety of sacramental actions that have become common place without explicit sacramental connotations. All of these practices are held together by the notion of a manifest divine–human encounter central to the Pentecostal liturgy and symbolized by the altar.

---

57. Macchia, *Baptized in the Spirit*, 89–154; Green, *Toward a Pentecostal Theology*, 289–93.

58. Tomberlin, *Pentecostal Sacraments*, 93.

59. See Biddy, "Re-Envisioning the Pentecostal Understanding," 228–39.

The altar as a notion of sacred space and time delineates the manifest, even theophanic circumference of the divine–human encounter in Pentecostal worship. If the participation of the church in this encounter is called sacramental, and I know of no other Christian term to describe it, then this sacramentality among Pentecostals is defined by the manifestation of the Spirit that leads toward, makes possible, and carries further the meeting of the human being with God. In other words, the Holy Spirit is origin, medium, and goal of all sacramentality.[60] This pneumatological affirmation has a number of immediate consequences.

If the Spirit is the origin of all divine–human encounter, including sacramental action, then Pentecostals can avoid a Christomonism that reduces the ecclesial authority of the sacraments to their assumed institution at the hands of the historical Jesus.[61] Neither can "the sacraments appear . . . as the somehow static prolongations of the incarnation as such" but rather "as the major expression, in our own history, of the embodiment . . . of the risen One in the world through the Spirit."[62] Sacramental action in the church is the result of the presence of the glorified Christ who is dynamically working in the Spirit throughout the worship of the community. A Pentecostal liturgy therefore does not submit to any form of sacramentalism, since the Spirit is not bound to the sacraments alone but precedes and supersedes them. Neither can Pentecostals hold to a punctiliar notion of sacramental celebration at specific points in the worship of the church or through particular rituals. Pneumatology offers a rationale for the work of God in the human being beyond the participation in sacramental action.[63] At the same time, such experiences, celebrations, and rituals are moments on the lifelong journey of the Christian and of the renewal of the church toward their full realization in the kingdom of God. At the altar, the continuing call of God and the human response meet in a Spirit-filled embrace that extends to the entire Christian life.

The Holy Spirit as the medium of sacramentality makes possible the encounter with Christ in worship. The Holy Spirit, not the human person, is the mediator of the grace of God and the acting subject of the celebration, even if the sacramental action of the church requires the participation of the community.[64] The essence of sacramentality exists

60. See Gasecki, *Profil des Geistes*, 394–451.
61. Gasecki, *Profil des Geistes*, 401–6.
62. Chauvet, *Sacraments*, 160.
63. Chauvet, *Sacraments*, 435.
64. Chauvet, *Sacraments*, 421.

precisely in the acceptance of the necessity of this continued mediation of God's presence in the church, since the goal of all mediation is the revelation of God. When the Roman Catholic community speaks of the church as mediating the grace of the sacrament (a sacramental ecclesiology that allows for the Holy Spirit), the Pentecostal community speaks of the church as mediating the grace of the Holy Spirit (a pneumatological ecclesiology that allows for sacramentality). In this sense, for Pentecostals, the Holy Spirit mediates the grace of God and the church mediates the grace of the Holy Spirit. This dual mediation holds the central mechanism of Pentecostal sacramentality.

As "medium" the Spirit does not replace liturgical or sacramental representations in the church. Rather, in Pentecostal terminology, mediation seeks manifestation—the physical representation of the meeting between God, the church, and the Christian in the Spirit. This physicality of the church and the human being is constitutive of Pentecostal sacramentality, which seeks not only the corporeal but the charismatic manifestation of the human encounter with God.[65] Speaking in tongues, prophecy, words of knowledge, and divine healing are therefore sacramental in the same sense as confession, foot washing, water baptism, and the Lord's Supper.[66] These manifestations reinforce and are reinforced by the pneumatological foundation of sacramentality.[67] In a Pentecostal worldview, sacramental and charismatic practices presuppose one another.

Sacramental practices among Pentecostals, of course, are more diverse than this essay indicates, although the uncritical acceptance of the notion of ordinances has prevented a more nuanced sacramental Pentecostal theology. In terms of extreme positions, some Pentecostals are closer to the Augustinian notion of sacramentality, with its emphasis on the efficacy of the work itself (generally stated as a theology of grace), while others identify (unwittingly) with Donatist tendencies that rely on the efficacy of the person performing (and also participating in) the work (often expressed as a theology of sanctification). Both positions have shown to be problematic in Pentecostal praxis. A pneumatological perspective indicates that some Pentecostals are more Catholic in their emphasis on actual grace dispensed at the hand of Christ (through the Holy

---

65. Albrecht speaks of both types of rituals and modes of sensibility among Pentecostals; Albrecht, *Rites in the Spirit*, 177–95.

66. See Macchia, "Footwashing a Neglected Sacrament," 239–49; Macchia, "Tongues as a Sign," 61–76.

67. See Black, "Church as Eucharistic Fellowship," 78–89.

Spirit); some are more Lutheran with a close union between the sacrament and the word of God (linked by the Holy Spirit); others hold a more Reformed view of sacraments as earthly signs attached to a divine promise (mediated by the Holy Spirit); while again others are more Zwinglian in their emphasis on the solitary importance of faith (produced by the Holy Spirit) for the efficacy of the work. A way to resolve the apparent irreconcilable theological differences emerges from the pneumatological focus essential to all Pentecostal perspectives.

The pneumatological foundation of Pentecostal sacramentality allows Pentecostals to adopt the longstanding theological tradition with regard to the efficacy of the sacramental rites and to correct the differing positions: sacramental action is efficacious not by the performance of the work itself (*ex opere operato*) but when that work is mediated by the Spirit (*ex Spiritu operato*). The altar as a sacramental symbol establishes the ritual environment for that mediation even if it does not guarantee the divine–human encounter. The efficacy of the rite depends on the disposition of the person performing the work (*ex opere operantis*), although that disposition does not cause the efficacy of the rite but establishes only the possibility of the receptivity of the Spirit from which the divine grace is dispensed (*ex Spiritu operantis*). This adaptation and modification does not restrict but widens the possibility of sacramental encounter beyond the realm of particular rituals (and ordinances). Such expansion of the possible encounter with God is genuine to all Pentecostal (and Christian) theology.

CONCLUSION

In this essay, I have argued that the Pentecostal worldview is existentially sacramental on pneumatological and ecclesiological grounds. The operation of the Holy Spirit is never at the disposal of the church or the individual. At the same time, precisely because the work of the Spirit is the free work of God, certain sacramental rites can be considered efficacious each and every time they are performed by the community.[68] This efficacy is not contained in the elements or instruments of any particular rite but in the encounter of the human being with the Spirit of God. For many Pentecostals, the efficacy of this encounter is measured by the transformation manifested at the altar that is most evident in the desire to fulfil

---

68. See Biddy, "Re-Envisioning the Pentecostal," 244–45.

the church's commissioning into the world.[69] Theologically, this perspective cannot be maintained by the concept of ordinances but requires a more expansive sacramental worldview. This essay has suggested that, for Pentecostals, the altar is an opportunity for the experience of the immediacy of the Spirit and the manifestation of the gifts of the Spirit through various sacramental and charismatic means in the life of the community and the individual. The goal of that encounter, however, is not the church itself or the individual but the transformation of all creation into a witness to the gospel by the power of the Spirit.

The altar is a sacramental symbol and archetype of Pentecost that marks a place of gathering and sending—both for the Spirit of God and for the church into the world. The direction of Spirit and church is intertwined in eschatological orientation toward the heavenly altar. For Pentecostals, the glory of the coming kingdom of God is already manifested in the experience of the Spirit in the community.[70] Sacramentality, because it is rooted in and carried by the Holy Spirit, is therefore always eschatological. For Pentecostals, the Spirit not only accompanies the church to the kingdom but brings that kingdom into the church.[71] No sacramental or charismatic activity can contain this cosmic dimension of the Spirit. Sacramental action in the church is incomplete participation in the fullness of the divine life. Nonetheless, participation in the sacramental encounter with God is a celebration of the church as the altar of God built in the present for the coming salvation of the whole of creation.

---

69. See McClung, "We Have an Altar."
70. See Tomberlin, *Pentecostal Sacraments*, 23–27.
71. See Vondey, "Pentecostal Perspectives," 55–68.

9

The Materiality of Pentecostal Theology

Two of the most prolific developments in the study of Pentecostalism have been phenomenological accounts of Pentecostal practices (e.g., sociological, ethnographic, cultural, ecclesiological, liturgical, and ritual studies) and theological accounts of Pentecostal doctrine (e.g., Pentecostal distinctives, classical Pentecostal teachings, theological hermeneutics, comparative theological studies, systematic and constructive accounts). Yet, little attention has been paid to the possible link between both developments and their mutual significance for Pentecostal studies. While experience, spirituality, and praxis are widely considered normative sources for Pentecostal thought, efforts in constructing contemporary Pentecostal theology proceed at times with little consideration of foundational and formative embodied practices. The adoption of non-Pentecostal theological reasoning has further contributed to a speculative development in the West without consistent engagement and reengagement of original practices. The articulation of a comprehensive theology for the Pentecostal movement threatens to become a theoretical exercise contributing to an extinction of traditional Pentecostal practices and neglect of their importance for the embodiment of Pentecostal theology.

With embodiment, I refer to the physicality and materiality of religious practices, rites, and rituals that inform and are informed by the articulation of Pentecostal doctrine.[1] One of the most widely known

1. The notion of the materiality of salvation among Pentecostals was introduced by Volf, "Materiality of Salvation," 447–67.

frameworks for narrating Pentecostal experiences is the so-called full gospel, which emerged historically as a fourfold, or more inclusive fivefold pattern that proclaims Jesus as savior, sanctifier, Spirit baptizer, healer, and soon-coming king (see chapter 7).[2] This chapter traces the kinesthetic contours of the full gospel with the modest task to identify which embodied practices support the theological narrative. I suggest that the full gospel functions not as an alternative system of doctrine but as a descriptive mechanism of spiritual practices shaped by a range of personal and communal experiences: salvation, sanctification, Spirit baptism, divine healing, and the coming kingdom function as heuristic devices for Pentecostal theology because they emerge from and yield embodied practices.

Since no overall study exists of foundational practices formative for the traditionating of the full gospel, this essay aims to provide a phenomenological basis for a constructive assessment of each of the five patterns. The account is placed in the experiential context of the altar call and response, arguably the center and summit of Pentecostal worship and theology.[3] The following sections trace the kinesthetic contours of embodied practices existing among Pentecostals and identify their foundational and formative theological contributions to each of the themes of the full gospel. The result is intended as an empirical framework for the articulation of Pentecostal theology on the ground (i.e., at the altar) emerging from and reengaging such practices. Even if the applicability of the full gospel to the global Pentecostal movement remains debated, the following account suggests that the heart of Pentecostal theology can be succinctly identified as an embodied gospel.

EMBODYING SALVATION AT THE ALTAR

Pentecostals are recognized perhaps most readily for their worship, rituals, music, and spontaneous practices of embodied praise.[4] The basic "plot" of worship focuses on the human response in the Holy Spirit to the salvation offered by God in Jesus Christ.[5] Soteriology is embodied

---

2. Dayton, *Theological Roots of Pentecostalism*; Thomas, *Toward a Pentecostal Ecclesiology*; Yong, *In the Days*.

3. See Albrecht, *Rites in the Spirit*; Tomberlin, *Pentecostal Sacraments*.

4. See Albrecht, *Rites in the Spirit*; Miller and Yamamori, *Global Pentecostalism*; Ingalls and Yong, *Spirit of Praise*.

5. Gause, *Living in the Spirit*; Rybarczyk, *Beyond Salvation*; Erickson, *Pentecostal*

in various forms among Pentecostals in a foundational rite typically labeled the "altar call."[6] The altar is a theological metaphor for the human encounter with God; most Pentecostal churches do not have a physical altar, neither in the sacrificial sense of the biblical writings nor in the sacramental sense of the liturgical traditions.[7] Although historically and conceptually sometimes identified with a particular space and time of corporate worship, liturgy, or ritual, the Pentecostal altar is a symbol of the kingdom of God, which is "neither here nor there" (see Luke 17:21) but which comes into existence, as on the day of Pentecost, through the outpouring of the Holy Spirit and the participation of the community in response to the divine presence.

The altar as a soteriological metaphor for a meeting of the human being with God has transitioned throughout Pentecostal history. The call to the altar acknowledges the existence of a ritual space for embodying salvation that invites diverse forms of prayer, repentance, conversion, miracles, worship, and ministry. The altar call is typically an invitation issued by the pastor or evangelist to the congregation to "bring themselves" (i.e., their lives, faith, sins, circumstances, illnesses, problems, fears, hopes, etc.) to a meeting with God.[8] The call from the platform or the front of the church may be a general invitation or follow a specific emphasis of the service; at other times, the call may not be voiced explicitly from the leaders of worship but erupt spontaneously through a tongue, prophecy, or revelation in the congregation.[9] The acceptance of the invitation is displayed in some form of audible or visible response, often accompanied by other physical and charismatic manifestations of individuals or the entire congregation. The response of the worshipers includes sometimes a congregational move forward into the "holy place," sometimes a gradual reorientation of some, at other times a jumping and running of the aisle by individuals. Responses vary from the assembly of the entire congregation at the altar to some remaining in the pews, falling on their knees in the aisle, or stretching out their hands toward the perceived presence of God at the altar. The bringing of oneself to the altar may be the actual walk of a person or manifested only by a groaning in the spirit, a singing of the congregation into the

---

Worship.

6. Albrecht, *Rites in the Spirit*, 165–70.
7. Pocknee, *Christian Altar*, 33–55.
8. Streett, *Effective Invitation*.
9. Albrecht, *Rites in the Spirit*, 165–66.

presence of God, or the eruption of tongues and prophecies, prayers and songs, that in a manner of speaking bring the altar to the people.[10] Pentecostals flock to the altar in expectation of a divine, often supernatural, interruption of their circumstances and in that sense of an initiation or repetition or revival (sometimes all three) of Pentecost in their own lives. To welcome the altar call and to respond to the interruption of the Holy Spirit is to respond to the invitation of God and the proclamation of the gospel and to embark on a new life. This kind of conversion in the framework of the full gospel is perhaps best described as "initial salvation" or an "initial participation in salvation,"[11] an "entry level"[12] or "first work" of grace on the *via salutis*[13] to be followed by others as possible entrance points to the way of salvation.

EMBODYING SANCTIFICATION AT THE ALTAR

Situated within the soteriological environment of the altar space, the pursuit of sanctification is a threshold-practice, a transitional rite of passage identified by an initial stage of departure of the participants from their familiar world and a concluding state of the consummation of a new state of existence, joined by an intervening phase of tarrying. The response to the altar call manifests the initial departure typically by a physical action, a shift of position and movement of the individual or the corporate body toward the altar.[14] The altar space is accepted as a sacred space for tarrying, "a temporary 'container' of sorts for the sacred, for the human to engage the sacred."[15] In its ritual sense, sanctification is an active waiting for the encounter with Christ and an immersion into the sacred presence of the Holy Spirit. "Lingering" or "tarrying" and "laying" or "giving yourself" at the altar are dominant metaphors for the embodiment of sanctification among Pentecostals.

Lingering and laying yourself at the altar are metaphors for the prolonged presence of a person before God, a personal, physical, and communal expression of Pentecostal piety and spirituality. The embodiment

---

10. See Cartledge, *Testimony in the Spirit*, 55–80; Marina, *Getting the Holy Ghost*.
11. Jacobsen, *Thinking in the Spirit*, 174–79.
12. Sanders, *Saints in Exile*, 58.
13. Gause, *Living in the Spirit*, 15–24.
14. Albrecht, *Rites in the Spirit*, 166–69.
15. Albrecht, *Rites in the Spirit*, 133.

of sanctification is a form of active participation in the divine presence, even though the human "activity" implies waiting, travailing, prostrating, and submitting oneself to the holiness of God in the expectation that Christ would impart his holiness through the Holy Spirit to the life of the believer.[16] The rituals of sanctification at the altar recapitulate the apostles' tarrying in the upper room, reiterating the church's waiting for the promises of God, a lingering before the Lord, a seeking of and yielding to the Holy Spirit (Acts 1:13–14). For some Pentecostals, this tarrying evident in prayer, fasting, and seeking the Lord forms consistent ascetical practices that are indispensable conditions for lifelong spiritual growth.[17] Others see these practices as contemplative modes of "deep receptivity and a sense of openness to God"[18] that do not permeate the entire Pentecostal worship but are dominant during the altar call and response ritual. Again, others view these spiritual rituals as pragmatic and dramatic expressions of "an *active* waiting, anticipating the Spirit's intervention and activity."[19] Tarrying and lingering along with similar expressions are metaphors for the Pentecostal vision of the moral life.[20] The most dominant altar practices are the tarrying service among African American Pentecostals, the soaking prayer among charismatic and neo-Pentecostal congregations, and the practice of foot washing among many classical Pentecostal groups.

The practice of tarrying at the altar forms the core of the African American Pentecostal experience of conversion, sanctification, and Spirit baptism.[21] This practice is ritually structured and set in its own environment often outside the regular worship service.[22] Key elements include an active waiting upon God, repetition of a Christian phrase or word, concentration on these words, and entering into communion with God.[23] Tarrying embodies sanctification by means of verbal repetition, fervency, interiorization, diligence, letting go of oneself and holding on to the coming of God, anticipating a breakthrough to the participation

---

16. Castelo, "Tarrying on the Lord," 50–56.
17. Chan, *Pentecostal Theology*, 77.
18. Albrecht, *Rites in the Spirit*, 183–84.
19. Neumann, *Pentecostal Experience*, 115–16.
20. Castelo, "Tarrying on the Lord," 50–56.
21. Daniels, "Until the Power," 173–91.
22. Sanders, *Saints in Exile*, 58–59.
23. Daniels, "Until the Power," 175.

in the sanctifying presence of the Spirit.[24] Sanctification as a tarrying practice contains the confession of sin and the surrender of one's sinful nature to God as a physical and sometimes violent struggle of the flesh.[25] Believers tarry for Jesus, both in an active separation from the world and through participation in the sanctifying presence of Christ accompanied by the witness of the Holy Spirit in physical manifestations that can range from an inward sense of deliverance from sin to the dramatic exorcism of a demonic spirit.

Soaking prayer embodies the more contemplative activities of resting, receiving, beholding, and becoming.[26] Among classical Pentecostals, similar experiences of falling to the ground during prayer were often referred to as being "slain in the Spirit"—a description of the intense experience of the presence of God as if dead.[27] Unlike the explicitly verbal and petitioning tarrying service, soaking prayer relies on a nonverbal, meditative, and quiet posture.[28] Forms of prayer often take place within a group of individuals who "alternate periods of song and silence"[29] and pray in their native language or quietly in tongues. Soaking is an extended practice of lingering at the altar, a less structured but nonetheless ritual and embodied form of seeking the encounter with Christ through the Holy Spirit. Verbal activities, such as singing, praying, speaking in tongues, prophecy, and other charismatic manifestations can accompany the experience.[30] Sanctification here is an umbrella term for an array of embodied experiences associated with seeking the presence of God that range from the assurance of forgiveness to immediate deliverance, gradual purification, the sense of transformation, and the experience of renewal.

Among the embodied practices of sanctification, foot washing is the most overtly sacramental experience among many classical Pentecostals.[31] Typically following the end of an evening service or celebrated as a liturgical service in its own right, the congregation meets at the altar or designated spaces with prepared bowls or tubs of water and towels in

24. Daniels, "Until the Power," 180–84.
25. See Tinney, "Theoretical and Historical Comparison," 240–41.
26. Yadao and Hetland, *Soaking in God's Presence*, 39–54.
27. Venable, "Slain in the Spirit," 21–26.
28. Wilkinson and Althouse, *Catch the Fire*.
29. MacNutt, "Soaking Prayer," 184.
30. Wilkinson and Althouse, *Catch the Fire*, 3–11.
31. Tomberlin, *Pentecostal Sacraments*, 193–224; Driver, *Magic of Ritual*, 208.

front of pews or chairs. The washing is typically preceded by the reading of John 13 and can be carried out in a broader sacramental framework, including the celebration of the Lord's Supper. Foot washing has become an often literal practice of cleansing; the washing of sin and dirt with water is accompanied by mutual confession, forgiveness, prayer, and tears.[32] Central for the significance attributed to the washing of feet is both the cleansing effect of the washing itself on the one whose feet are washed, and the effect of the humility and cleaning act on the one who is doing the washing.[33] The experience of foot washing is sanctifying in its participation in the humility and forgiveness of Jesus, theologically interpreting the hands of the believer as the hands of Christ, the water as the Holy Spirit, and participants serving "as agents of cleansing and healing as well as recipients of that grace."[34] As a threshold practice, sanctification is not an isolated ritual but a preparation for and underlying foundation of engaging further in the way of salvation.

EMBODYING SPIRIT BAPTISM AT THE ALTAR

Arguably, the baptism in the Spirit occupies a central formative position in the identity of the Pentecostal movement. Yet, while Spirit baptism is often seen as the center of Pentecostal theology and doctrine, the actual practices among Pentecostals have hardly been studied.[35] Three dominant forms of embodiment can be identified: praying through, preaching, and the laying on of hands. While prayer is of course a central practice throughout the Christian life, praying through requires a focused attention and dedication to a particular request or desire.[36] For Pentecostals, praying through emerges from a tarrying heart in the "upper room"; the prayer is carried out by a soul yearning for fulfillment until the prayer is answered. This tarrying is intrinsically connected to and often contingent upon the quest for sanctification, which may explain why Spirit baptism and sanctification have become a single theme in the fourfold version of the full gospel. Although praying through frequently emerges from an attitude of lament, the perceived absence of God and emptiness of the human

---

32. Johns, "Transformed by Grace," 152–65.
33. Macchia, "Footwashing the Neglected Sacrament," 239–49.
34. Johns, "Transformed by Grace," 159.
35. Macchia, *Baptized in the Spirit*; Wheelock, "Spirit Baptism."
36. Dabney, *Pray Through*.

life, it eventually moves from anguish to praise.[37] The practice is a raw form of prayer, straight and firm to God.[38] Praying through, in this sense, is not so much a performed ritual than an embodied affection that is carried out as much in a mode of celebration as in contemplation, penitence, ceremony, ecstasy, pragmatism, or spontaneous improvisation.[39] The practice demands focused attention on God, decreases preoccupation with the self, intensifies sensitivity for others, lowers defensiveness and restraint, increases openness and spontaneity, and births a longing and expectation for the kingdom of God.[40] Praying through manifests the materiality of the baptism in the Spirit when it becomes an embodied ritual identified by a transformation of the practice itself as the praying for the Spirit becomes a praying in the Spirit (see Rom 8:16, 26).

The transformation from praying for the Spirit to praying in and with the Spirit manifests the baptism for Pentecostals most clearly in the disciples' speaking with other tongues (see Acts 2:4). Such tongues are a verbal and oral manifestation that the prayer for the Spirit has been answered by the giving of the Spirit. A twofold emphasis persists among Pentecostals by interpreting this materiality of Spirit baptism either in the terms of sanctification or of charismatic empowerment.[41] As an altar experience narrating the full gospel, praying through is both a sanctifying tarrying for and an empowering demonstration of the encounter with the Holy Spirit.

Similarly, preaching functions as verbal and oral embodiment of proclaiming the full gospel. While typically a focal point of the Pentecostal service as a whole, the pastoral message plays a particular role in conferring the baptism in the Spirit.[42] Preaching is a material practice that involves a narrative of speaking, hearing, and then, again, speaking and hearing.[43] The immediate goal of the sermon is an appeal to the affections (rather than the intellect), a directing of the audience's desire to the gift of God's Spirit. This appeal to the affections is also a transformational practice in which the initial proclamation of the outpouring of the Spirit

37. Melton, "Lessons of Lament," 68–80.
38. Moore, "Raw Prayer," 35–48.
39. Albrecht, *Rites in the Spirit*, 179–89.
40. Devol, "Ecstatic Pentecostal Prayer," 285–88.
41. Macchia, "Kingdom and the Power," 109–25.
42. Wheelock, "Spirit Baptism," 182–83; Yeung, "William Seymour's Sermons," 57–73.
43. Camery-Hogatt, "Word of God," 225–55.

(by the preacher) and the hearing of the message (by the audience) shifts in the actual baptism to a speaking by the audience (which has received the Spirit) and the hearing of that speaking (in tongues and exaltation) by the preacher. Preaching is thus seen as a charismatic ritual evidenced in the transformation of the practice itself, involving the joining of word and Spirit beginning with the proclamation of the gospel through the anointing of the preacher, directed to a reexperiencing of the biblical event, shifting to the anointing of the audience, the outpouring of the Spirit, and the response of the recipients.[44] The baptism in the Holy Spirit as the expected experience resulting from the act of proclamation is a distinctive characteristic of Pentecostal preaching.

Among the different altar practices, the laying on of hands, a long-standing Christian altar ritual, demands the most physical contact among believers. The biblical records identifying the laying on of hands as a ritual practice reveal no formal liturgical pattern other than the imposition of hands.[45] At the same time, this imposition is exceptionally concrete in its material, physical, physiological, spiritual, and relational dimensions. The ritual is further embedded in other practices, including prayer or proclamation, and it represents for many Pentecostals the most expressive and efficacious rite to confer the baptism in the Holy Spirit.[46] Echoing the events of Pentecost, the laying on of hands by the believer represents the unrepeatable outpouring of the Holy Spirit on all flesh at the hands of Jesus.[47] In the ritual, the hand of the believer is the hand of Christ who baptizes with the Spirit, and the touch of the hand is the Holy Spirit—evoking a strong appeal to the affections of all persons participating in the ritual. The baptism in the Spirit itself is the affective moment concentrated in the giving and receiving of the Spirit at the laying on of hands. Prayer, prophecy, speaking in tongues, and the use of anointing oil often accompany the ritual.[48] Although concentrated in the use of hands, the practice is a thoroughly charismatic rite in action and demonstration including characteristic Pentecostal behaviors such as shouting, jumping, dancing, swaying, bowing, praising, and falling in the Spirit.[49] As with the other

44. Albrecht, *Rites in the Spirit*, 162–64; Leoh, "Pentecostal Preacher," 35–58; Stackhouse, "Charismatic Utterance," 42–46.
45. González, "Laying-On of Hands," 161–71.
46. Kay, *Pentecostals in Britain*, 101.
47. González, "Laying-On of Hands," 161–71.
48. Hollenweger, *Pentecostals*, 330–41.
49. Albrecht, *Rites in the Spirit*, 171–76.

altar rites, the laying on of hands is transformative in the transformation of the rite itself, as the laying on of hands becomes a transferring of and endowment with the Holy Spirit. As a baptismal practice, this participation in the divine life is a transformative experience in which the passive-receptive believer becomes an active agent of the Spirit: the one who has come to the altar is now equipped to leave the altar.

EMBODYING DIVINE HEALING AT THE ALTAR

The global expansion of Pentecostalism and the accompanying diversification of race, gender, culture, and religious formation exert a broad dynamic on Pentecostal healing practices.[50] Central practices are the vocalization of faith, the laying on of hands, and the anointing with oil. The kinesthetic contours of these practices remain thoroughly connected to the altar while diversifying rapidly toward the margins of the global movement. Pentecostal healing practices are in the first place practices of faith, evident not only in the expectation that healing results from the act of faith, but that such acts require the active participation of the believer in the pursuit of divine healing. The verbalization of faith is the most immediate ritual expression of this participation, and at the most basic level can be understood as a vocalization of prayer.[51] Regular prayer for those sick, suffering, or dying is a standard practice among Pentecostals and range from short commands, simple prayers of faith, speaking in tongues, testimonies, and intercession to prolonged tarrying, fasting prayer, and praying through at the altar until healing is manifested.[52] The invocation of healing "in the name of Jesus" is a common affective exclamation across the movement.[53] It indicates belief in the abiding presence of Jesus and the continuing and consistent availability of his healing power.[54] The verbalization of this belief is not necessarily seen as producing immediate results. Instead, a longer process can involve the verbalization of faith in repeated testimonies and prayers.[55] Nonetheless, divine healing is a

50. See Miller and Yamamori, *Global Pentecostalism*; Gunther Brown, *Global Pentecostal and Charismatic*.

51. Poloma, "Pentecostal Prayer," 47–65.

52. Williams, *Spirit Cure*, 98–121; MacNutt, *Power to Heal*; Randi, *Faith Healers*; Alexander, *Pentecostal Healing*.

53. Warrington, "Path to Wholeness," 45–49.

54. Warrington, "Acts and the Healing," 189–217.

55. Jansen and Lang, "Transforming the Self," 542–51.

response to prayer, and prayer is seen as an embodiment of faith in the midst of opposing circumstances.

The diversified healing practices among Pentecostals require for many a relearning of the traditional gestures of faith.[56] The widespread use of television and other media has shaped new, more institutionalized practices, particularly in affluent Western nations, while rural and developing countries have seen unprecedented mass-healing practices.[57] Vocalized healing prayers are sometimes produced by the "healer" following a strict format and pattern that can be reproduced through various media.[58] Some Pentecostals take the vocalization of faith to heart and "yell" or shout—in a radical form of public expression—in order to reach from the realm of the word to the realm of the Spirit.[59] Equally important to the exclamation of healing on behalf of the sick is also the vocal participation by those who are suffering. Here, the word of faith is sometimes seen as a "positive confession" despite one's physical circumstances.[60] Practices can include a groaning in the spirit, prayerful agreement with the healer, shouts of praise, or a "claiming" of healing by the sick—often despite the lack of physical evidence.

A second influential practice of divine healing is the laying on of hands. Although primarily a ritual for the baptism in the Spirit, the significance attached to the laying on of hands as both a means of sanctification and empowerment have led Pentecostals to extend its realm of influence also to the embodiment of healing. While the actual practice does not differ, whether intended for the baptism in the Spirit or for healing, the experience of healing, both in its giving and receiving, is directly identified by the transfer of divine power through the imposition of hands. The immediacy of the touch itself is anticipated as the "remedy" where the Spirit of God engages the body of believers (individually and corporately) in the redemption and cleansing from sin and disease.[61] In the diverse contexts of global Pentecostalism, the imposition of hands ranges from quick touches to long embraces or repeated and prolonged

---

56. Combet and Fabre, "Pentecostal Movement," 106–10.
57. Gunther Brown, *Global Pentecostal*; Williams, *Spirit Cure*.
58. Jansen and Lang, "Transforming the Self," 542–51.
59. Tang, "'Yellers' and Healers," 379–94.
60. Anderson, "Pentecostal Approaches," 523–34; Hudson, "Early British Pentecostals," 283–301.
61. Baer, "Redeemed Bodies," 735–71; Alexander, "'How Wide Thy Healing,'" 63–76.

treatments, carried out by individuals to large groups, from healing evangelists and pastors to elders and entire congregations.[62]

The physical touch to heal the sick is paradigmatic for the experience of the power of God. The touch is a physical extension and intensification of the prayer of faith; its importance is equaled only by a further intensification through the anointing with oil. Typically applied to the skin, frequently on the forehead or hands and feet but also directly on the place of pain and illness, and often supplemented by fragrance added to the oil, the anointing is a multisensory experience.[63] The application of oil is seen as a gentle but penetrating exhibition of power and demonstration of the Spirit's anointing available to all Christians.[64]

Nonetheless, while often practiced in literal interpretation of biblical healing narratives, Pentecostals have put few restrictions on practicing (receiving and extending) the healing power of Christ through the Spirit. Healing practices in the global movement can expand beyond the sacramental environment of the church and readily connect with indigenous religious identities and practices to form enculturated rituals departing from strict biblical or apostolic patterns.[65] Commercially available anointing oils have obtained an almost institutionalized character in many places.[66] Handkerchiefs anointed with oil are sometimes sent to the sick as an extension of the healing ministry in the church.[67] Even devotional newspapers and magazines are laid on the sick and have been attributed to divine healing.[68] In many places, the materiality of healing includes not just bodily recuperation but remedies for unemployment, family disputes, racism, marital discord, and other problems thus drawn into the realm of embodiment.[69] The materiality and physicality of healing is sought as much for the human body as for the nation and the environment.[70] Divine healing thus functions

---

62. Hejzlar, *Two Paradigms*; Marostica, "Learning from the Master," 207–27.
63. Cartledge, "Pentecostal Healing," 501–22.
64. Hollenweger, *Pentecostals*, 353–62.
65. Oosthuizen et al., *Afro-Christian Religion*; Dongsoo, "Healing of Han," 123–39; Clatterbuck, "Healing Hills," 248–77.
66. Asamoah-Gyadu, "'Unction to Function,'" 231–56.
67. Wiegele, *Investing in Miracles*, 80–104, 142–69.
68. Griffith, "Female Suffering," 184–208.
69. Cox, "Healers and Ecologists," 1042–46.
70. Daneel, *African Earthkeepers*; Wightman, "Healing the Nation," 239–55.

as a soteriological metaphor for the restoration of the whole cosmos anticipating the renewal of all of creation.

EMBODYING THE KINGDOM AT THE ALTAR

Eschatological practices are in principle any practices acted out by the church for its mission to and transformation of the world. These practices are therefore also always experiences at the altar, although few of them happen at a physical altar in an ecclesiastical environment. Moreover, the outpouring of the Holy Spirit grasps Pentecostals with an apocalyptic vision of the presence, power, and person of Christ that demands "taking the altar" to the ends of the earth (in the spatial and temporal sense). It is this apocalyptic urgency that transforms ecclesial practices into eschatological ones. Pentecostals see themselves as agents of witness and worship in "a missionary fellowship where testimonies [are] given constantly in order to develop in the hearers the virtues, expectancy, attitudes, and experiences of those testifying."[71] The practices of this eschatological fellowship are organized along any of the central experiences of the full gospel discussed above, albeit now realized as an aspect of the imminent fullness of the kingdom of God. In this manner, the eschatological motif returns Pentecostal theology to all the elements of the full gospel and directs then toward the kingdom of God.

In the ecclesio-missiological framework of Pentecostals, to embody *salvation* eschatologically means "an entry into the training program of a missionary fellowship"[72] where one's life is reordered and redirected by the Spirit in radical discontinuity from and as a testimony to the world. The eschatological experience of *sanctification* means a radical break and transformation of the person from a life of the flesh to a life in the Spirit as a testimony to a Christ-like standard of living. The eschatological experience of *the baptism in the Spirit* means a radical equipping of the Christian for witness to the lost and spiritual battle with the enemies of God as a testimony to empowered and anointed service.[73] The eschatological experience of *divine healing* means a radical experience of encounter with the coming Christ already manifested in the physical life of believers as a testimony to the presence of the kingdom.

---

71. Land, *Pentecostal Spirituality*, 80.
72. Land, *Pentecostal Spirituality*, 82.
73. Land, *Pentecostal Spirituality*, 91–93.

These and other experiences of the full gospel, demonstrating an expectation of imminent fulfillment of the kingdom of God, reshape the practices of the church into eschatological actions that serve as signs, confirmations, and celebrations of the power and legitimacy of those experiences. Many of these practices appear in other Christian traditions, since they are in principle ecclesio-missiological actions, but the difference among Pentecostals is their "eschatological intensification"[74] manifested in the apocalyptic urgency, anticipation, and manifestations of the outpouring of the Spirit. The gifts of the Spirit radically distinguish Pentecostal eschatology from other traditions, above all the dramatic oral gifts of speaking with tongues, prophecy, words of knowledge and wisdom, teaching, exhortation, and interpretation of tongues, which are seen as the most significant eschato-missiological experiences of the apostolic church revived in the Pentecostal movement.[75]

Eschatological practices have experienced a shift during the twentieth century with regard to the interpretation, application, and intensity of spiritual gifts and their situatedness in an apocalyptic frame of reference. Early Pentecostals interpreted the revival of charismatic gifts as missiological tools of an apocalyptic movement, confirmed by worldwide testimonies of the ability to speak in an unlearned foreign language (*xenolalia*). Convinced of the power of "missionary tongues" and the ability to speak the languages of the nations, Pentecostals quickly set off on foreign missions to bring the gospel to the lost before the imminent return of Christ in judgment.[76] What Pentecostals had learned at the altars of the church was carried under the influence of an apocalyptic vision into the world in order to bring the nations before the altar of God. With the changes of apocalyptic urgency during the twentieth century, particularly in the West, many Pentecostal practices have shifted from evangelization to social action.[77] While for some Pentecostal groups, the apocalyptic urgency of a world facing judgment remains the motivation for eschatological practices, the general focus of Pentecostal eschatology has moved to the space *between* missiological and ecclesiological concerns, that is, to the space between the world and the altar: emergency services, medical assistance, mercy ministries, educational programs,

74. Land, *Pentecostal Spirituality*, 94.
75. Kay, *Pentecostals in Britain*; Menzies, "Role of Glossolalia," 47–72.
76. Anderson, *Spreading Fires*, 40–45; McGee, *Miracles, Missions*, 61–76.
77. Klaus, "Growing Edges Have Shifted," 65–81; Prakash, "Toward a Theology," 65–97.

counseling services, economic development, policy change, and services in the arts form the new face of eschatological social commitment.[78] Eschatological practices have redefined the materiality of Pentecostal theology in terms of political activism, racial reconciliation, concerns for pacifism, economic justice, and ecological liberation.[79] This materiality of eschatological practices is essential for the embodiment of the full gospel; the weakening of eschatology is likely to affect Pentecostal theology at the core not in its doctrines but its spirituality.

CONCLUSION

The modest goal of the preceding survey was the identification of central embodied practices foundational and formative for contemporary Pentecostal theology. The kinesthetic practices narrated above are necessarily selective; many practices overlap and hold meaning for different theological motifs among the diverse Pentecostal groups. Nonetheless, more than a purely phenomenological observation, the heuristic framework of the full gospel allows us to trace the materiality of Pentecostal theology across a range of the theological narrative. The context of the altar places doctrinal practices in the experiential environment of spirituality characteristic of the Pentecostal movement. This methodology affirms the importance of embodiment suggested by selective studies and proposes that Pentecostal theology can be said to exhibit consistent patterns of materiality indispensable to its constructive articulation. In other words, an inclusive reading of the full gospel, which is hospitable to other theological motifs beyond the four- or fivefold core treated in this essay, suggests that materiality is a central identifying distinctive of Pentecostal theology. Nonetheless, the importance of materiality and physicality should not be treated as an isolated attribute of Pentecostalism as if Pentecostals sought embodiment exclusively for its own sake. Rather, the consistency of emphasizing embodied experience and practice depends on the narrative framework: embodiment and the full gospel mutually inform and depend upon one another.

---

78. Miller and Yamamori, *Global Pentecostalism*, 41–43; Vondey, *Pentecostalism*, 90–97.

79. Kärkkäinen, "Mission, Spirit, and Eschatology," 73–94; Althouse, *Spirit*, 179–92; Smith, "Revolutionaries and Revivalists," 55–82.

10

A Liturgical Hermeneutic of Pentecost

THE "FULL GOSPEL" REFERS to a theological hermeneutic, a way of reading the world with reference to God, which takes account of Pentecostals' innate articulations of their own theological story. Narrative, story, and testimony are widely considered the native expressions of Pentecostal spirituality and theology. The most consistent methodological framework used for narrating the historically dominant set of Pentecostal spiritual experiences is known as the four- or fivefold gospel. The larger, fivefold pattern proclaims, usually in kerygmatic form, the good news that Jesus Christ brings: (1) salvation, (2) sanctification, (3) baptism in the Spirit, (4) divine healing, and (5) the impending arrival of the kingdom of God. This chapter critically examines the functional "logic" of the full gospel as a theological hermeneutic and analyzes its application as an organizing method in Pentecostal theology.

The full gospel depends as method on a theological narrative built around participation in foundational biblical experiences originating with the day of Pentecost, which functions as the theological symbol of the full gospel. This symbol arises from a Pentecostal scriptural hermeneutic, which seeks to transport the inquiring subject into the biblical story. The place where contemporary Pentecostal theology meets Pentecost can be identified with the metaphor of the altar (see chapter 8). The full gospel is essentially a liturgical narrative aiming at participation in Pentecost through a theological (hermeneutical but also experiential) move to and from the altar. In the three sections that follow, I first situate the hermeneutic of the full gospel in the context of the day of Pentecost and show how Pentecost functions as a theological symbol. I then detail how this symbol finds entrance in Pentecostal theology through an altar liturgy grounded in and leading toward concrete practices shaped by the encounter with the Spirit. Finally, I illustrate how this liturgical hermeneutic is narrated through the five dominant themes of the full gospel. I argue that the full gospel functions as a descriptive and organizing mechanism of altar practices shaped by a range of personal and communal experiences originating with the symbol of Pentecost and presenting a participatory liturgical hermeneutic that yields a biblically and theologically organized and embodied theology.

PENTECOST AS THEOLOGICAL SYMBOL

The biblical day of Pentecost is the foundational symbol of Pentecostal theology. Pentecost is significant for Pentecostals first and foremost because of the experiences and practices recorded in the biblical texts of Luke–Acts.[1] While Pentecostals also acknowledge a Johannine and Pauline Pentecost, its emergence as a theological symbol originates with the Lukan testimony. Nevertheless, this preference is not indicative of the broad hermeneutical interests of Pentecostal theology; the focus on Luke–Acts serves not to restrict Pentecostal exegesis but rather to indicate that the day of Pentecost offers the central hermeneutical lens for any broader theological conversations.

The experience of the outpouring of the Holy Spirit at Pentecost forms the archetype for practices and convictions of Pentecostal theology, multiplied and reshaped in diverse experiences of "Pentecost" today (see chapter 8). A theology of Pentecost is the thematic hermeneutical locus that elicits an experiential identification with the biblical events of the day. The "plot" of Pentecost, the spiritual experiences and internal "logic" of the practices of the event, forms the foundation for the Pentecostal theological narrative. The full gospel emerges only from the starting point of this original plot of the outpouring of the Spirit applied to contemporary theological concerns and conversations by way of participating in the original Pentecost.

---

1. Mittelstadt, *Reading Luke–Acts*, 18–45.

The logic of participating in Pentecost proceeds from the realm of spirit (*pneuma*) to that of word (*logos*): Pentecostal theology begins with a pneumatological imagination, which proceeds from the experience of Pentecost in a foundational pneumatological direction.[2] At the same time, the theology of Pentecost is expressed clearly in the original setting with a central thematic focus on Jesus Christ: Pentecost is a witness to the crucified Jesus who has been raised from the dead and exalted to the right hand of God from whence he has poured out the Holy Spirit (Acts 2:14–36). The Pentecostal imagination proceeds only by way of this Christological narrative construct: the gospel of Jesus Christ is continued at Pentecost! In turn, the call to Christ is followed again with a pneumatological promise: the outpouring of the Holy Spirit on the audience, their children, and "all who are far away" (Acts 2:39). The full gospel develops the terms of this Spirit-Christology without a dichotomy between the work of Christ and the Spirit.

The gospel of the Spirit of Christ "poured out on all flesh" (Acts 2:17) allows Pentecostal theology to reach deep into Pentecost, not just as a historical day but as a theological symbol by engaging the concrete beliefs and practices emerging with Pentecost reflected in an experiential spirituality believed by Pentecostals still to be available as a continuation, repetition, or expansion of that original experience. Pentecostal Spirit-Christology is thus not a generic hermeneutical device; the foundational connection to the day of Pentecost shapes the pneumatological and Christological imagination always from Pentecost to Pentecost, that is, in a contemporary encounter with the Spirit of Christ seen as a participation in the original event. As symbol, the biblical Pentecost is determinative for the entire hermeneutical focus of Pentecostal thought and praxis.[3] The goal of this theological hermeneutic is, in the first place, to preserve the availability of Pentecost, the validity of those experiences, and their perpetuation. The concrete theological and experiential realm for this availability is the altar.

ALTAR LITURGY

The altar arises from the expectation to participate in the experience of Pentecost despite spatial and temporal (or other) distance from the

---

2. Yong, *Spirit Poured Out*, 27–30.
3. Vondey, *Pentecostal Theology*, 283–88.

original event. Since Pentecostal theology seeks participation in the immediacy of the original experiences of the biblical story,[4] and because the biblical day of Pentecost already contains as symbol all subsequent experiences of Pentecost, the move back to and forward from Pentecost reverses the biblical hermeneutic of reading and interpreting the biblical text to being read and interpreted by the biblical story.[5] This hermeneutical reversal is the product of reenacting the biblical Pentecost through the foundational rite typically labeled the "altar call."[6] In principle, the call to Pentecost is a call to the altar (and vice versa). The altar functions as a participatory liturgical framework for contemporary Pentecostals, and the goal of this experiential "altar hermeneutics"[7] is the immediate encounter with Christ through the Spirit at the altar as the material perpetuation of Pentecost.

The altar call and response rite arguably forms the center and summit of Pentecostal worship and theology (see chapter 8).[8] The Pentecostal altar comes into existence, as on the day of Pentecost, through encounter with the outpouring of the Holy Spirit and the response to the divine activity. This altar can be seen in a walking of the aisle or jumping on pews or, less dramatically, the congregating of people in a "sacred" place of ministry, preaching, or prayer (see chapter 5). In charismatic churches with historical roots in the established liturgical traditions, the architectural space of the sanctuary often defines the spatial boundaries of the altar.[9] In neo-Pentecostal communities, the idea of the "sacred space" with a central focal point is shifting from strong architectural identifiers to the more symbolically and experientially identified center of worship.[10] In the diverse materiality of Pentecostal churches worldwide, the human–divine encounter is identified primarily by the community's altar activity. In this foundational theological action, Pentecost is profoundly and deeply changed from a theological symbol to a liturgical actualization of the possibility of an immediate encounter with God. Whether church or academy, the altar call invites a response from all realms and activities of Christian theology.

4. Land, *Pentecostal Spirituality*, 63–88.
5. Moore, "Pentecostal Approach to Scripture," 4–5, 11.
6. Albrecht, *Rites in the Spirit*, 165–70.
7. The term was first used by Moore, "Altar Hermeneutics," 148–59.
8. See also Albrecht, *Rites in the Spirit*, 150–70; Tomberlin, *Pentecostal Sacraments*.
9. Ryle, "Laying Our Sins," 68–97.
10. Gold, "From the 'Upper Room,'" 74–88.

In response to the altar call, Pentecostal theology brings itself, its goals, motivations, methods, and convictions to the encounter with the Spirit where theology is always a first-order discourse with God. Altar theology is doxology, worship, wonder, and praise—and a challenge to any second-order reflection of academic, scientific, or theoretical methods. Glossolalia and prophecy, visions and dreams, are ways that manifest this counter-establishment discourse.[11] Accepting the invitation to the altar usually entails some form of audible or visible response, often accompanied by other physical and charismatic manifestations.[12] At the altar, the person and the community (and thus their theology) are transformed in the encounter with God and empowered to leave the altar and to take the gospel into the world. This movement to and from the altar forms the liturgical heartbeat of Pentecostalism. The biblical, experiential, and liturgical path of this altar theology is charted by the theological narrative of the full gospel.

THE FULL GOSPEL

The full gospel functions as a theological narrative expression of a Pentecostal altar liturgy: salvation, sanctification, Spirit baptism, divine healing, and the coming kingdom mark the way to and from the altar of Pentecost. The order and content of the full gospel are not strictly defined and vary historically and geographically since the narrative functions as an outlet of Pentecostal spirituality shaped by a range of personal and communal experiences and is not the result of systematic theological reflection.[13] The phrase "full gospel" may not be used directly even though the elements of the narrative are readily visible. And Pentecostals sometimes adjust the theological pattern and combine or include other themes to speak of a "fullness" of the gospel.[14] In short, Pentecostal theology can employ the elements of the full gospel "in a creative and not always in a constant way."[15] Systematic proposals sometimes depart from the original narrative or emphasize individual elements rather than the entire narrative. The full gospel can therefore not be understood in a

11. Yong, "Academic Glossolalia," 61–80.
12. See Tomberlin, *Pentecostal Sacraments*, 1–88.
13. See Vondey, "Embodied Gospel," 102–19; Thomas, "Pentecostal Theology," 3–19.
14. Yong-gi Cho, *Five-Fold Gospel*.
15. Kärkkäinen, "Encountering Christ," 5–19.

strict manner as a definitive narrative of the Pentecostal story.[16] Rather, the full gospel is an expression of Pentecostal spirituality and praxis because it "is based on a passionate desire to 'meet' with Jesus Christ as he is being perceived of as the Bearer of the Full Gospel."[17] The elements of the full gospel are never logically isolated or adhere to a strict theological sequence, since the altar experiences underlying the narrative have occurred worldwide in diverse fashion since the day of Pentecost. Although the full gospel possesses an inherent narrative plot that proceeds through each of the five motifs, the connections between the different elements are not just linear but perhaps more akin to the stabilizing strands of a web that hold together the story of Pentecostal experiences and practices.[18] Entrance to the altar, and participation in Pentecost, is possible in principle from any strand of this narrative web.

As an altar narrative built on Pentecost, the full gospel tells the story of Christ identified by several primary experiences of the Holy Spirit that together form a heuristic framework for theological articulation.[19] The full gospel functions as both a biblical hermeneutic, as the themes shape the way Pentecostals read the Bible with the goal of participating in the biblical events, and a narrative of contemporary Pentecostal practices and experiences that reflect the biblical story. A systematic and constructive doctrinal formulation of Pentecostal theology must aim at holding together this kind of dynamic narrative of expression of the biblical and contemporary personal, communal, ecclesial, cultural and counter-cultural experiences in the diverse contexts of global Pentecostalism. The primary hermeneutical challenge of this narrative is that it is not based on isolated doctrines but on interconnected foundational Pentecostal experiences. Pentecostal theology unfolds along these experiences, and its primary aspiration to participate in the biblical Pentecost frees the theological task from the order, rules, and regulations of contemporary narrative theology. Instead, the full gospel emerges through a participatory hermeneutic that takes theology continually to and from the altar in theological activity that both originates with Pentecost and seeks Pentecost and that reaches Pentecost by way of an immediate encounter with God.

---

16. Archer, "Fivefold Gospel," 7–43.
17. Kärkkäinen, "Encountering Christ," 7.
18. Archer, "Pentecostal Story," 36–59.
19. See Vondey, *Pentecostal Theology*, 35–151; Yong, *In the Days*, 95–98.

The full gospel therefore originates in the liturgical space between the freedom of Pentecostal experiences and practices, on the one hand, and the demands for a narrative of theological reflection and doctrinal articulation on the other (see chapter 4). Therein lies the most immediate challenge of the realization of Pentecostal theology, which exists amid the tension between the idealized "pure" experiences of the gospel and their counterpart as the strict dogmatic devotion to propositional doctrines (see chapter 7). The full gospel is a liturgical narrative of foundational practices of the Spirit and acts as a unique hermeneutic because experience is viewed as lived affirmation of the revelation of God. Viewed through the lens of Pentecost, the liturgy of the full gospel unfolds on the basis of the altar experiences at the root of the narrative so that Pentecostals speak less about salvation, sanctification, Spirit baptism, divine healing, and eschatology than about being saved, sanctified, baptized in the Spirit, healed, and commissioned for God's kingdom.

SAVED

The dominant full gospel narrative begins with a foundational concern for salvation. Taking theology to the altar is at the core an embarkment on the path to meet Jesus Christ as savior. More precisely, therefore, salvation is not simply one moment of the full gospel but its underlying rationale. The entrance to the full gospel as liturgy signals that an encounter with God is always soteriological, always redemptive, transforming, converting, correcting, and delivering. Still, meeting Jesus at the altar marks only the beginning of the soteriological direction identified with Pentecost.[20] Soteriology is the broad liturgical foundation for Pentecostal theology as a whole, and the full gospel narrates its soteriological hospitality.

Consequently, Pentecostal practices of salvation extend across all individual, familial, ecclesial, social, material, cosmic, and eschatological dimensions of life.[21] Salvation is manifested in a move to the altar, the acceptance of the invitation of God and the response of the worshiper in a move forward into the "holy place," sometimes a gradual reorientation, at other times a jumping and running of the aisle. Responses vary from the assembly of the entire congregation at the altar to some remaining in the pews, falling on their knees in the aisle, or stretching out their hands

20. See Kärkkäinen, "Encountering Christ," 5–19.
21. Yong, *Spirit Poured Out*, 91–98.

toward the perceived presence of God. The bringing of oneself to the altar may be the actual walk of a person or manifested only by a groaning in the spirit, a singing of the congregation into the presence of God, or the eruption of tongues and prophecies, prayers, and songs.[22] Salvation is practiced in a myriad of ways reflecting the soteriological emphasis that penetrates all Pentecostal theological concerns.

The wide-ranging practices among Pentecostals suggest that all elements of the full gospel are works of grace and possible steps to the altar and the path of salvation. Theological concerns thus range from the liberation from sin to participation in the divine life,[23] regeneration, sanctification, divine healing, and personal piety,[24] supernatural deliverance from the powers of the devil and the world,[25] spiritual and ideological, economic and political deliverance,[26] empowerment,[27] and holistic salvation.[28] The scope of the full gospel extends toward complete salvation, which reaches the soul through a whole range of experiences, marking the personal-spiritual, individual-physical, communal, socioeconomic, and ecological aspects of Pentecostal soteriology.[29] The symbol of Pentecost as the story of the redemptive activity of the Holy Spirit in the cosmos, world, society, the church, and the human person provides an archetype for narrating a broad Pentecostal liturgy that extends to the transformation and salvation of the whole of life.[30]

SANCTIFIED

A second motif in the narrative of the full gospel is sanctification, typically seen as a distinct work of grace and arguably the most contested teaching among Pentecostals: sanctification follows salvation in the account of the fivefold gospel but not in the fourfold pattern where it is subsumed under either salvation or Spirit baptism.[31] Nevertheless, within

22. Albrecht, *Rites in the Spirit*, 165–66; Cartledge, *Testimony in the Spirit*, 55–88.
23. Coulter, "Delivered by the Power," 447–67.
24. Alexander, *Black Fire*, 61–63.
25. See Covington, *Salvation on Sand Mountain*.
26. Chesnut, *Born Again in Brazil*.
27. Ngong, *Holy Spirit and Salvation*.
28. Anderson and Tang, *Asian and Pentecostal*.
29. Volf, "Materiality of Salvation," 447–67.
30. See Vondey, *Pentecostal Theology*, 153–280.
31. Dayton, *Theological Roots of Pentecostalism*, 17–23.

the soteriological emphasis of the altar call, sanctification recognizes both the call of God and the desire of the believer to holiness (see 1 Pet 1:15–16). Whereas salvation identifies the move of a person to the altar, the experience of sanctification is a remaining at the altar in anticipation of the coming Pentecost. In light of the foundational Pentecostal concern for the fullness of salvation, sanctification emphasizes the cleansing from sin and the seeking of perfection (see 2 Cor 7:1). As part of a soteriological liturgy, sanctification is not a forward moving into new territory (as with salvation) but a waiting and presentation of one's present circumstances, intentions, and convictions as the object of theological interpretation before God. The full gospel leads Pentecostal theology to the altar for the purpose of tarrying for the presence of Jesus and the outpouring of the Holy Spirit.[32] Sanctification is a threshold practice for both the subject and the object of theological inquiry.

The pursuit of sanctification is a transitional step identified by an initial departure from one's familiar world and a concluding state of reaching a new form of existence, joined by an intervening phase of tarrying. Theological hermeneutics as a way to the altar here creates a sacred space for tarrying, "a temporary 'container' of sorts for the sacred, for the human to engage the sacred."[33] "Lingering" or "tarrying" and "laying" or "giving yourself" at the altar are dominant activities that narrate this practice among Pentecostals. Sanctification is a form of active participation in the divine presence, even though the human "activity" implies waiting, travailing, prostrating, and submitting oneself to the holiness of God.[34] Pentecostal practices range from soaking prayer, falling or "being slain" in the Spirit, to more sacramental practices of footwashing. As a theological method, sanctification is an active waiting for the encounter with Christ and immersion in the sacred presence of the Holy Spirit. The full gospel is comfortable with this "unproductive" waiting for the prolonged presence of God as an expression of spiritual participation in the apostles' tarrying in the upper room (see Acts 1:13–14). As a theological hermeneutic, sanctification includes the possibilities of dissonance, grieving, and confession in order to be convicted and corrected.[35] Pentecostal theology is here at its darkest place; sanctification is not for the joyful explication of theological achievements and the praise of salvation

---

32. Wall, "Waiting on the Holy," 37–53.
33. Albrecht, *Rites in the Spirit*, 133.
34. Castelo, "Tarrying on the Lord," 50–56.
35. Johns, "Adolescence of Pentecostalism," 3–17.

but for humility, self-examination, and correction. It is through this critical gate that the full gospel can aim at empowerment, transformation, and liberation.

BAPTIZED IN THE SPIRIT

A third and typically central element of the full gospel is baptism in the Holy Spirit. A motif drawn from rich Jewish and Christian textual history,[36] to be baptized in the Spirit reflects a deep personal experience in which the regenerated and sanctified believer receives, in an extraordinary encounter with the Holy Spirit, empowerment for the Christian life. Widely viewed as the most distinctive practice of Pentecostals,[37] Spirit baptism is most intimately tied to the altar as a metaphor for the encounter with God to which the other elements point and from which they receive their meaning. Yet, this important position does not elevate Spirit baptism above the narrative. Rather, this transformative experience marks a turning point in the altar liturgy: after being baptized in the Spirit those who have come to the altar are transformed to leave the altar.

A theology baptized in the Spirit is attentive to this transformation both on the inside and the outside (subjectively and objectively). Spirit baptism occurs in the subject by means of the affections, abiding dispositions resulting from the encounter with the Holy Spirit and directing a person more fully toward God and neighbor.[38] On the outside, Spirit baptism ignites a passion directed beyond one's self to the church and to the world that seeks through participation in Pentecost God's promise of the redemption of all creation.[39] The baptism in the Spirit, therefore, is both a personal experience of grace and a communal, universal, and eschatological manifestation of the kingdom of God in the world.[40] Dominant forms of embodying this experience are praying through, preaching, and the laying on of hands, reflective of the apostles' practices on the day of Pentecost (see chapter 9). Arguably the most distinctive practice manifesting Spirit baptism for Pentecostals is the disciples' speaking with other tongues (see Acts 2:4). Such tongues are a verbal and oral manifestation

---

36. See Levison, *Filled with the Spirit*.
37. See Macchia, *Baptized in the Spirit*.
38. Land, *Pentecostal Spirituality*, 136.
39. Alexander et al., "Spirit Baptism," 27–47.
40. Macchia, *Baptized in the Spirit*, 85–88.

that the prayer for the Spirit has been answered by the reception of the Spirit. Similarly, preaching, the laying on of hands, prophecies, and other spiritual gifts are transformative sacramental rites manifesting the participation in the baptism with the Holy Spirit.

The theological motifs of this endowment are sanctification and charismatic empowerment. Through the baptism in the Spirit, the "church is allowed to participate in and bear witness to, the final sanctification of creation."[41] At the same time, the filling with the Spirit also opens up a socio-critical hermeneutic to empower a counter-critical church in the world through manifestation of the charismatic gifts of the Spirit while groaning in solidarity with the suffering creation for the fullness of redemption.[42] With the baptism in the Spirit, Pentecostal theology has arrived at the turning point of its own identity. As a baptismal practice, this transformative experience is manifested in the transformation of the passive-receptive believer into an active agent of the Spirit: Pentecostal theology that has come to the altar is now equipped to leave the altar.

HEALED

Divine healing signifies an important expansion of the experience of Pentecost and the baptism in the Spirit: healing marks a move from the altar into the world. This move is always tied to explicit practices of faith, evident in both the expectation that healing is a result of the act of faith and participation in the pursuit of divine healing. Central practices among Pentecostals are the vocalization of faith, the laying on of hands, and the anointing with oil (see chapter 9). Nonetheless, while healing practices are often literal interpretations of biblical narratives, there are few restrictions on receiving and extending healing, and activities often connect with indigenous religious practices to form enculturated rituals departing from strict biblical or apostolic patterns.[43] The expansion of these practices signals the realization that the experience of the fullness of salvation does not currently extend to all realms of creation. The vast demand for continued healing guards Pentecostal theology from becoming a romanticized or triumphalist exercise. The promise of divine healing challenges Pentecostals to leave the altar and to go into the world in an outward

---

41. Macchia, *Baptized in the Spirit*, 86.
42. Macchia, "Groans Too Deep," 149–73.
43. Vondey, *Pentecostal Theology*, 108–15.

orientation, and a liturgical praxis that embraces traditional concerns and methods and is open to improvised practices among all who need healing, restoration, liberation, and deliverance.

The gospel of divine healing thus proclaims that wholeness and restoration are the universal will of God for the salvation of all creation. Suffering, sickness, persecution, and dying are the consistent biblical themes that narrate the concerns for encountering the redeeming presence of God.[44] Pentecostals respond to these contexts with the symbol of Pentecost by proclaiming in broad terms healing through the power of God provided in the atoning work of Christ and the encounter with the Holy Spirit.[45] The liturgical contours of this theology remain thoroughly connected to the altar while diversifying rapidly through three intersecting dynamics: (1) those saved, sanctified, and filled with the Spirit come to the altar to find healing; (2) those who experience healing at the altar take the altar into the world; (3) and those in the world who receive healing come to the altar for salvation. On the one hand, healing can be seen as an extension of the gospel of salvation, sanctification, and Spirit baptism, while, on the other hand, healing practices translate this gospel into the present with often unprecedented interpretation and new forms of application.

A therapeutic and realistic proclamation of the full gospel acknowledges also that not all are healed. The existential tension between expectation and experience deeply shapes Pentecostal theology and has persuaded Pentecostals frequently to adjust their teachings in order to maintain the core belief in divine healing amid the often devastating effects of wars, natural disasters, national epidemics, and personal tragedies.[46] By maintaining the promise of divine healing, Pentecostal hermeneutics encounters not only its most material but also its most volatile demands as a liturgy insisting on the availability and extension of the experience of Pentecost "to the ends of the earth." As a theological emphasis of the full gospel, healing is as much based in the atonement as it is in search of atonement.[47] The full gospel resolves this hermeneutical tension with a pervasive eschatological orientation.

---

44. Mittelstadt, *Spirit and Suffering*; Thomas, *Devil*, 310–19.
45. Alexander, *Pentecostal Healing*.
46. Robinson, *Divine Healing*, 5–29, 39–68.
47. Holm, "Healing in Search," 50–67.

COMMISSIONED

Despite its place in the full gospel narrative, eschatology does not mark the "end" of Pentecostal theology. Rather, eschatology returns the full gospel to its central concerns for participation in Pentecost transformed by an apocalyptic urgency.[48] An apocalyptic emphasis on the kingdom of God projects Pentecostal theology back onto itself in critical reflection: eschatology not only draws Pentecostals from the altar to the ends of the earth but urges them to return to the altar and the encounter with God. Pentecostal eschatology culminates in an apocalyptic mandate to go and seek the lost, to proclaim Christ as king, and to bring the world into God's kingdom. This apocalyptic expectation of the inbreaking of the kingdom already manifested in the outpouring of the Holy Spirit (at Pentecost and beyond) permeates the reading and practices of the other gospel motifs. The events of Pentecost form an eschatological motivation for the proclamation of the whole of the full gospel, thereby continually expanding the Pentecostal theological narrative until it finds its full realization.

Eschatological practices are therefore, in principle, any altar practices acted out by the church for its mission to and transformation of the world (see chapter 8). The practices of the eschatological gospel are organized along any of the central experiences of Pentecost, albeit now realized as an aspect of the imminent fullness of the kingdom of God. In the altar narrative of the full gospel, to be saved means eschatologically "an entry into the training program of a missionary fellowship"[49] where Pentecostals see themselves as agents of witness and worship in the world. To be sanctified means an eschatological break and radical transformation from a life of the flesh to a life in the Spirit as a testimony to life in God's kingdom.[50] The eschatological baptism in the Spirit seeks to equip theology for a radical witness to the lost and spiritual battle with the enemies of God as a testimony to the empowered and anointed life resulting from Pentecost.[51] And the eschatological experience of divine healing points to a radical encounter with the coming kingdom already manifested in the physical life of believers as a testimony to the redeeming presence of God. These and other experiences reshape Pentecostal

---

48. Land, *Pentecostal Spirituality*, 58–70.
49. Land, *Pentecostal Spirituality*, 82.
50. Land, *Pentecostal Spirituality*, 88–90.
51. Land, *Pentecostal Spirituality*, 91–93.

theology into eschatological actions to serve as anticipation, confirmation, and celebration of an eternal Pentecost.

Pentecostal theology alerts Christianity to the ongoing significance of eschatology for ecclesiology and mission and the importance of cultivating eschatological practices in light of an apocalyptic vision.[52] The eschatological interpretation of the Pentecostal theological mission often includes both the ideas of urgent evangelization and long-term social transformation.[53] Outside the dominance of dispensational hermeneutics, the Pentecostal apocalyptic vision can be more exactly defined as an affective transformation conforming the church and the individual to the pathos of God,[54] instilled by the outpouring of the Holy Spirit through experiences of the charismatic gifts creating and shaping an eschatological liturgy.

CONCLUSION

The full gospel of salvation, sanctification, Spirit baptism, divine healing, and the kingdom of God elicits theological actions of the church through which God enables the participation of the world in the outpouring of the Spirit of Christ. The five dominant themes presented in this chapter chart the foundational logic of the Pentecostal theological narrative to which other themes could be added. A drive for the redemptive, transformative, and liberating "fullness" of the kingdom of God sustains the entire liturgy of the full gospel. The importance of this theological hermeneutic lies in its insistence on the full gospel as a liturgy of Pentecost that applies to the whole of the Christian life. Pentecostal theology is in this sense a participation in the day of Pentecost lived out in the charismatic, evangelistic, and socio-critical practices of the church around the altar. The full gospel is a curious, hospitable, and critical theological liturgy that points to an eternal Pentecost already captured by the experiences of Christ as savior, sanctifier, Spirit baptizer, divine healer, and coming king.

---

52. See Thompson, *Kingdom Come*.
53. Miller and Yamamori, *Global Pentecostalism*, 41–43.
54. See Land, *Pentecostal Spirituality*, 58–121.

Conclusion

The Liturgy of the Gospel as Theological Hermeneutics

THESE FINAL PAGES AIM at clarifying what the preceding chapters have achieved, where theological hermeneutics has arrived among Pentecostals, and what the nature of Pentecostal hermeneutics contributes more broadly to the Christian life. The heart of my claim concerning the nature of theological hermeneutics among Pentecostals has been its historical emergence as the liturgy of the gospel. The preceding chapters have traced this development by modifying the general path of hermeneutics proposed by Hans-Georg Gadamer as the question of truth extended to hermeneutical experience and eventually to the ontological shift guided by liturgy. During the rise of the Pentecostal movement with the twentieth century, the narrative of this liturgy has become expressed as the full gospel. If before I have studied the systematic doctrinal, experiential, and liturgical character of the full gospel,[1] here I want to identify specifically its hermeneutical character. What I have offered is not a hermeneutical model but a general theory of theological hermeneutics as it emerged in the history of the Pentecostal movement in light of the hermeneutical experiences afforded by the liturgy. The core of these experiences is the ontological transformation resulting from both a fusion and fission of the hermeneutical horizons narrated by the full gospel. With this shift, theological interpretation in Pentecostal perspective became interested equally in the sources of theological hermeneutics (i.e., gospel) and in the relationship of the sources to the interpreter and the world of the interpreter (i.e., liturgy).

---

1. See Vondey, *Pentecostal Theology*, 37–151.

The move from theological hermeneutics to theological method(s) among Pentecostals has proceeded along the pre-theoretical experiences of this shift. The semiotic contours of these methods have been convincingly described by others as the interplay of Spirit, word, and community.[2] The essays in this volume suggest that the theological experiences documenting this interplay among Pentecostals are mediated, broadly speaking, through liturgical participation in the effects of Pentecost. Put differently, it is the liturgical experience which correlates Spirit, word, and community because it awakens the theological enquiry in the correlation of the pneumatological, biblical, and communal imagination arising from the encounter with Christ. That the interpreter and the world of the interpreter are both subject and object of these experiences is supported by the hermeneutical fusion and fission of horizons that takes place in each of the correlative dimensions. The liturgy is the primary medium through which these hermeneutical experiences proceed, and the process of interpretation itself is documented in the history of Pentecostalism with the hermeneutic of the four- or fivefold gospel. These concluding pages offer a synthesis of the challenges theological hermeneutics faces with regard to the continuing influence of the full gospel, concentrating on its liturgical dimension and the nature of its form and experience.

PENTECOST AND THE HERMENEUTIC OF THE GOSPEL

The place of Pentecost in a theological hermeneutic narrated by *any* account of the gospel must engage the hermeneutical horizons in the light of Jesus Christ. In the first place, this task requires situating Pentecost in the Gospels and their respective narratives of Jesus of Nazareth. With the insistence on Pentecost as a primary horizon, theological hermeneutics in Pentecostal perspective is always a theological interpretation of Scripture (and its various narratives of Christ) from the vantage point of Pentecost.[3] The temptation is to view Pentecost as a horizon distinct from the gospel, or more specifically, to treat the book of Acts in a manner

---

2. See Archer, *Pentecostal Hermeneutic*; Yong, *Spirit-Word-Community*; Hanson, "Scripture, Community, and Spirit," 3–12.

3. For perspectives on this approach specific to Pentecostal hermeneutics, see Oliverio, "Pentecostal Philosophical-Theological Hermeneutic," 35–55; Yong, *Hermeneutical Spirit*, 27–78, 257–66; Keener, *Spirit Hermeneutics*, 39–56; Archer, *Pentecostal Hermeneutic*, 128–71.

distinct from the canonical Gospels that *subsequently* requires a fusion of their horizons. I have shown more recently that there are still few attempts in the history of biblical hermeneutics to identify and to reconcile the different texts that together construct Pentecost as a biblical event.[4] A limited focus on Acts 2 as the primary (if not the only) text documenting the historical event and its recognition and interpretation has isolated Pentecost from the rest of New Testament studies and placed the event often in the shadow of the Gospels, on the one hand, and either distanced from or interpreted through a dominant hermeneutical lens of the Pauline writings (with supposedly little interest in Pentecost) on the other. Although an oversimplification, the history of biblical hermeneutics among Pentecostals during the twentieth century can be characterized as an attempt to bridge the distance between Pentecost and the Gospels, with particular focus on the correlation of Luke–Acts.[5]

A corresponding temptation is to advocate for this integration of Pentecost exclusively through a fusion of horizons made possible by an interpretative reassessment. While a fusion of horizons through experiential, missiological, ethical, or eschatological reinterpretation (to name a few prominent examples) is certainly documented in the history of Pentecostal biblical hermeneutics, the day of Pentecost also requires a hermeneutical shift that is not simply contained in a hermeneutic *before* or *after* Pentecost. Gadamer's pervasive demand for a fusion of horizons is confronted not only with the problem of historical distance but also the rise of new horizons that can both extend and bridge that distance.[6] The essays in this book document that engaging the different horizons demands not only their recognition but the perpetual discernment of the fusion and fission of interpretive horizons in the light of Pentecost. That is, theological interpretation exists *between* the horizons (of the original Pentecost and its history of effects), and in the case of Pentecostal hermeneutics, it demands resisting not only the cessationist claim of the separation of the apostolic world from the present but also of the complete (and impossible) identity of the contemporary interpreter with the horizon of the historical Pentecost. The question that has emerged as the driving force in the Pentecostal history of theological hermeneutics is precisely "what" constitutes the *between* of interpretive horizons

4. Vondey, *Scandal of Pentecost*, 77–83.
5. See Mittelstadt, *Evolution*; Mittelstadt, *Reading Luke–Acts*; Oliverio, *Theological Hermeneutics*, 31–82.
6. See Thiselton, *New Horizons in Hermeneutics*; Thiselton, *Two Horizons*.

(theologically, experientially, conceptually, reflectively, etc.) and, equally important, "how" to remain in and reflect on that space between. The answer that arises from my observations about the Pentecostal tradition in the previous chapters is that this hermeneutical space between horizons is formed by participation in the Pentecostal liturgy. More precisely, while it is possible to say that theological hermeneutics among Pentecostals proceeds and functions liturgically, in practice the space between interpretive horizons has been identified as a functional hermeneutical place: the call to, tarrying at, transformation, release from, and return to the altar. In the life of Pentecostal congregations, theological interpretation takes the shape of an altar hermeneutic.

THE ALTAR AS A HERMENEUTICAL PLACE

Rather than viewing the liturgy itself as the conceptual frame that functions as a hermeneutical space (and thus "competing" with the valid practices and concepts of the liturgy in different hermeneutical traditions), it is more accurate to speak of the altar in the Pentecostal liturgy as the threshold of hermeneutical horizons. It is not unusual to identify the altar as a threshold in the wider Christian liturgy.[7] However, its significance in the Pentecostal tradition is complicated by the hermeneutical experience of both fusion and fission. The resulting "altar hermeneutic" has been described on the previous pages as the tension between a "this-is-that" and "this-is-not-that" interpretation. The particular hermeneutical challenge is that Pentecostals, as the interpreting subject, are not only comfortable with this tension but that the altar experience requires it in order to sustain an interpretation engaged in the effects of Pentecost.[8] Without this tension, the threshold collapses into either claims of an unmediated experience of Pentecost or an endless fragmentation of that experience in rituals designed to mediate the divine encounter. Instead, the altar constitutes the metaphysical, communal, aesthetic, and ethical commitments of interpretation that inform participation in the Pentecostal liturgy as the possibility of the intensifying presence of Christ.[9] This intensification is possible only if at the altar

---

7. See, e.g., Elliott, *Sculpted Thresholds*; Gerstel, *Thresholds of the Sacred*, 7–26, 53–72; Guardini, *Meditations Before Mass*, 39–45.

8. Nimi Wariboko has illustrated this tension with a different metaphor yet in the context of Pentecostal worship in *Split God*, 133–55, and *Pentecostal Hypothesis*, 115–54.

9. See Vondey, *Pentecostal Theology*, 194, 263.

occurs a necessary reversal of the subject and object of interpretation amid the fusion and fission of horizons. Because the altar is a threshold to Pentecost, this hermeneutical experience proceeds, not exclusively on epistemological grounds but also in ways that are incarnational (including both Christ's flesh and ours) and pneumatological (both through the gift of the Spirit and our manifestation of the Spirit's gifts). The full gospel narrates this hermeneutical reversal in the terms of five transformative experiences: salvation, sanctification, Spirit baptism, divine healing, and commissioning for the kingdom of God.

Salvation as a hermeneutical experience accentuates the shift away from exclusively epistemological models to soteriological accounts of inspiration and interpretation through a personal encounter with the God of biblical history, texts, narratives, and experiences. Sanctification identifies this encounter at the threshold of the human world and the divine by challenging, interpreting, and sanctifying human understanding for the sake of the formation and transformation of the whole person. Spirit baptism as a hermeneutical experience insists that the encounter with Christ in the act of interpretation is possible only through a hermeneutic that is open to disruption, overturning, and reorientation. Divine healing expands the Pentecostal hermeneutic to elucidate the role of Spirit, word, and community in the confrontation with human, spiritual, intellectual, psychological, and physical struggles. Through the lens of divine healing, theological hermeneutics becomes an opportunity to repair human suffering and loss in the experience of deliverance. Finally, an eschatological realism imbues Pentecostal hermeneutics with a passion for God's kingdom as both the beginning and destiny of the entire interpretive act. By endorsing an eschatological orientation, the altar hermeneutics narrated by the full gospel insists not only on the expectation of the kingdom of God but on its realization in the hermeneutical experience of the fusion and fission of horizons.

THE PLAYFULNESS OF LITURGICAL HERMENEUTICS

The liturgy of the full gospel documents that theological hermeneutics in Pentecostal perspective cannot be an instantaneous and comprehensive task. Conceptualizing and systematizing Pentecostal hermeneutics threatens to collapse the hermeneutical experiences of the full gospel into an interpretive "mechanism." I have described the resistance to instrumentalizing the hermeneutical experience in the history of Pentecostalism as an expression of play. That liturgical hermeneutics is guided by a playful imagination does not threaten the hermeneutical experience but complicates articulating the logic and method of Pentecostal interpretation. Immersed in the playful act, hermeneutics is both playing and being-played, acting and being acted upon by the fusion and fission of horizons. The insistence on the "fullness" of the gospel has indicated to Pentecostals that the hermeneutical task is extensive, and only the complete gospel narrates and constitutes the fullness of the experience of hermeneutical horizons. If Pentecostal theology, as I have insisted, is a way of *living* the full gospel, then theological hermeneutics for Pentecostals is the "understanding" and "interpretation" of that life through the transformation of the interpreter. A liturgical hermeneutics therefore refers not immediately or exclusively to the experience of Christian rituals or practices but to a successive and cumulative way of formation, reformation, and transformation. That this living hermeneutics is interpreted from the perspective of Pentecost highlights the continuous significance of a life redeemed by Christ for the witness of the Spirit. When theological hermeneutics joins Pentecost and the Gospels, this dual emphasis merges into the single act of seeking truth first and foremost in the Spirit manifested through the life of Jesus Christ: these are mutually informing hermeneutical experiences of the intensifying love of God.

The experience of liturgical hermeneutics as a form of play is defined by the fusion and fission of the hermeneutical horizons. The absence of play manifests the complete fission (or objectification) of the interpreter from Pentecost (and its history of effects), whereas their complete fusion (or subjectification) signals the loss of the object entirely in the mind of the interpreter. Both threats have been visible in the history of Pentecostal hermeneutics; they are characteristic of any desire to interpret one's hermeneutical experience as truth. In response, Pentecostals have sometimes overcorrected their hermeneutical method.[10] The previous chapters suggest that the correspondence of truth and method can be obtained liturgically, and for Pentecostals this means hermeneutical correction always takes place "at the altar." Both leaving and returning to the altar are necessary for the Christian life in order to engage redemptively and hermeneutically with the world and with God. The playfulness of this movement suggests that the place of the altar shifts, sometimes as the

---

10. The most prominent example is perhaps to either overemphasize or diminish the role of sanctification in the full gospel. See also Green, *Sanctifying Interpretation*.

deliberate endeavor of the interpreter, at other times in God's surprising and unexpected revelation through the act of interpretation. Hermeneutical method, and with it the subject, object, and medium of interpretation, therefore, does not always return to the same place. Instead, liturgical hermeneutics in Pentecostal perspective exists for the purpose of transforming all moments of the Christian life to be an (altar) place of the potential encounter with God.

The emphasis of the full gospel as an altar hermeneutic that is both liturgical and ludic must also maintain the distinction between liturgy and play. The liturgy is neither "ordinary" play nor a wholly different performance but a way of living between the horizons. The importance of a hermeneutical place, where the fusion and fission of horizons can occur in the life of the interpreter, suggests that the particular (not only Pentecostal) mode of living that combines liturgical and ludic forms is worship. Put differently, among Pentecostals, the full gospel is a biblical and theological model for a hermeneutical doxology. The spiritual and charismatic gifts that have come to characterize Pentecostalism during the twentieth century demonstrate more dramatically how the interpreter can feel constrained by liturgical forms. Hence, the full gospel is only a model, not an instruction, for how to enter into play with the divine presence at the altar. Conversely, the freedom of this encounter at the place of the altar is not unlimited and without boundaries. Therefore, theological hermeneutics is not everything Pentecostals want it to be as long as it seems justified by their hermeneutical experiences. I have described elsewhere the challenges faced historically by Pentecostals in the effort to maintain their own hermeneutical playfulness.[11] Liturgical hermeneutics encounters these challenges with particular force when the experience of the liturgy is confused with the liturgical form. That the place of theological hermeneutics in Pentecostal perspective is the altar signals that the hermeneutical challenges faced by Pentecostals exist not in the isolation of the performance of their liturgy but in the pursuit of their hermeneutical experiences throughout the liturgy of the entire Christian life and in the manner that life is lived.

---

11. Vondey, *Beyond Pentecostalism*, 171–201.

Bibliography

Adler, Hans, and Ernest A. Menze, eds. *Johann Gottfried Herder on World History: An Anthology.* Translated by Ernest A. Menze and Michael Palma. New York: Routledge, 1997.

Albrecht, Daniel E. "Pentecostal Spirituality: Looking Through the Lens of Ritual." *Pneuma: The Journal of the Society for Pentecostal Studies* 14 (1992) 107–25.

———. *Rites in the Spirit: A Ritual Approach to Pentecostal/Charismatic Spirituality.* Journal of Pentecostal Theology Supplement Series 17. Sheffield: Sheffield Academic, 1999.

Alexander, Bobby C. "Correcting Misinterpretations of Turner's Theory: An African-American Pentecostal Illustration." *Journal for the Scientific Study of Religion* 30 (1991) 32–41.

———. "Pentecostal Ritual Reconsidered: Anti-Structural Dimensions of Possession." *Journal of Religious Studies* 3 (1989) 109–28.

———. *Victor Turner Revisited: Ritual as Social Change.* American Academy of Religion Academy Series 74. Atlanta: Scholars, 1991.

Alexander, Estrelda Y. *Black Fire: One Hundred Years of African American Pentecostalism.* Downers Grove, IL: InterVarsity, 2011.

———. "Liturgy in Non-Liturgical Holiness Pentecostalism." *Wesleyan Theological Journal* 32 (1997) 158–93.

Alexander, Kimberly E. "'How Wide Thy Healing Streams Are Spread': Constructing a Wesleyan Pentecostal Model for Healing for the Twenty-First Century." *Asbury Theological Journal* 59 (2004) 63–76.

———. *Pentecostal Healing: Models in Theology and Practice.* Journal of Pentecostal Theology Supplement Series 29. Blandford Forum, UK: Deo, 2006.

Alexander, Kimberly E., et al. "Spirit Baptism, Socialization and Godly Love in the Church of God (Cleveland, TN)." *PentecoStudies* 11 (2006) 27–47.

Alexander, Paul. *Peace to War: Shifting Allegiances in the Assemblies of God.* Telford, PA: Cascadia, 2009.

Allen, William Francis, et al., eds. *Slave Songs of the United States.* 1867. Repr., Bedford, MA: Applewood, 1996.

Althouse, Peter. *Spirit of the Last Days: Pentecostal Eschatology in Conversation with Jürgen Moltmann.* Journal of Pentecostal Theology Supplement Series 25. London: Sheffield Academic, 2003.

Arteaga, William L., de. *Forgotten Power: The Significance of the Lord's Supper in Revival.* Grand Rapids: Zondervan, 2002.

Anderson, Allan H. "Pentecostal Approaches to Faith and Healing." *International Review of Mission* 91 (2002) 523–34.

———. *Spirit-Filled World: Religious Dis/Continuity in African Pentecostalism.* New York: Palgrave Macmillan, 2018.

———. *Spreading Fires: The Missionary Nature of Early Pentecostalism.* London: SCM, 2007.

———. *To the Ends of the Earth: Pentecostalism and the Transformation of World Christianity.* Oxford: Oxford University Press, 2013.

Anderson, Allan, and Edmund Tang, eds. *Asian and Pentecostal: The Charismatic Face of Christianity in Asia.* Oxford: Regnum, 2005.

Anderson, Gordon L. "Pentecostals Believe in More Than Tongues." In *Pentecostals from the Inside Out*, edited by Harold B. Smith, 53–64. Wheaton, IL: Victor, 1990.

Anderson, Robert Mapes. *Vision of the Disinherited: The Making of American Pentecostalism.* New York: Oxford University Press, 1979.

Andrews, Dale P. *Practical Theology for Black Churches: Bridging Black Theology and African American Folk Religion.* Louisville: Westminster John Knox, 2002.

Appold, Kenneth G. "Lutheran Reactions to Pentecostalism: A U.S. Case Study." In *Lutherans and Pentecostals in Dialogue*, 58–84. Strasbourg: Institute for Ecumenical Research, 2010.

Archer, Kenneth J. "The Fivefold Gospel and the Mission of the Church: Ecclesiastical Implications and Opportunities." In *Toward a Pentecostal Ecclesiology: The Church and the Fivefold Gospel*, edited by John Christopher Thomas, 7–43. Cleveland, TN: CPT, 2010.

———. "Nourishment for Our Journey: The Pentecostal Via Salutis and Sacramental Ordinances." *Journal of Pentecostal Theology* 13 (2004) 79–96.

———. *A Pentecostal Hermeneutic: Spirit, Scripture, and Community.* Cleveland, TN: CPT, 2009.

———. "Pentecostal Story: The Hermeneutical Filter for the Making of Meaning." *Pneuma: The Journal of the Society for Pentecostal Studies* 26 (2004) 36–59.

Arnesen, Eric. *Black Protest and the Great Migration: A Brief History with Documents.* Boston: Bedford/St. Martin's, 2003.

Arrington, French L. *Paul's Aeon Theology in 1 Corinthians.* Washington, DC: University Press of America, 1978.

Arthur, William. *The Tongue of Fire or the True Power of Christianity.* Columbia, NC: Pickett, 1891.

Asad, Talal. *Genealogies of Religion: Discipline and Reasons of Power in Christianity and Islam.* Baltimore: Johns Hopkins University Press, 1993.

Asamoah-Gyadu, J. Kwabena. "'Unction to Function': Reinventing the Oil of Influence in African Pentecostalism." *Journal of Pentecostal Theology* 13 (2005) 231–56.

Assmann, Jan. *Cultural Memory and Early Civilizations: Writing, Remembrance, and Political Imagination.* New York: Cambridge University Press, 2011.

———. *Das kulturelle Gedächtnis: Schrift, Erinnerung und politische Identität in frühen Hochkulturen.* C. H. Beck Kulturwissenschaft. Munich: Beck, 1997.

"The Augsburg Confession." In *The Book of Concord: The Confessions of the Evangelical Lutheran Church*, edited by Robert Kolb and Timothy J. Wengert and translated by Charles Arand et al., 27–106. Minneapolis: Fortress, 2000.

Augustine, Daniela C. *The Spirit and the Common Good: Shared Flourishing in the Image of God*. Grand Rapids: Eerdmans, 2019.

———. "The Spirit in Word and Sacrament: Reflections on Potential Contributions of Eastern Orthodoxy to the Development of Pentecostal Liturgical Theology." *Journal of Pentecostal Theology* 29 (2020) 56–72.

Baer, Hans A., and Merrill Singer. *African American Religion: Varieties of Protest and Accommodation*. 2nd ed. Knoxville: University of Tennessee Press, 2002.

Baer, Jonathan R. "Redeemed Bodies: The Functions of Divine Healing in Incipient Pentecostalism." *Church History* 70 (2001) 735–71.

Baer, Richard A., Jr. "Quaker Silence, Catholic Liturgy, and Pentecostal Glossolalia—Some Functional Similarities." In *Perspectives on the New Pentecostalism*, edited by Russell P. Spittler, 151–64. Grand Rapids: Baker, 1976.

Baier, Johann Wilhelm. *Compendium of Positive Theology*. Translated by C. F. W. Walther. St. Louis: Concordia, 1877.

Baker, Carolyn Denise. "Created Spirit Beings. Angels." In *Systematic Theology: A Pentecostal Perspective*, edited by Stanley M. Horton, 179–94. Springfield, MO: Logion, 1994.

Balthasar, Hans Urs von. *Truth Is Symphonic: Aspects of Christian Pluralism*. San Francisco: Ignatius, 1987.

Barfoot, Charles H., and Gerald T. Sheppard. "Prophetic vs. Priestly Religion: The Changing Role of Women Clergy in Classical Pentecostal Churches." *Review of Religious Research* 22 (1980) 2–17.

Barratt, Thomas Ball. *In the Days of the Latter Rain*. London: Elim, 1928.

Battle, Michael. *The Black Church in America: African American Christian Spirituality*. Religious Life in America. Oxford: Wiley-Blackwell, 2006.

Baudrillard, Jean. *For a Critique of the Political Economy of the Sign*. Translated by Charles Levin. St. Louis: Telos, 1981.

———. *Pour une critique de l'économie politique du signe*. Paris: Galimard, 1972.

———. *Symbolic Exchange and Death*. Translated by Iain Hamilton Grant. Theory, Culture & Society. London: Sage, 1993.

Beaty, James M. "A New Song in My Mouth." *Church of God, History and Heritage* (1998) 4.

Beckman, David M. "Trance: From Africa to Pentecostalism." *Concordia Theological Monthly* 45 (1974) 11–26.

Bente, F., and W. H. T. Dau, eds. *Triglot Concordia: The Symbolical Books of the Evangelical Lutheran Church*. St. Louis: Concordia, 1921.

Bergunder, Michael. "Pfingstbewegung, Globalisierung und Migration." In *Migration und Identität: Pfingstlich-charismatische migrationsgemeinden in Deutschland*, edited by Michael Bergunder and Jörg Haustein, 155–69. Frankfurt: Lembeck, 2006.

Bernard, David K. *Oneness and Trinity, A.D. 100–300: The Doctrine of God in Ancient Christian Writings*. Hazelwood, MO: Word Aflame, 1991.

———. *The Oneness View of Jesus Christ*. Hazelwood, MO: Word Aflame, 1994.

———. *The Trinitarian Controversy in the Fourth Century*. Hazelwood, MO: Word Aflame, 1993.

Bialecki, Jon. "Affect: Intensities and Energies in the Charismatic Language, Embodiment, and Genre of a North American Movement." In *The Anthropology of Global Pentecostalism and Evangelicalism*, edited by Simon Coleman and Rosalind I. J. Hackett, 95–108. New York: New York University Press, 2015.

Biddy, Wesley Scott. "Re-Envisioning the Pentecostal Understanding of the Eucharist: An Ecumenical Proposal." *Pneuma: The Journal of the Society for Pentecostal Studies* 28 (2006) 228–51.

Bittlinger, Arnold. *Papst und Pfingstler: Der römischpfingstliche dialog und seine ökumenische Relevanz*. Frankfurt: Lang, 1978.

Black, Jonathan. "The Church as Eucharistic Fellowship: A British Apostolic Contribution Toward a Pentecostal Ecclesiology." *Journal of the European Pentecostal Theological Association* 29 (2009) 78–89.

Bloch-Hoell, Nils. *The Pentecostal Movement: Its Origin, Development and Distinctive Character*. London: Allen & Unwin, 1964.

Blomquist, Karen L., ed. *Lutherans Respond to Pentecostalism*. Minneapolis: Lutheran University Press, 2008.

Bock, Darrell L. *A Theology of Luke and Acts: God's Promised Program, Realized for All Nations*. Grand Rapids: Zondervan, 2012.

Bonhoeffer, Dietrich. *Act and Being: Transcendental Philosophy and Ontology in Theology*. Edited by Wayne Whitson Floyd Jr. Translated by H. Martin Rumscheidt. Dietrich Bonhoeffer Works 2. Minneapolis: Fortress, 1996.

Bosworth, F. F. "Do All Speak in Tongues?" In *A Reader in Pentecostal Theology: Voices from the First Generation*, edited by Douglas Jacobsen, 142. Bloomington: Indiana University Press, 2006.

Boyer, Pascal. *Tradition as Truth and Communication: A Cognitive Description of Traditional Discourse*. Cambridge Studies in Social Anthropology 68. Cambridge: Cambridge University Press, 1990.

Braaten, Carl E. "Can We Still Hold the Principle of 'Sola Scriptura'?" *Dialog* 20 (1981) 189–90.

Bridgeman Davis, Valerie. "Go Play with God: Reclaiming Liturgy for Spiritual Formation." In *Companion to the Africana Worship Book*, edited by Valerie Bridgeman Davis, 26–32. Nashville: Discipleship Resources, 2008.

Brodwin, Paul. "Pentecostalism in Translation: Religion and the Production of Community in the Haitian Diaspora." *American Ethnologist* 30 (2003) 85–101.

Brown, Kenneth O. *Holy Ground: A Study of the American Camp Meeting*. Garland Reference Library of Social Science 717. New York: Garland, 1992.

———. *Holy Ground Too: The Camp Meeting Family Tree*. Hazelton, PA: Holiness Archives, 1997.

Brumback, Carl. *"What Meaneth This?" A Pentecostal Answer to a Pentecostal Question*. Springfield, MO: Gospel, 1947.

Bundy, David. "Bibliography and Historiography of Pentecostalism Outside North America." In *The New International Dictionary of Pentecostal and Charismatic Movements*, edited by Stanley M. Burgess and Eduard van der Maas, 405–17. Grand Rapids: Zondervan, 2002.

Burgess, Stanley M., and Eduard van der Maas, eds. *The New International Dictionary of Pentecostal and Charismatic Movements*. Grand Rapids: Zondervan, 2002.

Burghardt, Gordon M. "Defining and Recognizing Play." In *The Oxford Handbook of the Development of Play*, edited by Anthony D. Pellegrini, 9–18. Oxford: Oxford University Press, 2011.

Butler, Daniel L. *Oneness Pentecostalism: A History of the Jesus Name Movement*. Bellflower, CA: International Pentecostal Church, 2004.

Butler, Jon. "Disquieted History in *A Secular Age*." In *Varieties of Secularism in a Secular Age*, edited by Michael Warner and Jonathan Van Antwerpen, 193–216. Cambridge, MA: Harvard University Press, 2010.
Camery-Hogatt, Jerry. "The Word of God from Living Voices: Orality and Literacy in the Pentecostal Tradition." *Pneuma: The Journal of the Society for Pentecostal Studies* 27 (2005) 225–55.
Campbell, Ted A. *The Gospel in the Christian Traditions*. Oxford: Oxford University Press, 2009.
Cardona, Carlos. "La 'Jerarquía de las verdades' y el orden de lo real." *Scripta Theologica* 4.1 (1972) 123–44.
Cartledge, Mark J. *Charismatic Glossolalia: An Empirical-Theological Study*. Ashgate New Critical Thinking in Theology & Biblical Studies. Aldershot, UK: Ashgate, 2002.
———. "The Early Pentecostal Theology of Confidence Magazine (1908–1926): A Version of the Five-Fold Gospel?" *Journal of the European Pentecostal Theological Association* 28 (2008) 117–30.
———. "Pentecostal Healing as an Expression of Godly Love: An Empirical Study." *Mental Health, Religion, and Culture* 16 (2013) 501–22.
———. *Testimony in the Spirit: Rescripting Ordinary Pentecostal Theology*. Explorations in Practical, Pastoral and Empirical Theology. Surrey, UK: Ashgate, 2010.
Castelo, Daniel. "Tarrying on the Lord: Affections, Virtues, and Theological Ethics in Pentecostal Perspective." *Journal of Pentecostal Theology* 13 (2004) 50–56.
Catechism of the Catholic Church. 2nd ed. Vatican, 1997.
Cerillo, Augustus, Jr., and Grant Wacker. "Bibliography and Historiography of Pentecostalism in the United States." In *The New International Dictionary of Pentecostal and Charismatic Movements*, edited by Stanley M. Burgess and Eduard M. van der Maas, 382–405. Grand Rapids: Zondervan, 2002.
Cessario, Romanus. "The Sacraments of the Church." In *Vatican II: Renewal Within Tradition*, edited by Matthew L. Lamb and Matthew Levering, 129–44. Oxford: Oxford University Press, 2008.
Chalfant, William B. "The Fall of the Ancient Apostolic Church." In *Symposium on Oneness Pentecostalism, 1988 and 1990*, edited by United Pentecostal Church International, 351–85. Hazelwood, MO: Word Aflame, 1990.
Chan, Simon. "The Church and the Development of Doctrine." *Journal of Pentecostal Theology* 13 (2004) 57–77.
———. *Pentecostal Ecclesiology: An Essay on the Development of Doctrine*. Journal of Pentecostal Theology Supplement Series 38. Blandford Forum, UK: Deo, 2011.
———. *Pentecostal Theology and the Christian Spiritual Tradition*. Sheffield: Sheffield Academic, 2000.
Chauvet, Louis-Marie. *The Sacraments: The Word of God at the Mercy of the Body*. Collegeville, MN: Liturgical, 2001.
———. *Symbol and Sacrament: A Sacramental Reinterpretation of Christian Existence*. Translated by Patrick Madigan and M. Beaumont, 409–46. Collegeville, MN: Liturgical, 1995.
———. *Symbole et Sacrament: Un relecture sacramentelle de l'existence chrétienne*. Paris: Cerf, 1987.
Chesnut, R. A. *Born Again in Brazil: The Pentecostal Boom and the Pathogens of Poverty*. New Brunswick: Rutgers University Press, 1997.

Chiurazzi, Caetano. "Truth." In *The Gadamerian Mind*, edited by Theodore George and Gert-Jan van der Heiden, 93–105. Routledge Philosophical Minds. London: Routledge, 2021.

Christenson, Larry. *The Charismatic Renewal Among Lutherans*. Minneapolis: Lutheran Charismatic Renewal Services, 1976.

Church Hymnal. Cleveland, TN: Tennessee Music and Printing, 1951.

"The Church's Privileges." *The Pentecost* 2 (1910) 14.

Clatterbuck, Mark S. "Healing Hills and Sacred Songs: Crow Pentecostalism, Anti-Traditionalism, and Native Religious Identity." *Spiritus* 12 (2012) 248–77.

Clifford, Catherine E., ed. *For the Communion of the Churches: The Contributions of the Groupe des Dombes*. Grand Rapids: Eerdmans, 2010.

Clifton, Shane. "The Spirit and Doctrinal Development: A Functional Analysis of the Traditional Pentecostal Doctrine of the Baptism in the Holy Spirit." *Pneuma: The Journal of the Society for Pentecostal Studies* 29 (2007) 5–23.

Clynes, Raphael. *Liturgy and Christian Life*. Paterson, NJ: St. Anthony Guild, 1960.

Coffey, David. *Deus Trinitas: The Doctrine of the Triune God*. Oxford: Oxford University Press, 1999.

Cohn-Sherbok, Dan. *The Jewish Messiah*. Edinburgh: T. & T. Clark, 1997.

Collins, Mary, and David Power, eds. *Liturgy: A Creative Tradition*. New York: Seabury, 1983.

Combet, Georges, and Laureat Fabre. "The Pentecostal Movement and the Gift of Healing." In *Experience of the Spirit*, edited by Peter Huizing and William Bassett, 106–10. New York: Seabury, 1976.

Comblin, José. *The Holy Spirit and Liberation*. Translated by Paul Burns. Theology and Liberation Series. Maryknoll, NY: Orbis, 1989.

Congar, Yves. "Articles fondamentaux." *Catholicisme*. Vol. 1. Paris: Cerf, 1948.

———. *Diversity and Communion*. Translated by John Bowden. London: SCM, 1984.

———. *The Revelation of God*. Translated by A. Manson and L. C. Sheppard. New York: Herder and Herder, 1968.

Conklin, Paul K. *Cane Ridge: America's Pentecost*. Madison: University of Wisconsin Press, 1990.

Conn, Charles W. *Like a Mighty Army: A History of the Church of God*. Cleveland, TN: Pathway, 1996.

Cooley, Steven D. "Manna and the Manual: Sacramental and Instrumental Constructions of the Victorian Methodist Camp Meeting During the Mid-Nineteenth Century." *Religion and American Culture* 6 (1996) 131–59.

Costen, Melva Wilson. *African American Christian Worship*. Nashville: Abingdon, 1993.

Costen, Melva Wilson, and Darius Leander Swann, eds. *The Black Christian Worship Experience*. Rev. and enlarged ed. Atlanta: ITC, 1992.

Coulter, Dale. "'Delivered by the Power of God': Toward a Pentecostal Understanding of Salvation." *International Journal of Systematic Theology* 10 (2008) 447–67.

Covington, Dennis. *Salvation on Sand Mountain: Snake Handling and Redemption in Southern Appalachia*. Reading, MA: Addison-Wesley, 1995.

Cox, Harvey. *Festival of Fools: A Theological Essay on Festivity and Fantasy*. Cambridge, MA: Harvard University Press, 1969.

———. *Fire from Heaven: The Rise of Pentecostal Spirituality and the Reshaping of Religion in the Twenty-First Century*. New York: Addison-Wesley, 1995.

———. "Healers and Ecologists: Pentecostalism in Africa." *Christian Century* 111 (1994) 1042–46.

———. "Personal Reflections on Pentecostalism." *Pneuma: The Journal of the Society for Pentecostal Studies* 15 (1993) 29–34.

———. *Religion in the Secular City: Toward a Postmodern Theology*. New York: Simon & Schuster, 1984.

———. *The Secular City*. Rev. ed. New York: MacMillan, 1966.

Cox, Raymond L., ed. *The Four-Square Gospel*. Los Angeles: Foursquare, 1969.

Cullmann, Oscar. "Comments on the Decree on Ecumenism Enacted in the Second Vatican Council and Promulgated on N 21 1964." *Ecumenical Review* 17 (1965) 93–112.

———. "Einheit in der Vielfalt im Lichte der 'Hierarchie der Wahrheiten.'" *Glaube im Prozeß: Christsein nach dem II. Vatikanum*, edited by Elmar Klinger and Klaus Wittstadt, 356–64. Freiburg: Herder, 1984.

Cummings, George C. L. "The Slave Narratives as a Source of Black Theological Discourse: The Spirit and Eschatology." In *Cut Loose Your Stammering Tongue: Black Theology in the Slave Narrative*, edited by D. N. Hopkins and George C. L. Cummings, 33–46. Louisville: Westminster John Knox, 2003.

Dabney, D. Lyle. "Saul's Armor: The Problem and the Promise of Pentecostal Theology Today." *Pneuma: The Journal of the Society for Pentecostal Studies* 23 (2001) 115–46.

Dabney, E. J. *What It Means to Pray Through*. Memphis, TN: COGIC, 1987.

Dahl, Nils Alstrup. *Jesus in the Memory of the Early Church: Essays*. Minneapolis: Augsburg, 1976.

"Daily Portion from the King's Bounty." *The Weekly Evangel* (1916) 9.

Daneel, Marthinus L. *African Earthkeepers: Wholistic Interfaith Mission*. Maryknoll, NY: Orbis, 2001.

Daniels, David D., III. "'Everybody Bids You Welcome': A Multicultural Approach to North American Pentecostalism." In *The Globalization of Pentecostalism: A Religion Made to Travel*, edited by Murray W. Dempster et al., 222–52. Oxford: Regnum, 1999.

———. "'Gotta Moan Sometime': A Sonic Exploration of Earwitnesses to Early Pentecostal Sound in North America." *Pneuma: The Journal of the Society for Pentecostal Studies* 30 (2008) 5–32.

———. "'Until the Power of the Lord Comes Down': African American Spirituality and Tarrying." In *Contemporary Spiritualities: Social and Religious Contexts*, edited by Clive Erricker and Jane Erricker, 173–91. London: Continuum, 2001.

Darrand, Tom Craig. *Metaphors of Social Control in a Pentecostal Sect*. Studies in Religion and Society 6. Lewiston, NY: Mellen, 1983.

Dayton, Donald W. *Theological Roots of Pentecostalism*. Peabody, MA: Hendrickson, 1987.

———. "Theological Roots of Pentecostalism." *Pneuma: The Journal of the Society for Pentecostal Studies* 2 (1980) 3–49.

Del Colle, Ralph. "A Catholic Response." *Pneuma: The Journal of the Society for Pentecostal Studies* 30 (2008) 255–62.

———. *Christ and the Spirit: Spirit-Christology in Trinitarian Perspective*. Oxford: Oxford University Press, 1994.

———. "Spirit-Christology: Dogmatic Foundations for Pentecostal-Charismatic Spirituality." *Journal of Pentecostal Theology* 3 (1993) 91–112.

———. "Trinity and Temporality: A Pentecostal/Charismatic Perspective." *Journal of Pentecostal Theology* 8 (1996) 99–113.

Dempster, Murray W. "The Search for Pentecostal Identity." *Pneuma: The Journal of the Society for Pentecostal Studies* 15 (1993) 1–8.

Dempster, Murray, et al., eds. *The Globalization of Pentecostalism: A Religion Made to Travel*. Oxford: Regnum, 1999.

Devol, Thomas I. "Ecstatic Pentecostal Prayer and Meditation." *Journal of Religion and Health* 13 (1974) 285–88.

Dews, Peter. *Logics of Disintegration: Post-Structuralist Thought and the Claims of Critical Theory*. London: Verso, 1987.

Diekmann, Godfrey. "The Place of Liturgical Worship." In *Concilium Theology in the Age of Renewal*, edited by Johannes Wagner and Helmut Hucke, 2:67–107. New York: Paulist, 1965.

Dieter, Melvin E. *The Holiness Revival of the Nineteenth Century*. 2nd ed. Studies in Evangelicalism 1. Lanham, MD: Scarecrow, 1996.

Dietzfelbinger, Wolfgang. "Die Hierarchie der Wahrheiten." In *Die Autorität der Freiheit*, edited by J. C. Hampe, 2:619–24. Munich: Kösel, 1967.

Dijk, R. A. van. "Religion, Reciprocity, and Restructuring Family Responsibility in the Ghanaian Pentecostal Diaspora." In *The Transnational Family: New European Frontiers and Global Networks*, edited by D. F. Bryceson and U. Vuorela, 173–96. Cross-Cultural Perspectives on Women 25. Oxford: Berg, 2001.

Dongsoo, Kim. "The Healing of Han in Korean Pentecostalism." *Journal of Pentecostal Theology* 15 (1999) 123–39.

Draper, Jonathan A. "Christian Self-Definition Against the 'Hypocrites' in Didache 8." In *Society of Biblical Literature 1992 Seminar Papers*, edited by Eugene H. Lovering Jr., 362–77. Atlanta: Scholars, 1992.

Driver, Tom. *The Magic of Ritual*. San Francisco: Harper & Row, 1991.

Droogers, André. "Methodological Ludism Beyond Religionism and Reductionism." In *Conflicts in Social Science*, edited by Anton van Harskamp, 44–67. Routledge Studies in Social & Political Thought 2. London: Routledge, 1996.

———. "The Third Bank of the River: Play, Methodological Ludism and the Definition of Religion." In *The Pragmatics of Defining Religion: Contexts, Concepts, and Contents*, edited by J. G. Platvoet and A. L. Molendijk, 285–313. Studies in the History of Religions 84. Leiden: Brill, 1999.

Duitsman Cornelius, Janet. *Slave Missions and the Black Church in the Antebellum South*. Columbia: University of South Carolina Press, 1999.

Durasoff, Steve. *Bright Wind of the Spirit: Pentecostalism Today*. Englewood Cliffs, NJ: Prentice-Hall, 1972.

Eberhard, Philippe. *The Middle Voice in Gadamer's Hermeneutics: A Basic Interpretation with Some Theological Implications*. Tübingen: Mohr Siebeck, 2004.

Elliott, Gillian B. *Sculpted Thresholds and the Liturgy of Transformation in Medieval Lombardy*. New York: Routledge, 2022.

Erickson, Gary D. *Pentecostal Worship: A Biblical and Practical Approach*. Springfield, MO: Word Aflame, 2011.

Eslinger, Ellen. *Citizens of Zion: The Social Origins of Camp Meeting Revivalism*. Knoxville: University of Tennessee Press, 1999.

Faupel, D. William. *The Everlasting Gospel: The Significance of Eschatology in the Development of Pentecostal Thought.* Journal of Pentecostal Theology Supplement Series 10. Sheffield: Sheffield Academic, 1996.

———. "The Function of 'Models' in the Interpretation of Pentecostal Thought." *Pneuma: The Journal of the Society for Pentecostal Studies* 2 (1980) 51–71.

Fenwick, John R. K., and Bryan D. Spinks. *Worship in Transition: The Liturgical Movement in the Twentieth Century.* New York: Continuum, 1995.

Flanagan, Kieran. "Liturgy as Play: A Hermeneutics of Ritual Re-Presentation." *Modern Theology* 4 (1988) 346–72.

Flannery, Austin, ed. *Vatican Council II. The Basic Sixteen Documents.* Northport, NY: Costello, 1996.

Fletcher, John. *The Doctrines of Grace and Justice Equally Essential to the Pure Gospel.* Stockbridge: Herald Office, 1810.

Flower, Alice Reynolds. "The Spirit of Life." *The Weekly Evangel* (1916) 10.

Floy-Thomas, Stacey, et al. *Black Church Studies: An Introduction.* Nashville: Abingdon, 2007.

Föller, O. "Martin Luther on Miracles, Healing, Prophecy, and Tongues." *Studia Historiae Ecclesiasticae* 32 (2005) 333–51.

"Formula of Concord." In *Triglot Concordia: The Symbolical Books of the Evangelical Lutheran Church*, edited and translated by F. Bente and W. H. T. Dau, 775–843. St. Louis: Concordia, 1921.

Foucault, Michel. *The Archaeology of Knowledge; and The Discourse on Language.* Translated by A. M. Sheridan Smith. Social Theory. London: T. & T. Clark, 1972.

———. *The Order of Things: An Archaeology of the Human Sciences.* Translated by Alan Sheridan. New York: Pantheon, 1970.

———. *Surveiller et punir: Naissance de la prison.* Paris: Gallimard, 1975.

———. *This Is Not a Pipe.* Translated by James Harkness. Berkeley: University of California Press, 1983.

Frazier, E. Franklin. *The Negro Church in America.* New York: Schocken, 1974.

Friesen, Aaron T. *Norming the Abnormal: The Development and Function of the Doctrine of Initial Evidence in Classical Pentecostalism.* Eugene, OR: Pickwick, 2013.

———. "Pentecostal Antitraditionalism and the Pursuit of Holiness: The Neglected Role of Tradition in Pentecostal Theological Reflection." *Journal of Pentecostal Theology* 23 (2014) 191–215.

Frodsham, Stanley H. *With Signs Following: The Story of the Pentecostal Revival in the Twentieth Century.* Springfield, MO: Gospel, 1946.

Froitzheim, Dieter. "Logische Vorüberlegungen zum Thema 'Hierarchie der Wahrheiten.'" *Stimmen der Zeit* 188 (1971) 424–32.

Gabler, Johann Philipp. Review of *Summa theologiae Christianae*, by Christoph Friedrich von Ammon. *Journal für auserlesene theologische Literatur* 5 (1810) 587–600.

Gadamer, Hans-Georg. *The Relevance of the Beautiful and Other Essays.* Edited by R. Bernasconi. Translated by Nicholas Walker. Cambridge: Cambridge University Press, 1986.

———. *Truth and Method.* Translated by Joel Weinsheimer and Donald G. Marshall. 2nd ed. London: Continuum, 2004.

Gaede, Charles. "Pentecost and Praise: A Pentecostal Ritual?" *Paraclete* 22 (1988) 5–8.

Ganoczy, Alexandre. *Einführung in die katholische Sakramentenlehre*. Darmstadt: Wissenschaftliche Buchgesellschaft, 1979.

Gasecki, Krzysztof. *Das Profil des Geistes in den Sakramenten: Pneumatologische Grundlagen der Sakramentenlehre. Darstellung und Reflexionen ausgewählter katholischer Entwürfe*. Münster: Aschendorff, 2009.

Gause, R. Hollis. *Living in the Spirit: The Way of Salvation*. Cleveland, TN: Pathway, 1980.

Gennrich, Paul. *Der Kampf um die Schrift in der Deutsch-Evangelischen Kirche des neunzehnten Jahrhunderts*. Berlin: Reuther & Reichard, 1898.

Gerlach, Luther P., and Virginia H. Hine. *People, Power, Change: Movements of Social Transformation*. Indianapolis, IN: Bobbs-Merrill, 1970.

Gerstel, E. J. *Thresholds of the Sacred: Architectural, Art Historical, Liturgical, and Theological Perspectives on Religious Screens, East and West*. Washington, DC: Dumbarton Oaks, 2006.

Giddens, Anthony. "Living in a Post-Traditional Society." In *Reflexive Modernization: Politics, Tradition and Aesthetics in the Modern Social Order*, edited by Ulrich Beck et al., 56–109. Malden, MA: Polity, 1994.

Gold, Malcolm. "From the 'Upper Room' to the 'Christian Centre': Changes in the Use of Sacred Space and Artefacts in a Pentecostal Assembly." In *Materializing Religion: Expression, Performance, and Ritual*, edited by E. Arweck and W. Keenan, 74–88. Aldershot, UK: Ashgate, 2006.

González, Rudolph D. "Laying-On of Hands in Luke and Acts: Theology, Ritual, and Interpretation." PhD diss., Baylor University, 1999.

Goodwin, Thomas. *A Discourse of the True Nature of the Gospel: Demonstrating That It Is No New Law, But a Pure Doctrine of Grace*. London: Darby, 1695.

Green, Chris E. W. *Sanctifying Interpretation: Vocation, Holiness, and Scripture*. 2nd ed. Cleveland, TN: CPT, 2020.

———. *Toward a Pentecostal Theology of the Lord's Supper: Foretasting the Kingdom*. Cleveland, TN: CPT, 2012.

Griffith, R. Marie. "Female Suffering and Religious Devotion in American Pentecostalism." In *Women and Twentieth Century Protestantism*, edited by Margaret Lamberts Bendroth and Virginia Lieson Brereton, 184–208. Urbana: University of Illinois Press, 2002.

Gritsch, Eric W., and Robert Jenson. *Lutheranism: The Theological Movement and Its Confessional Writings*. Philadelphia: Fortress, 1976.

Groupe des Dombes. *The Gift of Authority: Authority in the Church III. An Agreed Statement by the Anglican–Roman Catholic International Commission*. New York: Church, 1999.

———. "The Holy Spirit, the Church, and the Sacraments." *One in Christ* 16 (1980) 234–64.

Guardini, Romano. *Meditations Before Mass*. Translated by Elinor Castendyk Briefs. Westminster: Newman, 1956.

Gunstone, John. *Pentecost Comes to Church: Sacraments and Spiritual Gifts*. London: Darton, Longman & Todd, 1994.

———. "The Spirit's Freedom in the Spirit's Framework." In *Liturgy Reshaped*, edited by Kenneth W. Stevenson, 4–16. Garden City, NY: Anchor, 1982.

Gunther Brown, Candy. *Global Pentecostal and Charismatic Healing*. Oxford: Oxford University Press, 2011.

Guthrie, Joseph Randall. "Pentecostal Hymnody: Historical, Theological, and Musical Influences." DMA diss., Southwestern Baptist Theological Seminary, 1992.

Hägglund, Bengt. *Die Heilige Schrift und ihre Deutung in der Theologie Johann Gerhards: Eine Untersuchung über das altlutherische Schriftverständnis.* Lund: Gleerup, 1951.

Haney, Kenneth. "A Brief Oneness Pentecostal Response." *Pneuma: The Journal of the Society for Pentecostal Studies* 30 (2008) 227.

Hanson, Paul. "Scripture, Community, and Spirit: Biblical Theology's Contribution to a Contextualized Christian Theology." *Journal of Pentecostal Theology* 3 (1995) 3–12.

Harris, Roy. *Reading Saussure: A Critical Commentary on the Cours de linguistique générale.* La Salle, IL: Open Court, 1987.

Hejzlar, Pavel. *Two Paradigms for Divine Healing: Fred F. Bosworth, Kenneth E. Hagin, Agnes Sanford, and Francis MacNutt in Dialogue.* Global Pentecostal and Charismatic Studies 4. Leiden: Brill, 2010.

Henn, W. "The Hierarchy of Truths Twenty Years Later." *Theological Studies* 48 (1987) 439–71.

Hesser, Garry, and Andrew J. Weigert. "Comparative Dimensions of Liturgy: A Conceptual Framework and Feasibility Application." *Sociological Analysis* 41 (1980) 215–29.

Hinson, Glenn. *Fire in My Bones: Transcendence and the Holy Spirit in African American Gospel.* Contemporary Ethnography. Philadelphia: University of Pennsylvania Press, 2000.

———. "The Significance of Glossolalia in Church History." In *Speaking in Tongues: A Guide to Research in Glossolalia*, edited by Watson E. Mills, 189–96. Grand Rapids: Eerdmans, 1986.

Hodges, Melvin L. *A Theology of the Church and Its Mission: A Pentecostal Perspective.* Springfield, MO: Gospel, 1977.

Hollenweger, Walter. "The Black Roots of Pentecostalism." In *Pentecostals After a Century: Global Perspectives on a Movement in Transition*, edited by Allan H. Anderson and Walter J. Hollenweger, 40–49. Journal of Pentecostal Theology Supplement Series 15. Sheffield: Sheffield Academic, 1999.

———. "The Critical Tradition of Pentecostalism." *Journal of Pentecostal Theology* 1 (1992) 7–17.

———. *Enthusiastisches Christentum: Die Pfingstbewegung in Geschichte und Gegenwart.* Zurich: Zwingli, 1969.

———. *Pentecostalism: Origins and Developments Worldwide.* Peabody, MA: Hendrickson, 1997.

———. *The Pentecostals: The Charismatic Movement in the Churches.* Minneapolis: Augsburg, 1972.

———. "The Social and Ecumenical Significance of Pentecostal Liturgy." *Studia Liturgica* 8 (1971) 207–15.

Hollingsworth, Andrea. "Spirit and Voice: Toward a Feminist Pentecostal Pneumatology." *Pneuma: The Journal of the Society for Pentecostal Studies* 29 (2007) 189–213.

Holm, Randall. "Healing in Search of Atonement." *Journal of Pentecostal Theology* 23 (2014) 50–67.

Hopkins, Dwight N. "Slave Theology in the 'Invisible Institution.'" In *Cut Loose Your Stammering Tongue: Black Theology in the Slave Narrative*, edited by D. N. Hopkins and George C. L. Cummings, 1–32. Louisville: Westminster John Knox, 2003.

Horbury, William. *Jewish Messianism and the Cult of Christ.* London: SCM, 1998.

Horn, Nico. "From Human Rights to Human Wrongs: The Dramatic Turn-About of the South African Pentecostal Movement." In *Christianity and Human Rights*, edited by Frederick M. Shepherd, 213–27. Lanham, MD: Lexington, 2009.

Houtepen, Anton. "*Hierarchia Veritatum* and Orthodoxy." In *Orthodoxy and Heterodoxy*, edited by Johan-Baptist Metz and E. Schillebeeckx, 39–52. Concilium 192. Edinburgh: T. & T. Clark, 1987.

Hudson, Neil. "Early British Pentecostals and Their Relationship to Health, Healing and Medicine." *Asian Journal of Pentecostal Studies* 6 (2003) 283–301.

Hughes, George. *Days of Power in the Forest Temple: A Review of the Wonderful Work of God at Fourteen National Camp-Meetings from 1867 to 1872*. Boston: Best, 1873.

Hughes, Robert. *The Shock of the New*. New York: Random House, 1981.

Hummel, Horace D. "Are Law and Gospel a Valid Hermeneutical Principle?" *Concordia Theological Quarterly* 46 (1982) 181–207.

Ingalls, Monique M., and Amos Yong, eds. *The Spirit of Praise: Music and Worship in Global Pentecostal-Charismatic Christianity*. University Park: Pennsylvania State University Press, 2015.

Jackson, Pamela E. J. "Theology of the Liturgy." In *Vatican II: Renewal Within Tradition*, edited by Matthew L. Lamb and Matthew Levering, 101–28. Oxford: Oxford University Press, 2008.

Jackson, Thomas, ed. *The Works of John Wesley*. 14 vols. Grand Rapids: Zondervan, 1959.

Jacobsen, Douglas. *Thinking in the Spirit: Theologies of the Early Pentecostal Movement*. Bloomington: Indiana University Press, 2003.

Jager, Colin. "After the Secular: The Subject of Romanticism." *Public Culture* 18 (2006) 301–22.

———. "This Detail, This History: Charles Taylor's Romanticism." In *Varieties of Secularism in a Secular Age*, edited by Michael Warner and Jonathan Van Antwerpen, 166–92. Cambridge, MA: Harvard University Press, 2010.

Jansen, Eva, and Claudia Lang. "Transforming the Self and Healing the Body Through the Use of Testimonies in a Divine Retreat Center, Kerala." *Journal of Religion and Health* 51 (2012) 542–51.

Jelly, Frederick. "Marian Dogmas Within Vatican II's Hierarchy of Truths." *Marian Studies* 27 (1976) 19–40.

———. "St. Thomas' Theological Interpretation of the 'Theotokos' and Vatican II's Hierarchy of Truths of Catholic Doctrine." In *Tommaso d'Aquino nel suo settimo centenario: Atti del congresso internazionale*, edited by S. Lynnet, 4:221–30. Naples: Edizioni Domenicane Italiane, 1976.

Jernegan, Marcus W. "Slavery and Conversion in the American Colonies." *American Historical Review* 21 (1916) 505–27.

Ji, Won Yong. "The Work of the Holy Spirit and the Charismatic Movements, from Luther's Perspective." *Concordia Journal* 11 (1985) 204–13.

Johns, Cheryl Bridges. "The Adolescence of Pentecostalism: In Search of a Legitimate Sectarian Identity." *Pneuma: The Journal of the Society for Pentecostal Studies* 17 (1995) 3–18.

———. "Transformed by Grace: The Beauty of Personal Holiness." In *Holiness Manifesto*, edited by Kevin W. Mannoia and Don Thorsen, 152–65. Grand Rapids: Eerdmans, 2008.

Johns, Jackie David, and Cheryl Bridges Johns. "Yielding to the Spirit." *Journal of Pentecostal Theology* 1 (1992) 109-32.
Johnson, Charles A. *The Frontier Camp Meeting: Religion's Harvest Time*. Dallas: Southern Methodist University Press, 1955.
Johnson, James. "A Brief Oneness Pentecostal Response." *Pneuma: The Journal of the Society for Pentecostal Studies* 30 (2008) 225-26.
Johnson, James Weldon, and J. Rosamond Johnson. *The Books of the American Negro Spirituals*. 1925. Repr., New York: DaCapo, 2002.
Johnson, Todd M., et al. "Christianity 2010: A View from the New Atlas of Global Christianity." *International Bulletin of Missionary Research* 34 (2010) 29-36.
Johnstone, Patrick, and Jason Mandryk. *Operation World: 21st Century Edition*. Updated and rev. ed. Carlisle, UK: Paternoster, 2001.
Joint International Commission Between the Roman Catholic Church and the Orthodox Church. "The Mystery of the Church and the Eucharist in the Light of the Mystery of the Holy Trinity." *One in Christ* 19 (1983) 188-97.
Jones, Charles Edwin. *Perfectionist Persuasion: The Holiness Movement and American Methodism, 1867-1936*. ATLA Monograph Series 5. Metuchen, NJ: Scarecrow, 1974.
Joyner, Charles. "'Believer I Know': The Emergence of African-American Christianity." In *African American Christianity: Essays in History*, edited by Paul E. Johnson, 25-36. Berkeley: University of California Press, 1994.

———. *Down by the Riverside: A South Carolina Community*. Urbana: University of Illinois Press, 1984.

Jungkuntz, Theodore. "Sectarian Consequences of Mistranslation in Luther's Smalcald Articles." *Currents in Theology and Mission* 4 (1977) 166-67.
Jungmann, Joseph Andreas. "Constitution on the Sacred Liturgy." In *Commentary on the Documents of Vatican II*, edited by Herbert Vorgrimler, 1:1-87. New York: Herder & Herder, 1966.
Kalu, Ogbu. *African Pentecostalism: An Introduction*. Oxford: Oxford University Press, 2008.

———. "Changing Tides: Some Currents in World Christianity at the Opening of the Twenty-First Century." In *Interpreting Contemporary Christianity: Global Processes and Local Identities*, edited by Ogbu U. Kalu and Alaine M. Low, 3-23. Grand Rapids: Eerdmans, 2008.

Kärkkäinen, Veli-Matti. "Are Pentecostals Oblivious to Social Justice? Theological and Ecumenical Perspectives." *Missionalia* 29 (2001) 387-404.

———. "Beyond Augsburg: Faith Alone and Full Gospel." *Lutheran Forum* 41 (2007) 45-48.

———. "'Encountering Christ in the Full Gospel Way': An Incarnational Pentecostal Spirituality." *Journal of the European Pentecostal Theological Association* 27 (2007) 5-19.

———. *An Introduction to Ecclesiology: Ecumenical, Historical, and Global Perspectives*. Downers Grove, IL: InterVarsity, 2002.

———. "Mission, Spirit, and Eschatology: An Outline of a Pentecostal-Charismatic Theology of Mission." *Mission Studies* 16 (1999) 73-94.

———. "Prayer, Liturgy, and Sacramentality: Pentecostal Intimations and Reflections." *Journal of Pentecostal Theology* 34 (2025) 24-43.

Kay, William K. *Pentecostals in Britain*. Carlisle, UK: Paternoster, 2001.

Keener, Craig S. *Spirit Hermeneutics: Reading Scripture in the Light of Pentecost*. Grand Rapids: Eerdmans, 2016.

Kelsey, Morton T. *Tongue Speaking*. Garden City, NY: Waymark, 1968.

Kiesling, Christopher. "The Sacramental Character and the Liturgy." In *Vatican II: The Theological Dimension*, edited by Anthony D. Lee, 385–412. Washington, DC: Thomist, 1963.

Kilmartin, Edward J. *Christian Liturgy: Theology and Practice*. Kansas City, MO: Sheed & Ward, 1988.

Kim, Ig-Jin. *History and Theology of Korean Pentecostalism: Sunbogeum (Pure Gospel) Pentecostalism: An Attempt to Research the History of the Largest Congregation in Church History and the Theology of Its Pastor Yonggi Cho*. Missiological Research in the Netherlands 35. Zoetermeer: Uitgeverij Boekencentrum, 2003.

Klaus, Byron. "Growing Edges Have Shifted: Pentecostal Mission in the 21st Century." *Journal of the European Pentecostal Theological Association* 30 (2010) 65–81.

Knight, Cecil B. *Pentecostal Worship*. Cleveland, TN: Pathway, 1974.

Kossie, Karen Lynell. "The Move Is On: African American Pentecostal-Charismatics in the Southwest." PhD diss., Rice University, 1998.

Kropatscheck, Friedrich. *Das Schriftprinzip der lutherischen Kirche: Geschichtliche und dogmatische Untersuchungen*. Vol. 1 of *Die Vorgeschichte: Das Erbe des Mittelalters*. Leipzig: Böhme, 1904.

Land, Steven J. "A Living Faith: Divine Healing." *Ministry Now Profiles* 2 (1997) 14–15.

———. *Pentecostal Spirituality: A Passion for the Kingdom*. Sheffield: Sheffield Academic, 1991.

Le Corbusier. *Towards a New Architecture*. Translated by Frederick Etchells. New York: Pauson & Clarke, 1927.

Lee, Paul D. "Pneumatological Ecclesiology in the Roman Catholic–Pentecostal Dialogue: A Catholic Reading of the Third Quinquennium (1985–1989)." PhD diss., Pontificiam Universitatem S. Thomae, 1994.

Leoh, Vincent. "A Pentecostal Preacher as an Empowered Witness." *Asian Journal of Pentecostal Studies* 9 (2006) 35–58.

Levison, John R. *Filled with the Spirit*. Grand Rapids: Eerdmans, 2009.

Lindberg, Carter. *The Third Reformation? The Charismatic Movement and the Lutheran Tradition*. Macon, GA: Mercer University, 1983.

Loewenich, Walther von. "Luthers Auslegung der Pfingstgeschichte." In *Vierhundertfünfzig Jahre lutherische Reformation: 1517–1967, Festschrift für Franz Lau*, edited by Helmar Junghans et al., 181–90. Göttingen: Vandenhoek and Ruprecht, 1967.

Lord, Andy. *Network Church: A Pentecostal Ecclesiology Shaped by Mission*. Global Pentecostal and Charismatic Studies 11. Leiden: Brill, 2012.

Lovett, Leonard. "Black Origins of the Pentecostal Movement." In *Aspects of Pentecostal-Charismatic Origins*, edited by Vinson Synan, 123–41. Plainfield, NJ: Logos International, 1975.

Lowery, Mark. "The Hierarchy of Truths and Doctrinal Particularity." PhD diss., Marquette University, 1988.

Luther, Martin. "Disputation of Doctor Martin Luther on the Power and Efficacy of Indulgences by Dr. Martin Luther (1517)." In *Works of Martin Luther*, edited and translated by Adolph Spaeth et al., 1:29–38. Philadelphia: A. J. Holman, 1915.

———. *Lectures on Galatians, 1535: Chapters 1–4*. Vol. 26 of *Luther's Works*. Edited and translated by Jaroslav Pelikan and Walter A. Hansen. St. Louis: Concordia, 1963.

———. "Preface to the New Testament, 1522." In *Martin Luther: Selections from His Writings*, edited by John Dillenberger, 14–18. New York: Random House, 1962.

———. "Smalcald Articles." In *The Book of Concord: The Confessions of the Evangelical Lutheran Church*, edited by Robert Kolb and Timothy J. Wengert and translated by Charles Arand et al., 295–328. Minneapolis: Fortress, 2000.

Lutheran Church—Missouri Synod, ed. *The Charismatic Movement and Lutheran Theology: A Report of the Commission on Theology and Church Relations of the Lutheran Church—Missouri Synod*. St. Louis: Commission on Theology and Church Relations, 1972.

———. *Gospel and Scripture: The Interrelationship of the Material and Formal Principles in Lutheran Theology: A Report*. St. Louis: Commission on Theology and Church Relations, 1972.

Lutherans and Pentecostals in Dialogue. Strasbourg: Institute for Ecumenical Research, 2010.

Lyotard, Jean-Francois. *Discours, figure*. Collection d'esthétique 7. Paris: Klincksieck, 1971.

———. *Économie libidinale*. Collection "Critique." Paris: Minuit, 1974.

Macchia, Frank D. *Baptized in the Spirit: A Global Pentecostal Theology*. Grand Rapids: Zondervan, 2006.

———. "Created Spirit Beings. Repudiating the Enemy: Satan and Demons." In *Systematic Theology*, edited by Stanley M. Horton, 194–213. Rev. ed. Springfield, MO: Logion, 1994.

———. "Discerning the Truth of Tongues Speech: A Response to Amos Yong." *Journal of Pentecostal Theology* 6 (1998) 67–71.

———. "Groans Too Deep for Words: Towards a Theology of Tongues as Initial Evidence." *Asian Journal of Pentecostal Studies* 1 (1998) 149–73.

———. "Is Footwashing the Neglected Sacrament? A Theological Response to John Christopher Thomas." *Pneuma: The Journal of the Society for Pentecostal Studies* 19 (1997) 239–49.

———. *Justified by the Spirit: Creation, Redemption, and the Triune God*. Grand Rapids: Eerdmans, 2010.

———. "The Kingdom and the Power: Spirit Baptism in Pentecostal and Ecumenical Perspective." In *The Work of the Spirit: Pneumatology and Pentecostalism*, edited by Michael Welker, 109–25. Grand Rapids: Eerdmans, 2006.

———. "The Nature and Purpose of the Church: A Pentecostal Reflection on Unity and *Koinonia*." In *Pentecostalism and Christian Unity: Ecumenical Documents and Critical Assessments*, edited by Wolfgang Vondey, 243–55. Eugene, OR: Pickwick, 2010.

———. "Repudiating the Enemy: Satan and Demons." In *Systematic Theology: A Pentecostal Perspective*, edited by Stanley M. Horton, 194–213. Springfield, MO: Logion, 1994.

———. "Sighs Too Deep for Words: Toward a Theology of Glossolalia." *Journal of Pentecostal Theology* 1 (1992) 47–73.

———. "Tongues as a Sign: Towards a Sacramental Understanding of Pentecostal Experience." *Pneuma: The Journal of the Society for Pentecostal Studies* 15 (1993) 61–76.

MacNutt, Francis. *The Power to Heal*. Notre Dame, IN: Ave Maria, 1977.

———. "The Soaking Prayer." In *Touching the Heart of God*, edited by Leonard E. LeSourd, 183–86. Old Tappan, NJ: Chosen, 1990.

MacRobert, Iain. *The Black Roots and White Racism of Early Pentecostalism in the USA*. New York: St. Martin's, 1988.

———. "The Black Roots of Pentecostalism." In *African American Religion: Interpretive Essays in History and Culture*, edited by Timothy E. Fulop and Albert J. Raboteau, 295–309. New York: Routledge, 1997.

Magesa, Laurenti. *Anatomy of Inculturation: Transforming the Church in Africa*. Maryknoll, NY: Orbis, 2004.

Maier, Paul L. "Fanaticism as a Theological Category in the Lutheran Confessions." *Concordia Theological Quarterly* 44 (1980) 173–81.

Marina, Peter. *Getting the Holy Ghost: Urban Ethnography in a Brooklyn Pentecostal Tongue-Speaking Church*. Plymouth, MA: Lexington, 2013.

Marks, Carole. *Farewell—We're Good and Gone*. Bloomington: Indiana University Press, 1989.

Marostica, Matthew. "Learning from the Master: Carlos Annacondia and the Standardization of Pentecostal Practices in and Beyond Argentina." In *Global Pentecostal and Charismatic Healing*, edited by Candy Gunther Brown, 207–27. Oxford: Oxford University Press, 2011.

Marshall, Ruth. *Political Spiritualities: The Pentecostal Revolution in Nigeria*. Chicago: University of Chicago Press, 2009.

Martin, Bernice. "The Aesthetic of Latin American Pentecostalism: The Sociology of Religion and the Problem of Taste." In *Materializing Religion: Expression, Performance, and Ritual*, edited by Elisabeth Arweck and William Keenan, 138–60. Theology and Religion in Interdisciplinary Perspective Series. Aldershot, UK: Ashgate, 2006.

———. "The Pentecostal Gender Paradox: A Cautionary Tale for the Sociology of Religion." In *The Blackwell Companion to Sociology of Religion*, edited by Richard K. Fenn, 52–66. Blackwell Companions to Religion 2. Oxford: Blackwell, 2001.

Martin, David. *The Future of Christianity: Reflections on Violence and Democracy, Religion and Secularization*. Surrey, UK: Ashgate, 2011.

———. *A General Theory of Secularization*. Oxford: Blackwell, 1978.

———. *On Secularization: Towards a Revised General Theory*. Aldershot, UK: Ashgate, 2005.

———. *Secularisation, Pentecostalism, and Violence: Receptions, Rediscoveries, and Rebuttals in the Sociology of Religion*. New York: Routledge, 2017.

———. *Tongues of Fire: The Explosion of Protestantism in Latin America*. Oxford: Blackwell, 1993.

Martin, Joan. "By Perseverance and Unwearied Industry." In *Cut Loose Your Stammering Tongue: Black Theology in the Slave Narrative*, edited by D. N. Hopkins and George C. L. Cummings, 107–30. Louisville: Westminster John Knox, 2003.

Maynard-Reid, Peditro U. *Diverse Worship: African American, Caribbean, and Hispanic Perspectives*. Downers Grove, IL: InterVarsity, 2000.

Mbiti, John S. *Introduction to African Religion*. Rev. ed. Oxford: Heinemann, 1991.

McClendon, Gwyneth H., and Rachel Beatty Riedl. "Individualism and Empowerment in Pentecostal Sermons: New Evidence from Nairobi, Kenya." *African Affairs* 115 (2015) 119–44.

McClung, Grant. "We Have an Altar (Hebrews 13:10)." *Enrichment Journal* (2009). https://enrichmentjournal.ag.org/Issues/2009/Summer-2009/We-Have-an-Altar-Hebrews-13-10.

McDonnell, Kilian, ed. *Presence, Power, Praise: Documents on Charismatic Renewal.* 3 vols. Collegeville, MN: Liturgical, 1980.

McGee, Gary B. *Miracles, Missions, and American Pentecostalism.* American Society of Missiology Series 45. Maryknoll, NY: Orbis, 2010.

Mead, Amos P. *Manna in the Wilderness, or, the Grove and Its Altar, Offerings, and Thrilling Incidents. Containing a History of the Origin and Rise of Camp Meetings, and a Defence of This Remarkable Means of Grace; Also, an Account of the Wyoming Camp Meeting. Together with Sketches of Sermons and Preachers.* 3rd ed. Philadelphia: Perkinpine & Higgins, 1860.

Medina, Néstor. "Orality and Context in a Hermeneutical Key: Toward a Latina/o-Canadian Pentecostal Life-Narrative Hermeneutics." *PentecoStudies* 14 (2015) 97–123.

Meier, F. E. "The Formal and Material Principles of Lutheran Confessional Theology." *Concordia Theological Monthly* 24 (1953) 545–50.

Melton, Narelle Jane. "Lessons of Lament: Reflections on the Correspondence Between the Lament Psalms and Early Australian Pentecostal Prayer." *Journal of Pentecostal Theology* 20 (2011) 68–80.

Menzies, Robert P. "The Role of Glossolalia in Luke-Acts." *Asian Journal of Pentecostal Studies* 15 (2012) 47–72.

Menzies, William W. "Frontiers in Theology: Issues at the Close of the First Pentecostal Century." In *Theological Symposium for Asian Church Leaders: Asian Issues on Pentecostalism, September 21, 1998*, edited by the 18th Pentecostal World Conference, 15–30. Seoul: Pentecostal World Conference, 1998.

———. "A Trinitarian Pentecostal Response." *Pneuma: The Journal of the Society for Pentecostal Studies* 30 (2008) 229–32.

Metz, Johann Baptist. *Faith in History and Society: Toward a Practical Fundamental Theology.* Translated by David Smith. London: Burns & Oates, 1980.

Meyer, Birgit. "Make a Complete Break with the Past: Memory and Postcolonial Modernity in Ghanaian Pentecostal Discourse." In *Memory and the Postcolony: African Anthropology and the Critique of Power*, edited by Richard Werbner, 182–208. London: Zed, 1998.

———. "Pentecostalism and Globalization." In *Studying Global Pentecostalism: Theories and Methods*, edited by Allan Anderson et al., 113–30. Berkeley: University of California Press, 2010.

———. "Religious and Secular, 'Spiritual' and 'Physical' in Ghana." In *What Matters? Ethnographies of Value in a Not So Secular Age*, edited by Courtney Bender and Ann Taves, 86–118. New York: Columbia University Press, 2012.

———. *Translating the Devil: Religion and Modernity Among the Ewe in Ghana.* Edinburgh: Edinburgh University Press, 1999.

Miller, Albert G. "Pentecostalism as a Social Movement: Beyond the Theory of Deprivation." *Journal of Pentecostal Theology* 9 (1996) 97–114.

Miller, Donald E., and Tetsunao Yamamori. *Global Pentecostalism: The New Face of Christian Social Engagement.* Berkeley: University of California Press, 2007.

Mittelstadt, Martin W. *The Evolution of a Pentecostal Scholar: Twenty Years in Luke-Acts.* Global Pentecostal and Charismatic Studies 50. Leiden: Brill, 2024.

———. *Reading Luke–Acts in the Pentecostal Tradition*. Cleveland: CPT, 2010.
———. *The Spirit and Suffering in Luke-Acts: Implications for a Pentecostal Pneumatology*. London: T. & T. Clark, 2004.
Moltmann, Jürgen. "A Response to My Pentecostal Dialogue Partners." *Journal of Pentecostal Theology* 4 (1994) 59–70.
Moltmann, Jürgen, and Karl-Josef Kuschel, eds. *Pentecostal Movements as an Ecumenical Challenge*. Concilium 1966/3. Maryknoll, NY: Orbis, 1996.
Moore, Rickie D. "Altar Hermeneutics: Reflections on Pentecostal Biblical Interpretation." *Pneuma: The Journal of the Society for Pentecostal Studies* 38 (2016) 148–59.
———. "A Pentecostal Approach to Scripture." *Seminary Viewpoint* 8 (1987) 4–5, 11.
———. "Raw Prayer and Refined Theology: 'You Have Not Spoken Straight to Me, as My Servant Job Has.'" In *The Spirit and the Mind: Essays in Informed Pentecostalism*, edited by Terry L. Cross and Emerson Powery, 35–48. Lanham, MD: University Press of America, 2000.
Morrill, Bruce T. *Anamnesis as Dangerous Memory: Political and Liturgical Theology in Dialogue*. Collegeville, MN: Pueblo, 2004.
Mühlen, Heribert. "Die Bedeutung der Differenz zwischen Zentraldogmen und Randdogmen für den ökumenischen Dialog." In *Freiheit in der Begegnung: Zwischenbilanz des Ökumenischen Dialogs*, edited by J. L. Leuba, 191–227. Frankfurt: Knecht, 1969.
———. *Der Heilige Geist als Person. In der Trinität bei der Inkarnation und im Gnadenbund. Ich-Du-Wir*. Münster: Aschendorff, 1963.
———. "Kirche in Bewegung—Keine neue Bewegung in der Kirche." *Erneuerung in Kirche und Gesellschaft* 2 (1977) 22–25.
———. "Die Lehre des Vaticanum II über die *Hierarchia veritatum* und ihre Bedeutung für den ökumenischen Dialog." *Theologie und Glaube* 56 (1966) 303–35.
———. *Una Mystica Persona. Die Kirche als das Mysterium der heilsgeschichtlichen Identität des Heiligen Geistes in Christus und den Christen: Eine Person in vielen Personen*. Münster: Aschendorff, 1967.
Murray, Ian H. *Revival and Revivalism: The Making and Marring of American Evangelicalism 1750–1858*. London: Banner of Truth Trust, 1994.
Mutungu, Derek B. "A Response to M. L. Daneel." In *All Together in One Place: Theological Papers from the Brighton Conference on World Evangelization*, edited by Harold D. Hunter and Peter D. Hocken, 127–31. Journal of Pentecostal Theology Supplement Series 4. Sheffield: Sheffield Academic, 1993.
Nel, Marius. "A Distinctive Pentecostal Hermeneutic: Possible and/or Necessary?" *Acta Theologica* 37 (2017) 86–103. https://journals.ufs.ac.za/index.php/at/article/view/3336/3200.
Neumann, Peter. *Pentecostal Experience: An Ecumenical Encounter*. Eugene, OR: Pickwick, 2012.
Newburn, Armon. "The Significance of the Altar Service." In *Conference on the Holy Spirit Digest*, edited by Gwen Jones, 2:168–74. Springfield, MO: Gospel, 1983.
Ngong, David Tonghou. *The Holy Spirit and Salvation in African Christian Theology: Imagining a More Hopeful Future for Africa*. Bible & Theology in Africa 8. New York: Lang, 2010.
Nichol, John Thomas. *Pentecostalism*. New York: Harper & Row, 1966.
Nichols, Terrence L. *That All May Be One: Hierarchy and Participation in the Church*. Collegeville, MN: Liturgical, 1997.

Nielsen, Cynthia R. "Gadamer on Play and the Play of Art." In *The Gadamerian Mind*, edited by Theodore George and Gert-Jan van der Heiden, 139–54. Routledge Philosophical Minds. London: Routledge, 2021.

"The Notion of Hierarchy of Truths—An Ecumenical Interpretation. A Study Document Commissioned and Received by the Joint Working Group, 1990." In *Deepening Communion: International Ecumenical Documents with Roman Catholic Participation*, edited by William G. Rusch and J. Gros, 561–71. Washington, DC: US Catholic Conference, 1998.

Oberman, Heiko A. *The Dawn of the Reformation: Essays in Late Medieval and Early Reformation Thought*. Edinburgh: T. & T. Clark, 1986.

O'Connell, Patrick. "Hierarchy of Truths." In *The Dublin Papers on Ecumenism*, edited by P. S. de Achutegui, 83–115. Manila: Ateneo University Publications, 1972.

Oliverio, L. William, Jr. "Contours of a Constructive Pentecostal Philosophical-Theological Hermeneutic." *Journal of Pentecostal Theology* 29 (2020) 35–55.

———. *Pentecostal Hermeneutics in the Late Modern World*. Eugene, OR: Pickwick, 2022.

———. *Theological Hermeneutics in the Classical Pentecostal Tradition: A Typological Account*. Global Pentecostal and Charismatic Studies 12. Leiden: Brill, 2012.

"Oneness-Trinitarian Pentecostal Final Report, 2002–2007." *Pneuma: The Journal of the Society for Pentecostal Studies* 30 (2008) 203–24.

Ong, Walter J. *Orality and Literacy*. 3rd ed. London: Routledge, 2012.

Oosthuizen, G. C., et al., eds. *Afro-Christian Religion and Healing in Southern Africa*. African Studies 8. Lewiston, NY: Mellen, 1989.

Pangrazio, Andrea. "The Mystery of the History of the Church." In *Council Speeches of Vatican II*, edited by Hans Küng et al., 188–92. Glen Rock, NJ: Paulist, 1964.

Parham, Charles F. "Sermons by Charles F. Parham." *The Apostolic Faith* (1925) 9–10.

Paris, Arthur E. *Black Pentecostalism: Southern Religion in an Urban World*. Amherst: University of Massachusetts Press, 1982.

Paul VI. *Gaudium et Spes*. Vatican, 1965. https://www.vatican.va/archive/hist_councils/ii_vatican_council/documents/vat-ii_const_19651207_gaudium-et-spes_en.html.

———. *Sacrosanctum Concilium*. Vatican, 1963. https://www.vatican.va/archive/hist_councils/ii_vatican_council/documents/vat-ii_const_19631204_sacrosanctum-concilium_en.html.

Pelikan, Jaroslav, and Walter A. Hansen, eds. *Luther's Works*. St. Louis: Concordia, 1963.

"The Pentecostal Baptism Restored." *The Apostolic Faith* 1 (1906) 1.

"Perspectives on *Koinonia*: Final Report of the Dialogue Between the Roman Catholic Church and Some Classical Pentecostal Churches and Leaders, 1985–1989." In *Pentecostalism and Christian Unity: Ecumenical Documents and Critical Assessments*, edited by Wolfgang Vondey, 133–58. Eugene, OR: Pickwick, 2010.

Pew Research Center. "Spirit and Power: A 10-Country Survey of Pentecostals." Oct. 5, 2006. https://www.pewresearch.org/religion/2006/10/05/spirit-and-power/.

Pinnock, Clark H., and Barry Callen. *The Scripture Principle: Reclaiming the Full Authority of the Bible*. 2nd ed. Grand Rapids: Baker, 2006.

Plüss, Jean-Daniel. "Globalization of Pentecostalism or Globalization of Individualism? A European Perspective." In *The Globalization of Pentecostalism: A Religion Made to Travel*, edited by Murray W. Dempster et al., 170–82. Oxford: Regnum, 1999.

———. *Therapeutic and Prophetic Narratives in Worship: A Hermeneutic Study of Testimony and Visions. Their Potential Significance for Christian Worship and Secular Society.* Studies in the Intercultural History of Christianity 54. Bern: Lang, 1988.

Pocknee, Cyril E. *The Christian Altar: In History and Today.* London: Mowbray, 1963.

Poewe, Karla, ed. *Charismatic Christianity as a Global Culture.* Columbia: University of South Carolina Press, 1994.

Poewe-Hexham, Karla, and Irving Hexham. "Charismatic Churches and Apartheid in South Africa." In *All Together in One Place: Theological Papers from the Brighton Conference on World Evangelization*, edited by Harold D. Hunter and Peter D. Hocken, 73–83. Journal of Pentecostal Theology Supplement Series 4. Sheffield: Sheffield Academic, 1993.

Polanyi, Michael. *Knowing and Being: Essays.* Edited by Marjorie Grene. Chicago: Chicago University Press, 1969.

Poloma, Margaret. "Pentecostal Prayer Within the Assemblies of God: An Empirical Study." *Pneuma: The Journal of the Society for Pentecostal Studies* 31 (2009) 47–65.

———. "A Reconfiguration of Pentecost." In *"Toronto" in Perspective: Papers on the New Charismatic Wave of the Mid-1990s*, edited by David Hilborn, 99–128. Carlisle, UK: ACUTE, 2001.

———. "The Symbolic Dilemma and the Future of Pentecostalism: Mysticism, Ritual, and Revival." In *The Future of Pentecostalism in the United States*, edited by Eric Patterson and Edmund J. Rybarczyk, 105–22. Lanham, MD: Lexington, 2007.

Prakash, Dhan. "Toward a Theology of Social Concern: A Pentecostal Perspective." *Asian Journal of Pentecostal Studies* 13 (2010) 65–97.

"A Proposed Description of the Nature and Purpose of a Dialogue Between a Group of Pentecostals and Roman Catholics Under the Sponsorship of the Secretariat for Promoting Christian Unity." Unpublished report. J. Rodman Williams Collection. Regent University Library, Virginia Beach, VA.

Qualls, Joy E. A. *God Forgive Us for Being Women: Rhetoric, Theology, and the Pentecostal Tradition.* Eugene, OR: Pickwick, 2018.

Quiroz, Sitna. "Relating as Children of God: Ruptures and Continuities in Kinship Among Pentecostal Christians in the South-East of the Republic of Benin." PhD diss., London School of Economics and Political Science, 2015.

Raboteau, Albert J. *Slave Religion: The "Invisible Institution" in the Antebellum South.* New York: Oxford University Press, 1978.

Rahner, Karl. "Dogma. Wesen und Einteilung." *Lexikon für Theologie und Kirche*, edited by Josef Hofer and Karl Rahner, 3:439–41. 2nd ed. Freiburg: Herder, 1995.

———. *Foundations of Christian Faith: An Introduction to the Idea of Christianity.* Translated by William V. Dych. New York: Seabury, 1978.

———. "Geheimnis." *Lexikon für Theologie und Kirche*, edited by Josef Hofer and Karl Rahner, 4:593–97. Freiburg: Herder, 1960.

———."Kirche und Welt." In *Sacramentum Mundi: Theologisches Lexikon für die Praxis*, edited by Karl Rahner and Adolf Darlap, 2:1336–57. Freiburg: Herder, 1968.

———. *The Later Writings.* Theological Investigations 5. Translated by K. H. Kruger. New York: Seabury, 1982.

———. "On the Theology of Worship." In *Theological Investigations.* Translated by E. Quinn, 19:141–49. New York: Crossroads, 1983.

———. "Überlegungen zum personalen Vollzug des sakramentalen Geschehens." *Geist und Leben* 43 (1970) 282–301.
Rahner, Karl, and Herbert Vorgrimler. "Anamnesis." In *Dictionary of Theology*, 9–10. 2nd ed. New York: Crossroads, 1990.
Ramírez, Daniel. "A Historian's Response." *Pneuma: The Journal of the Society for Pentecostal Studies* 30 (2008) 245–54.
Randi, James. *The Faith Healers*. Buffalo, NY: Prometheus, 1987.
Ratschow, Carl-Heinz. "Einleitende Analyse der Themafrage." In *Sola Scriptura? Ringvorlesung der theologischen Fakultät der Philipps-Universität*, edited by Carl-Heinz Ratschow, 1–21. Marburg, Germ.: Elwert, 1977.
Readings, Bill. *Introducing Lyotard: Art and Politics*. Critics of the Twentieth Century. London: Routledge, 1991.
Reed, David A. "An Anglican Response." *Pneuma: The Journal of the Society for Pentecostal Studies* 30 (2008) 263–69.
———. *"In Jesus' Name": The History and Beliefs of Oneness Pentecostals*. Journal of Pentecostal Theology Supplement Series 31. Blandford Forum, UK: Deo, 2008.
Richardson, Thos. J. "Sainthood—Be and Live." *The Church of God Evangel* 12 (1921) 2.
Risser, James. "Philosophical Hermeneutics, Language, and the Communicative Event." In *The Cambridge Companion to Gadamer*, edited by Robert Dostal, 93–116. 2nd ed. Cambridge Companions to Philosophy. Cambridge: Cambridge University Press, 2021.
Ritschl, Albrecht. "Ueber die beiden Principien des Protestantismus: Antwort auf eine 25 Jahre alte Frage." *Zeitschrift für Kirchengeschichte* 1 (1876) 397–413.
Robeck, Cecil M., Jr. *Azusa Street Mission and Revival: The Birth of the Global Pentecostal Movement*. Nashville: Thomas Nelson, 2017.
———. "Global and Local." *Christian Century* 123 (2006) 34.
———. "Making Sense of Pentecostalism in a Global Context." Paper presented at the Meeting of the Society for Pentecostal Studies. Springfield, MO, March 1999.
———. "The Past: Historical Roots of Racial Unity and Division in American Pentecostalism." *Cyberjournal for Pentecostal and Charismatic Research* 14 (2005). http://www.pctii.org/cyberj/cyberj14/robeck.html.
———. "Taking Stock of Pentecostalism: The Personal Reflections of a Retiring Editor." *Pneuma: The Journal of the Society for Pentecostal Studies* 15 (1993) 35–60.
Robertson, Roland. *Globalization: Social Theory and Global Culture*. Theory, Culture & Society 16. London: Sage, 1992.
———. "Glocalization: Time-Space and Homogeneity-Heterogeneity." In *Global Modernities*, edited by Mike Featherstone, Scott Lash, and Roland Robertson, 25–44. Theory, Culture & Society. London: Sage, 1995.
Robinson, James. *Divine Healing: The Years of Expansion, 1906–1930. Theological Variation in the Transatlantic World*. Eugene, OR: Pickwick, 2014.
Rocha, Pedro Romano. "The Principal Manifestation of the Church (SC 41)." In *Vatican II: Assessment and Perspectives Twenty-Five Years After (1962–1987)*, edited by René Latourelle, 3–26. New York: Paulist, 1989.
Rosin, Robert. "Luther Discovers the Gospel: Coming to the Truth and Confessing the Truth." *Concordia Journal* 32 (2006) 147–60.
Rusch, William G., and J. Gros, eds. *Deepening Communion: International Ecumenical Documents with Roman Catholic Participation*. Washington, DC: US Catholic Conference, 1998.

Rybarczyk, Edmund J. *Beyond Salvation: Eastern Orthodoxy and Classical Pentecostalism on Becoming Like Christ*. Milton Keynes, UK: Paternoster, 2004.

Ryle, Jacqueline. "Laying Our Sins and Sorrows on the Altar: Ritualizing Catholic Charismatic Reconciliation and Healing in Fiji." In *Practicing the Faith: The Ritual Life of Pentecostal-Charismatic Christians*, edited by Martin Linhardt, 68–97. New York: Berghahn, 2011.

Samarin, William J. *Tongues of Men and Angels: The Religious Language of Pentecostalism*. New York: Macmillan, 1972.

Sanders, Cheryl J. "African American Worship in the Pentecostal and Holiness Movements." *Wesleyan Theological Journal* 32 (1997) 105–20.

———. *Saints in Exile: The Holiness-Pentecostal Experience in African American Religion and Culture*. New York: Oxford University Press, 1996.

"Satan and Martin Luther." *The Weekly Evangel* 194 (1917) 2.

Saussure, Ferdinand de. *Cours de linguistique générale*. Edited by Charles Bally and Albert Sechehaye. Paris: Payot, 1955.

———. *Course in General Linguistics*. Translated by Wade Baskin. New York: Philosophical Library, 1959.

Schiller, Friedrich. *Letters on the Aesthetic Education of Man*. Translated by Elizabeth Wilkinson and L. A. Willoughby. Oxford: Clarendon, 1967.

Schlink, Edmund. "Die Hierarchie der Wahrheiten und die Einigung der Kirchen." *Kerygma und Dogma* 21 (1975) 36–48.

———. *Theology of the Lutheran Confessions*. Translated by Paul F. Koehneke and Herbert J. A. Bouman. 3rd ed. Philadelphia: Fortress, 1961.

Schmemann, Alexander. *Introduction to Liturgical Theology*. Translated by Asheleigh E. Moorhouse. Crestwood, NY: St. Vladimir's Seminary Press, 1986.

Schmidt, Herman. *La constitution de la sainte liturgie: Texte, genèse, commentaire, documents*. Bruxelles: Lumen Vitae, 1966.

———, ed. *Liturgy: Self-Expression of the Church*. New York: Herder & Herder, 1972.

Schoeps, H. J. *Paul: Theology of the Apostle in Light of Jewish Religious History*. Philadelphia: Westminster, 1966.

Schoonenberg, Piet. "Historiciteit en interpretatie van het dogma." *Tijdschrift voor Theologie* 8 (1968) 293–98.

Schützeichel, Heribert. "Das hierarchische Denken in der Theologie." *Catholica* 30.1 (1976) 96–111.

Seasoltz, Kevin. "Anthropology and Liturgical Theology." In *Liturgy and Human Passage*, edited by David Power and Luis Maldonado, 3–13. New York: Seabury, 1979.

Segraves, Daniel. "A Oneness Pentecostal Response." *Pneuma: The Journal of the Society for Pentecostal Studies* 30 (2008) 233–39.

Senn, Frank C. *Christian Liturgy: Catholic and Evangelical*. Minneapolis: Fortress, 1997.

Sernett, Milton C. *Bound for the Promised Land: African American Religion and the Great Migration*. Durham, NC: Duke University Press, 1997.

Seymour, W. J. Untitled editorial. *Apostolic Faith* 1 (1907) 2.

Shaka, Richard. "A Trinitarian Pentecostal Response." *Pneuma: The Journal of the Society for Pentecostal Studies* 30 (2008) 240–44.

Sheldrake, Rupert. *The Presence of the Past: Morphic Resonance and the Habits of Nature*. New York: Times, 1988.

Shields, Guy. "Camp-Meeting Special." In *Pentecostal and Charismatic Studies: A Reader*, edited by William K. Kay and Anne E. Dyer, 18–19. London: SCM, 2004.

Shils, Edward. *Tradition*. Chicago: University of Chicago Press, 1981.

Simpson, A. B. *The Four-Fold Gospel*. Harrisburg, PA: Christian Alliance, 1925.
Skelley, Michael. *The Liturgy of the World: Karl Rahner's Theology of Worship*. Collegeville, MN: Liturgical, 1991.
Slessarev-Jamir, Helene. *Prophetic Activism: Progressive Religious Justice Movements in Contemporary America*. New York: New York University Press, 2011.
Smith, Calvin L. "Revolutionaries and Revivalists: Pentecostal Eschatology, Politics, and the Nicaraguan Revolution." *Pneuma: The Journal of the Society for Pentecostal Studies* 30.1 (2008) 55–82.
Smith, James K. A. *How (Not) to Be Secular: Reading Charles Taylor*. Grand Rapids: Eerdmans, 2014.
———. *Thinking in Tongues: Pentecostal Contributions to Philosophy*. Grand Rapids: Eerdmans, 2010.
Smith, James K. A., and Amos Yong, eds. *Science and the Spirit: A Pentecostal Engagement with the Sciences*. Bloomington: Indiana University Press, 2010.
Smith, Timothy L. *Revivalism and Social Reform in Mid-Nineteenth-Century America*. Nashville: Abingdon, 1957.
Solivan, Samuel. *The Spirit, Pathos, and Liberation: Toward an Hispanic Pentecostal Theology*. Journal of Pentecostal Theology Supplement Series 14. Sheffield: Sheffield Academic, 1998.
Spaeth, Adolph et al., eds. *Works of Martin Luther*. 6 vols. Philadelphia: Holman, 1915.
Spurling, Richard G. *The Lost Link*. Published by the author, 1920.
Stackhouse, Ian. "Charismatic Utterance: Preaching as Prophecy." In *The Future of Preaching*, edited by Geoffrey Stevenson, 42–46. London: SCM, 2010.
Stephens, Randall J. *The Fire Spreads: Holiness and Pentecostalism in the American South*. Cambridge, MA: Harvard University Press, 2008.
Stephenson, Christopher A. "The Rule of Spirituality and the Rule of Doctrine: A Necessary Relationship in Theological Method." *Journal of Pentecostal Theology* 15 (2006) 83–105.
Stoltzfus, Michael. "Martin Luther: A Pure Doctrine of Faith." *Journal of Lutheran Ethics* 3 (2003). https://learn.elca.org/jle/martin-luther-a-pure-doctrine-of-faith/.
Streett, R. Alan. *The Effective Invitation*. Old Tappan, NJ: Revell, 1984.
Stringer, Martin. "Text, Context, and Performance: Hermeneutics and the Study of Worship." *Scottish Journal of Theology* 53 (2000) 365–79.
Studebaker, Steven. "Pentecostal Soteriology and Pneumatology." *Journal of Pentecostal Theology* 11 (2003) 248–70.
Sutton, Matthew Avery. *Aimee Semple McPherson and the Resurrection of Christian America*. Cambridge, MA: Harvard University Press, 2007.
Suurmond, Jean-Jacques. "The Church at Play: The Pentecostal/Charismatic Renewal of the Liturgy as Renewal of the World." In *Pentecost, Mission, and Ecumenism: Essays on Intercultural Theology. Festschrift in Honour of Professor Walter Hollenweger*, edited by Jan A. B. Jongeneel et al., 247–59. Studies in the Intercultural History of Christianity 75. Frankfurt: Lang, 1992.
———. *Word and Spirit at Play: Towards a Charismatic Theology*. Grand Rapids: Eerdmans, 1994.
Synan, Vinson, ed. *Aspects of Pentecostal-Charismatic Origins*. Plainfield, NJ: Logos International, 1975.
———. "Classical Pentecostalism." In *The New International Dictionary of Pentecostal and Charismatic Movements*, edited by Stanley M. Burgess and Eduard van der Maas, 219–22. Grand Rapids: Zondervan, 2002.

———. *The Holiness-Pentecostal Movement in the United States.* Grand Rapids: Eerdmans, 1971.

———. *In the Latter Days: The Outpouring of the Holy Spirit in the Twentieth Century.* Ann Arbor, MI: Servant Books, 1984.

Tang, Edmond. "'Yellers' and Healers—Pentecostalism and the Study of Grassroots Pentecostalism in China." In *Asian and Pentecostal,* edited by Allan Anderson and Edmond Tang, 379–94. Oxford: Regnum, 2005.

Tavard, George. "Hierarchia Veritatum: A Preliminary Investigation." *Theological Studies* 32 (1971) 278–89.

Taves, Ann, and Courtney Bender. "Introduction." In *What Matters? Ethnographies of Value in a Not So Secular Age,* edited by Courtney Bender and Ann Taves, 1–33. New York: Columbia University Press, 2012.

Taylor, Charles. "The Future of the Religious Past." In *Religion: Beyond a Concept,* edited by Hent de Fries, 178–244. New York: Fordham University Press, 2008.

———. *Modern Social Imaginaries.* Durham, NC: Duke University Press, 2004.

———. *A Secular Age.* Cambridge, MA: Belknap, 2007.

———. "Western Secularity." In *Rethinking Secularism,* edited by Craig Calhoun et al., 31–53. Oxford: Oxford University Press, 2011.

Thils, Gustave. "Un colloque sur le thème: La 'hiérarchie des vérités' de la foi." *Revue théologique de Louvain* 10 (1979) 245–49.

Thiselton, Anthony C. *New Horizons in Hermeneutics.* Grand Rapids: Zondervan, 1992.

———. *The Two Horizons: New Testament Hermeneutics and Philosophical Description with Special Reference to Heidegger, Bultmann, Gadamer, and Wittgenstein.* Exeter, UK: Paternoster, 1980.

Thomas, John Christopher, ed. *The Devil. Disease and Deliverance: Origins of Illness in New Testament Thought.* Sheffield: Sheffield Academic, 1998.

———. *Footwashing in John 13 and the Johannine Community.* Sheffield: JSOT Press, 1991.

———. "Pentecostal Theology in the Twenty-First Century." *Pneuma: The Journal of the Society for Pentecostal Studies* 20 (1998) 3–19.

———. *Toward a Pentecostal Ecclesiology: The Church and the Fivefold Gospel.* Cleveland, TN: CPT, 2010.

Thompson, Matthew K. *Kingdom Come: Revisioning Pentecostal Eschatology.* Journal of Pentecostal Theology Supplement Series 37. Blandford Forum, UK: Deo, 2010.

Thompson, William Oscar, Jr. "The Public Invitation as Method of Evangelism: Its Origin and Development." PhD diss., Southwestern Baptist Theological Seminary, 1979.

Tillich, Paul. "The Meaning and Justification of Religious Symbols." In *The Interpretation of Texts,* edited by David Klemm, 1:165–71. Atlanta: Scholars, 1986.

———. *The Protestant Era.* Chicago: University of Chicago Press, 1947.

Tinney, James S. "A Theoretical and Historical Comparison of Black Political and Religious Movements." PhD diss., Howard University, 1978.

Tomberlin, Daniel. *Pentecostal Sacraments: Encountering God at the Altar.* Cleveland, TN: Center for Pentecostal Leadership and Care, 2010.

Tomlinson, A. J. *The Last Great Conflict.* Cleveland, TN: Walter E. Rodgers, 1913.

Torczyner, Harry. *Magritte: Ideas and Images.* New York: Abrams, 1977.

Tugwell, Simon. "The Speech-Giving Spirit, a Dialogue with 'Tongues.'" In *New Heaven? New Earth? An Encounter with Pentecostalism,* edited by Simon Tugwell et al., 119–59. Springfield, IL: Templegate, 1976.

Tupamahu, Ekaputra. "Tongues as a Site of Subversion: An Analysis from the Perspective of Postcolonial Politics of Language." *Pneuma: The Journal of the Society for Pentecostal Studies* 38 (2016) 294–311.

Turner, Victor. *Dramas, Fields, and Metaphors*. Ithaca, NY: Cornell University Press, 1978.

———. *The Forest of Symbols: Aspects of Ndembu Ritual*. Ithaca, NY: Cornell University Press, 1967.

Valeske, Ulrich. *Hierarchia Veritatum: Theologiegeschichtliche Hintergründe und mögliche Konsequenzen eines Hinweises im Ökumenismusdekret des II. Vatikanischen Konzils zum zwischenkirchlichen Gespräch*. Munich: Claudius, 1968.

Venable, Jerry Don. "Slain in the Spirit: Another View." *Paraclete* 22 (1988) 21–26.

Vest, Lamar. *Spiritual Balance: Reclaiming the Promise*. Cleveland, TN: Pathway, 1994.

Vilhauer, Monica. "Beyond the 'Fusion of Horizons': Gadamer's Notion of Understanding as 'Play.'" *Philosophy Today* 53 (2009) 359–64.

Vincent, Hebron. *A History of the Wesleyan Grove, Martha's Vineyard, Camp Meeting: From the First Meeting Held There in 1835 to That of 1858*. 1858. Repr., Charleston, SC: Bibliolife, 2009.

Volf, Miroslav. *After Our Likeness: The Church as the Image of the Trinity*. Grand Rapids: Eerdmans, 1998.

———. "Materiality of Salvation: An Investigation into the Soteriologies of Liberation and Pentecostal Theologies." *Journal of Ecumenical Studies* 26 (1989) 447–67.

———. *Trinität und Gemeinschaft: Eine ökumenische Ecclesiologie*. Neukirchen-Vlyun: Neukirchener, 1996.

Vondey, Wolfgang. *Beyond Pentecostalism: The Crisis of Global Christianity and the Renewal of the Theological Agenda*. Grand Rapids: Eerdmans, 2010.

———, ed. *Continuing and Building Relationships*. Vol. 2 of *Pentecostalism and Christian Unity*. Eugene, OR: Pickwick, 2013.

———. "The Denomination in Classical and Global Pentecostal Ecclesiology: A Historical and Theological Contribution." In *Denomination: Assessing an Ecclesiological Category*, edited by Paul M. Collins and Barry Ensign-George, 100–116. London: Continuum, 2011.

———. "Embodied Gospel: The Materiality of Pentecostal Theology at the Altar." In *Pentecostals and the Body*, edited by Michael Wilkinson and Peter Althouse, 102–19. Annual Review of the Sociology of Religion 8. Leiden: Brill, 2017.

———. *God and Play*. Elements in Religion and Monotheism. Cambridge: Cambridge University Press, forthcoming.

———. *Heribert Mühlen: His Theology and Praxis: A New Profile of the Church*. Lanham, MD: University Press of America, 2004.

———. "The Making of a Black Liturgy: Pentecostal Worship and Spirituality from African Slave Narratives to Urban City Scapes." *Black Theology* 10 (2012) 147–68.

———. "Oneness and Trinitarian Pentecostalism: Critical Dialogue on the Ecumenical Creeds." *One in Christ* 44 (2010) 86–102.

———. "Pentecostal Identity and Christian Discipleship." *Cyberjournal of Pentecostal-Charismatic Research* 6 (1999). http://www.pctii.org/cyberj/cyber6.html.

———. *Pentecostalism: A Guide for the Perplexed*. London: Bloomsbury, 2013.

———, ed. *Pentecostalism and Christian Unity: Ecumenical Documents and Critical Assessments*. Eugene, OR: Pickwick, 2010.

———. "Pentecostal Perspectives on *The Nature and Mission of the Church*: Challenges and Opportunities for Ecumenical Transformation." In *"The Nature and Mission of the Church": Ecclesial Reality and Ecumenical Horizons for the Twenty-First*

Century, edited by Paul M. Collins and Michael A. Fahey, 55–68. New York: Continuum, 2008.

———. "Pentecostals and Ecumenism: Becoming the Church as a Pursuit of Christian Unity." *International Journal for the Study of the Christian Church* 11 (2011) 318–30.

———. *Pentecostal Theology: Living the Full Gospel*. London: T. & T. Clark, 2017.

———. *People of Bread: Rediscovering Ecclesiology*. New York: Paulist, 2008.

———. "Point de vue pentecôstiste (Dossier à propos du document Nature et Mission de L'Église)." *Unité des Chrétiens* 149 (2008) 23–26.

———. "Presuppositions for Pentecostal Engagement in Ecumenical Dialogue." *Exchange: Journal of Ecumenical and Missiological Research* 30 (2001) 344–58.

———. *The Scandal of Pentecost: A Theology of the Public Church*. London: T. & T. Clark, 2024.

———. "Spirit and Nature as Ultimate Concern: Tillich's 'Radical' Ontology in Conversation with Contemporary Pentecostalism." *Bulletin of the North American Paul Tillich Society* 39 (2013) 30–35.

———. "The Symbolic Turn: A Symbolic Conception of the Liturgy of Pentecostalism." *Wesleyan Theological Journal* 36 (2001) 223–47.

———. "The Theology of the Altar and Pentecostal Sacramentality." In *Scripting Pentecost: A Study of Pentecostals, Worship, and Liturgy*, edited by Mark J. Cartledge and A. J. Swoboda, 94–107. Explorations in Practical, Pastoral, and Empirical Theology. Aldershot, UK: Ashgate, 2016.

———. "La théologie pentecôtiste selon une perspective œcuménique: Défis et opportunités pour son integration." *Istina* 57 (2012) 369–87.

———. "Wesleyan Theology and the Disjointing of the Protestant Scripture Principle." *Wesleyan Theological Journal* 46 (2011) 70–85.

Vondey, Wolfgang, and Chris W. Green. "Between This and That: Reality and Sacramentality in the Pentecostal Worldview." *Journal of Pentecostal Theology* 19 (2010) 243–64.

Wacker, Grant. *Heaven Below: Early Pentecostals and American Culture*. Cambridge, MA: Harvard University Press, 2001.

Wall, Robert W. "Waiting on the Holy Spirit (Acts 1:4): Extending a Metaphor to Biblical Interpretation." *Journal of Pentecostal Theology* 22 (2013) 37–53.

Wallace, Adam. *A Modern Pentecost: Embracing a Record of the Sixteenth National Camp-Meeting for the Promotion of Holiness Held at Landisville, Pa., July 23d to August 1st, 1873*. Philadelphia: Methodist Home Journal, 1873.

Walther, C. F. W. *The Proper Distinction Between Law and Gospel*. Translated by W. H. T. Dau. St. Louis, MO: Concordia, 1928.

Ward, Horace S. "The Anti-Pentecostal Argument." In *Aspects of Pentecostal-Charismatic Origins*, edited by Vinson Synan, 99–122. Plainfield, NJ: Logos International, 1975.

Wariboko, Nimi. *The Charismatic City and the Public Resurgence of Religion: A Pentecostal Social Ethics of Cosmopolitan Urban Life*. New York: Palgrave, 2014.

———. "Fire from Heaven: Pentecostals in the Secular City." *Pneuma: The Journal of the Society for Pentecostal Studies* 33 (2011) 391–408.

———. *The Pentecostal Hypothesis: Christ Talks, They Decide*. Eugene, OR: Cascade, 2020.

———. *The Pentecostal Principle: Ethical Methodology in New Spirit*. Grand Rapids: Eerdmans, 2011.

———. *The Split God: Pentecostalism and Critical Theory*. New York: SUNY Press, 2018.

Warrington, Keith. "Acts and the Healing Narratives: Why?" *Journal of Pentecostal Theology* 14 (2006) 189–217.

———. "The Path to Wholeness: Beliefs and Practices Relating to Healing in Pentecostalism." *Evangel* 21 (2003) 45–49.

Wasserman, Earl. *The Subtler Language*. Baltimore: Johns Hopkins University Press, 1968.

Weinsheimer, Joel C. *Gadamer's Hermeneutics: A Reading of Truth and Method*. New Haven, CT: Yale University Press, 1985.

Weiss, Paul. "The Living Systems." In *Beyond Reductionism*, edited by A. Koestler and J. R. Smyth, 3–55. Boston: Beacon, 1971.

Welker, Michael. *God the Spirit*. Translated by John F. Hoffmeyer. Minneapolis: Fortress, 1994.

Wells Davies, Wilma. *The Embattled but Empowered Community: Comparing Understandings of Spiritual Power in Argentine Popular and Pentecostal Cosmologies*. Global Pentecostal and Charismatic Studies 5. Leiden: Brill, 2010.

Wells, Samuel. *Improvisation: The Drama of Christian Doctrine*. Grand Rapids: Brazos, 2004.

Wertz, William F., Jr. "A Reader's Guide to Schiller's Letters on the Aesthetical Education of Man." *Fidelio* 14 (2005) 80–104.

Wesche, Percival A. "The Revival of the Camp-Meeting by the Holiness Groups." MA thesis, University of Chicago, 1945.

Westerfield Tucker, Karen B. "North America." In *The Oxford History of Christian Worship*, edited by Geoffrey Wainwright and Karen B. Westerfield Tucker, 586–632. Oxford: Oxford University Press, 2006.

Wheelock, Donald R. "Spirit Baptism in American Pentecostal Thought." PhD diss., Emory University, 1983.

Wiegele, Katharine L. *Investing in Miracles: El Shaddai and the Transformation of Popular Catholicism in the Philippines*. Honolulu: University of Hawaii Press, 2005.

Wightman, Jill M. "Healing the Nation: Pentecostal Identity and Social Change in Bolivia." In *Conversion of a Continent: Contemporary Religious Change in Latin America*, edited by Timothy J. Steigenga and Edward L. Cleary, 239–55. New Brunswick: Rutgers University Press, 2007.

Wilkinson, Michael. "Pentecostals and the World: Theoretical and Methodological Issues for Studying Global Pentecostalism." *Pneuma: The Journal of the Society for Pentecostal Studies* 38 (2016) 373–93.

Wilkinson, Michael, and Peter Althouse. *Catch the Fire: Soaking Prayer and Charismatic Renewal*. De Kalb: Northern Illinois University Press, 2014.

Williams, Jack. "Playing Church: Understanding Ritual and Religious Experience Resourced by Gadamer's Concept of Play." *International Journal of Philosophy and Theology* 79 (2018) 323–36.

Williams, Joseph W. *Spirit Cure: A History of Pentecostal Healing*. Oxford: Oxford University Press, 2013.

Williams, Melvin D. *Community in a Black Pentecostal Church: An Anthropological Study*. Pittsburgh: University of Pittsburgh Press, 1974.

Williams, Robert C. "Worship and Anti-Structure in Thurman's Vision." In *The Black Christian Worship Experience*, edited by Melva Wilson Costen and Darius Leander Swann, 161–74. Rev. ed. Atlanta: ITC, 1992.

Wilson Bridges, Flora. *Resurrection Song: African American Spirituality*. Maryknoll, NY: Orbis, 2001.

Winsett, R. E., ed. *Songs of Pentecostal Power*. Dayton, TN: Winsett, 1908.
Witte, Henk. *"Alnaargelang hun band met het fundament van het christelijk geloof verschillend is": Wording en verwerling van de uitspraak over de 'hierarchie' van waarheden van Vaticanum II*. Tilburg: Tilburg University Press, 1986.
Womack, David A. *The Wellsprings of the Pentecostal Movement*. Springfield, MO: Gospel, 1968.
Wood, A. Skevington. "Luther's Concept of Revelation." *Evangelical Quarterly* 35 (1963) 149–59.
Wood, George. "A Brief Trinitarian Pentecostal Response." *Pneuma: The Journal of the Society for Pentecostal Studies* 30 (2008) 228.
Wood, Peter H. "'Jesus Christ Has Got Thee at Last': Afro-American Conversion as a Forgotten Chapter in Eighteenth Century Southern Intellectual History." *Bulletin of the Center for the Study of Southern Culture and Religion* 3 (1979) 1–7.
Woodson, Carter Godwin. *The History of the Negro Church*. 2nd ed. Washington, DC: Associated, 1922. Reprint, 1992.
Woodworth-Etter, Maria Beulah. "Signs and Wonders God Wrought in the Ministry for Forty Years." In *A Reader in Pentecostal Theology: Voices from the First Generation*, edited by Douglas Jacobsen, 26–30. Bloomington: Indiana University Press, 2006.
"The World's Supreme Need." *The Pentecostal Evangel* 880 (1921) 18.
Yadao, Paul, and Leif Hetland. *Soaking in God's Presence*. Peachtree City, GA: Global Mission Awareness, 2011.
Yeung, Timothy. "The Characteristics of William Seymour's Sermons: A Reflection on Pentecostal Ethos." *Asian Journal of Pentecostal Studies* 14 (2011) 57–73.
Yong, Amos, ed. "Academic Glossolalia? Pentecostal Scholarship, Multidisciplinarity, and the Science–Religion Conversation." *Journal of Pentecostal Theology* 14 (2005) 61–80.
———. "The Demise of Foundationalism and the Retention of Truth: What Evangelicals Can Learn from C. S. Peirce." *Christian Scholar's Review* 29 (2000) 563–88.
———. *The Hermeneutical Spirit: Theological Interpretation and Scriptural Imagination for the 21st Century*. Eugene, OR: Cascade, 2017.
———. *In the Days of Caesar: Pentecostalism and Political Theology*. Grand Rapids: Eerdmans, 2010.
———. *The Spirit of Creation: Modern Science and Divine Action in the Pentecostal-Charismatic Imagination*. Grand Rapids: Eerdmans, 2011.
———. *The Spirit Poured Out on All Flesh: Pentecostalism and the Possibility of Global Theology*. Grand Rapids: Baker Academic, 2005.
———. *The Spirit Renews the Face of the Earth: Pentecostal Forays in Science and Theology of Creation*. Eugene, OR: Pickwick, 2009.
———. *Spirit-Word-Community: Theological Hermeneutics in Trinitarian Perspective*. Ashgate New Critical Thinking in Religion, Theology, and Biblical Studies. 2002. Repr., Eugene, OR: Wipf & Stock, 2006.
———. "'Tongues of Fire' in the Pentecostal Imagination: The Truth of Glossolalia in Light of R. C. Neville's Theory of Religious Symbolism." *Journal of Pentecostal Theology* 6 (1998) 39–65.
Yong, Amos, and Estrelda Y. Alexander, eds. *Afro-Pentecostalism: Black Pentecostal and Charismatic Christianity in History and Culture*. New York: New York University Press, 2011.
Yong-gi Cho, David. *The Five-Fold Gospel and The Three-fold Blessing*. Seoul: Logos, 1997.

Index

affections, 17, 61–63, 96, 97, 120, 167–69, 184, 188, 193
altar, 7, 62, 63, 100, 101, 104, 105, 145, 146, 151–56, 158, 159, 161–65, 167–69, 172–88, 192–95
altar call, 15, 59, 61, 62, 92, 109, 111, 146, 147, 151–54, 156, 161–64, 177–79, 183, 192
anthropology, 20, 56, 57, 67, 79, 119, 120, 122, 123, 126, 138

baptism in the Spirit, 7, 18, 19, 29, 30, 43, 44, 58–60, 82–88, 105, 140, 141, 161, 164, 166–68, 170, 172, 175, 179, 181, 182, 184–88, 193
Bible. *See* Scripture
Black liturgy, 5, 31, 61, 90–98, 102, 106, 107, 112, 145, 157, 182. *See also* liturgy

charismata. *See* spiritual gifts
Christology, 7, 16–21, 26, 28, 30, 34, 37–40, 42–49, 53, 55, 57–59, 62, 63, 67, 73, 76, 77, 79– 81, 83–85, 87, 88, 89, 94, 113, 129, 131–35, 138, 140–43, 146, 147, 149, 150, 154–57, 161, 163–66, 168, 169, 171–73, 175, 177–81, 183, 186–88, 190, 192–94. *See also* Jesus Christ
church. *See* ecclesiology
community, 14, 17, 25, 27, 34, 40, 49, 50, 53, 54, 56, 59, 60, 62, 67, 68, 71, 72, 74, 75, 79, 86, 92, 95, 98, 100–103, 106, 107, 111–13, 120, 140, 146, 150, 151, 153–59, 161–63, 176, 178–80, 182, 184, 190,192, 193. *See also* ecclesiology
cosmology, 110, 116, 117, 118, 123, 172, 182. *See also* anthropology; creation
creation, 12, 18–19, 28, 29, 30, 31, 52, 95, 117, 118, 146, 151, 159, 172, 184, 185, 186
cross, 18, 40, 73, 79, 81, 87, 121, 142, 177
culture, 11, 14, 15, 22, 29–32, 35, 36, 55, 60, 68–69, 92, 94, 102, 104–6, 121, 160, 169, 180

doctrine, 4, 5, 11, 16–23, 33, 38–40, 43, 44, 50, 52, 58, 59, 60, 61, 78, 83, 106, 117, 131–41, 143, 160, 161, 166, 174, 180, 181, 189

ecclesiology, 12, 22–27, 29, 30, 37, 38–40, 47, 53–55, 60, 67–69, 77, 78, 80–82, 84–86, 88–89, 92, 95, 100, 116, 132, 133, 137–39, 142, 144, 145, 147–53, 155–59, 162, 164, 171–73, 178, 182, 184, 185, 187, 188
ecumenism, 5, 11–15, 18, 22–28, 33, 34, 36, 37, 39–42, 44, 69, 85, 107, 130, 132, 137

embodiment, 5, 7, 26, 30, 34, 42, 44, 56–59, 62, 77, 92, 108, 111–13, 119, 156, 160, 161, 163, 165, 166, 167, 170, 171, 174, 176
empowerment, 12, 18, 19, 28, 29, 45, 48, 49, 55, 57, 58, 60, 61, 63, 67, 72, 73, 74, 82, 92, 95, 97, 101, 110, 112, 119, 129, 133, 134, 144, 146, 147, 149, 159, 167, 169–73, 182, 184–86
enchantment, 110–13, 116–18, 120
encounter, 7, 12, 21, 30, 46, 56–58, 62, 63, 68, 71, 78, 91–93, 103–5, 111, 113, 116, 124, 129, 140, 146, 147, 151–59, 162, 163, 165, 167, 172, 176–81, 183, 184, 186, 187, 190, 192, 193, 195
epistemology, 6, 56, 60, 62, 74, 123, 157, 173
eschatology, 7, 18, 22–24, 28, 54, 55, 63, 82, 85, 88, 95, 97, 113, 115, 116, 118, 140, 141, 144, 156, 159, 161, 162, 167, 172–75, 179, 181, 184, 186–88, 191, 193
ethics, 14, 30, 31, 32, 61, 77, 121, 164, 191, 192
experience, 1, 3, 4, 5, 6, 12, 16, 17, 18, 21, 25, 27, 33, 36, 43–48, 55, 59, 78, 79, 83–85, 92, 94, 95, 97, 98, 99, 104, 106, 108, 113, 116, 117, 122–23, 133, 139–43, 154–56, 159–61, 164–74, 175–95

faith, 2, 16, 17, 19, 26, 38, 40, 48, 52, 61, 68, 76, 77, 81, 92, 95, 107, 109, 113, 130, 131, 135, 136, 139, 148, 149, 152, 158, 162, 169, 170, 171, 185
full gospel, 4, 7, 17, 30, 37, 56, 59, 62, 75, 79, 80, 95, 105, 113, 119, 120, 129, 130, 139–43, 150, 154, 156, 161, 163, 166, 167, 172–77, 179–84, 186–90, 193–95

Gadamer, Hans-Georg, 1–6, 189, 191

globalization, 11–15, 25, 27, 33–36, 49–60, 62, 63, 81, 86, 93, 125, 142, 145, 161, 169–71, 180
glossolalia, 17, 43, 44, 46, 50, 56, 58, 59, 60, 61, 62, 63, 72, 83, 84, 86, 87, 114, 115, 131, 147, 153, 157, 163, 165, 167, 168, 169, 173, 182, 184
gospel, 2, 4, 7, 17, 18, 26, 29, 30, 38, 45, 53, 55, 56, 59, 61, 62, 70, 71, 78, 94, 113, 115, 123, 125, 129, 130–47, 159, 161, 163, 166–68, 172–77, 179–84, 186–90, 193–95
grace, 68, 78–80, 84, 123, 124, 132, 133, 142, 153, 154, 156–58, 163, 166, 182, 184

healing, 7, 17, 18, 28, 30, 43–45, 47, 59, 62, 83, 113, 116, 134, 140, 141, 142, 152–54, 157, 161, 166, 169–72, 175, 179, 181, 182, 185–88, 193
hermeneutics, 1–7, 14, 37, 46, 52, 57, 68, 69, 72–75, 79, 83–85, 88, 89, 133, 140, 145–47, 160, 171, 173, 175–78, 180–81, 183, 185, 186, 188, 189–95
hierarchy. See truths, hierarchy of
history, 2, 3, 4, 7, 11, 18, 22, 25, 26, 30, 36–38, 41–43, 48, 52, 53, 63, 68, 69, 73, 74, 79, 89, 90, 94, 99, 109, 118–26, 130, 133, 135–37, 140, 142, 148, 150, 151, 156, 162, 177, 178, 184, 189–91, 193, 194
holiness, 18, 77–80, 82, 100, 153, 162, 164, 181, 183. See also sanctification
Holy Spirit, 1, 12, 16, 18–23, 25, 26, 28–30, 34, 40, 44, 45, 47, 49, 55, 56, 68, 73, 79–81, 83–85, 87, 92, 95, 97, 101, 104, 105, 113, 116, 130, 133, 140, 144, 146, 147, 150, 151, 153–59, 161–69, 172, 176–78, 180, 182–88. See also pneumatology
Horizon, 1–7, 34, 104, 189–95. See also Gadamer, Hans-Georg

INDEX 227

Jesus Christ, 7, 16–21, 26, 28, 30, 34, 37, 39, 40, 42–45, 47–49, 53, 55, 57–59, 62, 63, 67, 73, 76, 77, 79–81, 83–85, 87–89, 94, 113, 129, 131–35, 138, 140–43, 146, 147, 149, 150, 154–57, 161, 163–66, 168, 169, 171–73, 175, 177–81, 183, 186–88, 190, 192–94. *See also* Christology

kingdom of God, 7, 23, 63, 85, 95, 113, 116, 140, 141, 144, 156, 159, 161, 162, 167, 172, 173, 175, 179, 181, 184, 187, 188, 193. *See also* eschatology

language, 3, 5, 6, 14, 19, 48, 56–59, 70, 74–76, 79, 81, 87, 94, 96, 98, 99, 101, 117, 122, 146, 152, 165, 173
laying on of hands, 47, 115, 152, 166, 168, 169, 170, 184, 185
liturgy, 2–7, 11, 40, 47, 53–55, 67–69, 71, 72, 74–77, 81–94, 96–107, 116, 144–46, 148–52, 154–57,160, 162, 165, 168, 175, 176, 178, 179, 181–84, 186, 188–00, 192–95

materiality, 57–59, 62, 112, 113, 117, 122, 135–40, 143, 151, 160, 167, 168, 171, 174, 178, 181, 186
miracles, 12, 43, 118, 144, 148, 162
mission, 22, 23, 30, 85, 93, 105, 131, 145, 172, 173, 187, 188, 191
modernity, 1, 11, 14, 15, 22, 28, 32, 39, 42, 43, 46, 50–53, 88, 99, 107–11, 113–15, 118, 119, 121, 122, 125, 126, 140

narrative, 4, 5, 7, 16, 17, 52, 55, 59, 60, 63, 73, 92, 96, 108, 110, 117–19, 121, 124–26, 131, 133, 136, 140, 141, 143, 146, 161, 167, 174–82, 184, 187–89

ontology, 4, 5, 6, 38, 60, 62, 87, 122, 123, 124, 126, 189

Pentecost, 1–4, 6, 7, 15, 18, 28, 29, 54–63, 76, 81, 84, 85, 88, 99, 105, 113–16, 118, 126, 133, 144–48, 150, 151, 159, 163, 168, 175–94
play, 3, 5, 6, 33, 96, 108, 109, 113–16, 118–26, 145, 194, 195
pneumatology, 4, 19, 25, 45, 62, 95, 97, 111, 116, 123, 125, 131, 142, 145, 146, 150, 154–58, 177, 190, 193. *See also* Holy Spirit
political theology, 11, 14, 28, 29, 30, 31, 32, 57, 60, 61, 73, 74, 75, 78, 110, 131, 145, 174, 182
power, 12, 18, 29, 45, 48, 49, 55, 57, 58, 61, 63, 67, 72, 73, 74, 82, 95, 101, 110, 112, 129, 133, 134, 144, 146, 147, 149, 159, 169, 170, 171, 172, 173, 186. *See also* empowerment
practices, Pentecostal, 21, 42, 55, 58, 106, 109, 142, 145, 149, 152, 163–71, 174, 182, 183, 184, 185, 192. *See also* embodiment, liturgy, ritual, sacraments
prayer, 5, 16, 17, 44, 92, 94, 95–98, 100, 102, 104, 107, 115, 146, 151–53, 162, 164–71, 178, 183, 184, 185
preaching, 30, 47, 56, 92, 96, 104, 114, 133, 152, 166, 167, 168, 178, 184, 185
prophecy, 1, 17, 29, 30, 32, 44, 56, 60, 61, 92, 131, 157, 162, 165, 168, 173, 179

reason, 19, 70, 71, 86, 108, 120, 121, 149
redemption, 30, 67, 117, 149, 153, 170, 184, 185, 194
religion, 3, 11, 13, 14, 27, 29, 30, 31, 36, 44, 50, 57, 63, 81, 85, 90, 93–98, 103–6, 109–12, 114–26, 131, 135, 143, 145, 148, 160, 169, 171, 185
revelation, 20, 21, 37, 38, 73, 130–32, 134, 137, 141, 143, 153, 157, 162, 181, 195
revival, 11, 26, 50, 63, 76, 81, 82, 83, 86, 87, 93, 98, 100, 103, 104, 106, 115, 124, 133, 163, 173

ritual, 5, 6, 47, 52, 54–60, 62, 84, 90, 91, 94–96, 98, 102–4, 106, 107, 113, 114, 145, 146, 148, 150, 152–58, 160–71, 185, 192, 194

sacramentality, 43, 46, 47, 48, 53, 54, 56, 57–62, 69, 88–89, 99, 100, 101, 107, 145, 146, 148–59, 162, 165, 166, 171, 183, 185
sacraments, 46, 47, 48, 49, 54, 68, 101, 138, 149, 150, 153, 154, 155, 156, 158
salvation. *See* soteriology
sanctification, 7, 18, 28, 29, 47, 77–80, 82–84, 99, 100, 101, 104, 105, 113, 116, 117, 139, 140, 141, 157, 161, 163–67, 170, 172, 175, 179, 181–88, 193, 194
Scripture, 1, 2, 18, 20–23, 30, 40, 45, 47, 78, 84, 88, 114, 116, 131, 132, 134, 136, 139, 142, 145, 146, 148, 151, 162, 168, 171, 175–80, 185, 186, 190, 191, 193, 195
secular age, 5, 85, 108–26
secularization, 32, 107, 108–11, 115, 117–19, 121, 124, 126
sin, 77, 79, 83, 96, 132, 135, 165, 166, 170, 182, 183
society, 12, 14, 15, 27–33, 60, 61, 68, 72, 74–76, 78, 79, 81, 85, 92, 94, 98, 99, 103, 105, 109, 111–14, 122, 123, 173, 174, 181, 182, 188
soteriology, 7, 17, 18, 20, 28, 29, 38, 40, 43, 62, 63, 78, 79, 83, 87, 101, 113, 116, 117, 130, 131, 135, 139–42, 149, 150, 155, 159, 160–63, 166, 172, 175, 179, 181–88, 193
Spirit-Christology, 18, 19, 85, 87, 133, 144, 177, 188
spiritual gifts, 3, 12, 16, 19, 25, 26, 30, 42, 43, 52, 54, 61, 77, 114–16, 129, 130, 131, 143, 148, 150–53, 157, 159, 162, 164, 165, 167, 168, 173, 178, 179, 185, 188, 195
spirituality, 14, 17, 18, 21, 77, 90, 91, 92, 93, 94, 100, 104, 106, 107, 111, 140, 152, 160, 163, 174, 175, 177, 179, 180
story. *See* narrative
symbol, 5, 43, 57–59, 68, 69–77, 79, 81–89, 99, 106, 113, 120, 147, 151, 154, 158, 159, 162, 175–78, 182, 186
symbolic turn, 5, 69, 72–77, 82, 83, 85–88

testimony, 17, 79, 84, 104, 105, 152, 172, 175, 176, 187
tongues, speaking with. *See* glossolalia
tradition, 1, 2, 3, 4, 5, 16, 19, 20, 24, 28, 30, 33, 37, 40, 50–69, 73, 77, 84, 85, 87, 88, 91, 94, 96–99, 101, 103, 104, 106, 111, 112, 114, 131, 145, 148, 155, 158, 160, 170, 186, 192
transcendence, 20, 116, 117, 123, 125
Trinity, 16, 19, 20, 21, 24, 38, 40, 45, 46, 61, 155
truth, 3, 4, 5, 6, 37–39, 41, 42, 46, 52, 57–59, 71, 85, 136, 138, 150, 189, 194
truths, hierarchy of, 5, 36–42, 86, 87, 117

urbanization, 28, 61, 94, 102–7, 114, 115, 147

worldview, 19, 35, 50, 112, 117, 118, 121, 136, 145, 157, 158, 159
worship, 4, 14, 16, 21, 44, 47, 56, 58, 62, 90–92, 94–98, 100, 101, 104–7, 148, 150–56, 161–64, 172, 178, 179, 187, 192, 195